A RULE OF PROPERTY FOR BENGAL

HEDGEHOG AND FOX

ashoka UNIVERSITY HISTORY SERIES

The fox knows many things, but the hedgehog knows one big thing

GENERAL EDITOR: RUDRANGSHU MUKHERJEE

Steven I. Wilkinson
ARMY AND NATION

Thomas R. Trautmann
ELEPHANTS AND KINGS

Partha Chatterjee, Sudipta Kaviraj, Nivedita Menon
THE INDIAN IDEOLOGY

Nayanjot Lahiri
ASHOKA IN ANCIENT INDIA

Nicholas B. Dirks
AUTOBIOGRAPHY OF AN ARCHIVE

Vasudha Dalmia
HINDU PASTS

Dipesh Chakrabarty
THE CALLING OF HISTORY

Mahesh Rangarajan
NATURE AND NATION

Bhavani Raman
DOCUMENT RAJ

Sumit Guha
BEYOND CASTE

Iqtidar Alam Khan
INDIA'S POLITY IN THE AGE OF AKBAR

Linda Hess
BODIES OF SONG

Charu Gupta
THE GENDER OF CASTE

Ajay Skaria
UNCONDITIONAL EQUALITY

Uday Kumar
WRITING THE FIRST PERSON

INDIAN HISTORY CLASSICS

Ranajit Guha
A RULE OF PROPERTY FOR BENGAL

Romila Thapar
THE PAST BEFORE US

Muzaffar Alam
THE LANGUAGES OF POLITICAL ISLAM IN INDIA *c.*1200–1800

Asok Sen
ISVARCHANDRA VIDYASAGAR AND HIS ELUSIVE MILESTONES

RANAJIT GUHA

A Rule of Property for Bengal

An Essay on the Idea of Permanent Settlement

with Introductory Essays by

PARTHA CHATTERJEE and
RUDRANGSHU MUKHERJEE

Orient BlackSwan and permanent black
in association with
ashoka UNIVERSITY

Published by

PERMANENT BLACK
'Himalayana', Mall Road, Ranikhet Cantt,
Ranikhet 263645
perblack@gmail.com

and

ORIENT BLACKSWAN PRIVATE LTD
Bangalore Bhopal Bhubaneshwar Chandigarh Chennai
Ernakulam Guwahati Hyderabad Jaipur Kolkata
Lucknow Mumbai New Delhi Patna
www.orientblackswan.com

in association with

ashoka
UNIVERSITY

ISBN 978-81-7824-482-2

First published in 1963 by Mouton & Co.,
and the Ecole des Hautes Etudes.

Second edition published in 1982 by
Orient Longman Ltd.

Typeset in Adobe Garamond Pro
by Guru Typograph Technology, Crossings Republic,
Ghaziabad 201009
Printed and bound by Manipal Technologies Limited, Manipal

To my teacher

PROFESSOR SUSHOBHAN SARKAR

who stoked so many of my first doubts

Contents

ABBREVIATIONS

B.O.R. Board of Revenue
C.O.D. Court of Directors
G.G.C. Governor-General in Council
P.D. Cobbett's *Parliamentary Debates*
P.H.E. Hansard, *The Parliamentary History of England*
P. & M. Parkes & Merivale, *Memoirs of Sir Philip Francis*. 2 vols

Foreword

Mr Guha's book is focused on the most disputed step in the agrarian field ever taken in India under British rule, the Permanent Settlement of Bengal. By Lord Cornwallis's proclamation of 1793 the State renounced for all time its right to raise the assessments already made upon the landholders. Cornwallis thus assured the proprietors that the amount of revenue to be paid by them each year would remain fixed 'for ever'. Mr Guha is concerned primarily with the intellectual origins of this bold innovation in imperial policy. The basic idea of a permanent settlement, he demonstrates, came from France, from the writings of the Physiocrats. It was sponsored in England in the 1770s and 1780s by several persons, but most particularly by the highly controversial Sir Philip Francis. What was hoped and intended was that the Permanent Settlement would have the effect of promoting the development in Bengal of a prosperous capitalist type of agriculture of the kind that had just grown up in England. But, as Mr Guha indicates, even before 1793 there were voices of warning that in India things could conceivably work out quite differently.

Mr Guha has thus shown us how French physiocratic principles were taken up by British governors with the intention of transforming a vast Asian countryside. It is a pleasure to give his concise, illuminating essay a place among the publications of the VIème Section (Sciences Economiques et Sociales) of the Ecole Pratique des Hautes Etudes, Sorbonne.

DANIEL THORNER

Directeur d'Etudes
à l'Ecole Pratique des Hautes Etudes

Preface to the Second Edition

IT IS GOOD TO SEE this humble essay come home. Conceived in a hostile academic climate on its native ground and declared as undesirable even before its birth, it saw the light of day in another land. It is entirely due to the initiative and persistence of Nirmal Chandra and Nirmalya Acharya that it has been possible at last for this orphan to return where it belongs.

Belonging is, however, a tricky notion, and the conflict of academic passions and interests could make even the best of scholars disagree about what belongs where. I am reminded, for instance, of that distinguished reviewer who found the first edition of this book wanting not so much in merit as in relevance to Indian history. If the historical origins of the concepts and theories relating to the first important – some would say, the most important – land law introduced by the British in India and the economic and political circumstances under which those were used to formulate a statute of permanent proprietary rights are of no relevance to the study of Indian history, I do not know what is.

This exercise may claim a modicum of relevance in another respect too. It addresses itself to the question of *colonialist knowledge* which Indian historiography and the social sciences will have to consider sooner or later. By tracing the intellectual ancestry of the Permanent Settlement to the very beginnings of Political Economy, it also helps to throw some light on the latter as it moves along an important, if obscure, part of its trajectory. Physiocratic thought, the precursor of Political Economy, was an implacable critique of feudalism in its native habitat and proved to be a real force in undermining the *ancien régime*. Ironically, however, while being grafted to India by the most advanced capitalist power of that age, it became instrumental in building a neo-feudal organization of landed property and in the absorption and reproduction of pre-capitalist elements in a colonial regime. In other words, a typically bourgeois form of knowledge was bent backwards to adjust itself to the relations of power in a semi-feudal society. It is this epistemological paradox that I have attempted to identify and explain in terms of the interaction between Bengal and its British rulers during the second half of the eighteenth century.

Political Economy was of course not the only body of knowledge to have suffered a sea change under conditions of colonialism. There were other systems of thought too which the western bourgeoisie had relentlessly used in their struggle against feudalism during the period of their ascendancy in their own societies but which they modified and compromised all too readily in order to find a social base for their power in the conquered lands of the Asian continent. Capitalism which had built up its hegemony in Europe by using the sharp end of Reason found it convenient to subjugate the peoples of the East by wielding the blunt head. This helped the indigenous elite as well to perpetuate their own authority in collaboration with colonialism and independently after decolonization. As the Indian experience shows, the formal termination of colonial rule, taken by itself, does little to end the government of colonialist knowledge. It has been the author's intention in this work to try and grasp some of the initial moments of that thraldom.

Canberra, April 1981 RANAJIT GUHA

Preface to the First Edition

IN HIS EARLY YOUTH the author, like many others of his generation in Bengal, grew up in the shadow of the Permanent Settlement: his livelihood, like that of his family, was derived from remote estates they had never visited; his education was orientated by the needs of a colonial bureaucracy recruiting its cadre from among the scions of Lord Cornwallis' beneficiaries; his world of culture was strictly circumscribed by the values of a middle class living off the fat of the land and divorced from the indigenous culture of its peasant masses. He had therefore learnt to regard the Permanent Settlement as a charter of social and economic stagnation. Subsequently, as a postgraduate student of Calcutta University he read about the anti-feudal ideas of Philip Francis and was at once faced with a question which the textbooks and the academics could not answer for him. How was it that the quasi-feudal land settlement of 1793 had originated from the ideas of a man who was a great admirer of the French Revolution? One could not know from the history books that such a contradiction existed and had to be explained. The manuals were satisfied that the good work England had done in India represented a series of successful experiments which had little to do with the ideas and prejudices inherited by the rulers from their European background. This view of British policy as a 'rootless blossom' is not confirmed by the history of the land law that had the longest life under the raj. The author hopes that he has been able to locate the origins of the Permanent Settlement in that confluence of ideas where the two mainstreams of English and French thought merged in the second half of the eighteenth century. There were still many local pundits in Calcutta who doubted the validity of the central thesis of this essay when it was first published as a series of articles in the Bengali journal *Parichaya* in 1956–7. Since then the publication of Professor Eric Stokes' work on the English utilitarian influence in India has made many converts. The author's own humble contribution will have served its purpose if, taken together with Professor Stokes' researches, it helps to some extent at least to redress the one-sided interpretation of British rule in India exclusively in terms of conflicts and coalitions of interests.

The author is grateful to the Department of Economics, University of Manchester, and particularly to Professor B.R. Williams for all the encouragement and facilities received for the completion of this work. He is indebted to Dr K.A. Ballhatchet, Dr George Blyn, Professor Asa Briggs, Professor Holden Furber, Dr Daniel Thorner and Dr Peter Wexler for having read through the manuscript and offering their comments.

Manchester, August 1962 RANAJIT GUHA

An Introduction to *A Rule of Property for Bengal*

PARTHA CHATTERJEE

THIS BOOK WAS FIRST published in Paris in 1963. Since then, it has been republished in separate editions in India in 1982 and the United States in 1996. That it is now being issued once more is testimony to the lasting value among scholars of Guha's first major work of historical research. *A Rule of Property for Bengal* is now a recognized classic of modern South Asian history.

In a note written in 2007, Guha explained the origins of his interest in the Permanent Settlement.[1] He was born in a middle-ranking landlord family in the district of Bakarganj, now in Bangladesh. His childhood playmates were the children of tenants and servants who mostly belonged to low, often ritually untouchable, castes. As a young boy, Guha noticed the elaborate code of authority and deference that marked the speech and comportment of the elders in his family – the masters – and those of their servants. But the innocent egalitarianism of childhood companionships hid from him the inevitable expectation that he too would one day have to join the ranks of the masters. In his early teens, however, he moved to the city of Calcutta where, after finishing high school, he joined

[1] 'Kaifiyat' (2007), reprinted in Ranajit Guha, *Chirasthayi bandobaster sutrapat* (Kolkata: Talpata, 2010), pp. 7–21.

Presidency College where he studied History and became active in the Communist Party. His childhood memories of growing up in a rural landlord's house receded into a remote corner of his mind. It was as a young communist in 1940 that he chanced upon the six volumes of the report of the Floud Commission in his father's study. Appointed by the provincial government of Fazlul Huq which had been swept into power by a massive wave of peasant agitations in eastern Bengal, the Floud Commission had recommended the abolition of the Permanent Settlement and the grant of ownership rights to tenants. Reading the report stoked the young Guha's curiosity about this colonial institution that had fundamentally shaped the contours of modern Bengali society.

Ranajit Guha spent the next decade and a half in India and Europe as a full-time member of the Communist Party of India. In 1956, when he quit the party after the Soviet invasion of Hungary, he decided to enter academic life. Looking for a project for doctoral research, he remembered the politically charged debates over the Permanent Settlement in the 1930s and 1940s. By then, the zamindari system had been abolished in both the eastern and western halves of Bengal, now constituent parts of the two independent nation-states of Pakistan and India, respectively. Theoretically at least, it was now possible to take a dispassionate view of the history of the Permanent Settlement.

It didn't quite turn out that way. Urged by a friend who was then on the editorial staff of *Parichay*, a distinguished Bengali literary journal closely associated with the Communist Party, Guha published in several instalments in 1956–7 the results of his research into the origins of the Permanent Settlement. The essays were enthusiastically received by Susobhan Sarkar, Guha's former teacher and the leading historian among leftist intellectuals in Bengal. But the party commissar charged with enforcing political correctness in the journal soon began to quibble about the relevance of all this talk about abstruse concepts of early political economy. Irked by the persistent meddling, Guha discontinued the series. When he proposed the project as a subject for doctoral research at the University of Calcutta, the leading economic historian in the History department was unimpressed. He did not think a study of mercantilist, physiocratic or free trade ideas was a fit subject of research in Indian history. As it happened, events conspired to move Ranajit Guha into an academic career in Britain. He wrote the book while holding a fellowship at the University of Manchester.

The structure of the Bengali series published in *Parichay* by and large anticipated that of *Rule of Property*, with the main focus on Philip Francis.[2] Guha found in the writings of Francis a clear, even if overly abstract, vision of a regenerated Bengali society ruled by bourgeois property holders. This was the plank on which Francis' 1776 plan for a permanent settlement with Bengal's zamindars rested. Yet the result of the permanent settlement as enacted by Cornwallis in 1793 was the creation of a quasi-feudal agrarian order of lazy, often absentee, landlords utterly uninterested in the productive improvement of their properties, squeezing the last drop of rent and illegal exactions out of their hapless tenants. Even when he took a first stab at resolving this paradox in 1956–7, Guha delved into the biographies of the key East India Company officials involved in the making of agrarian policy in Bengal. He noticed, for instance, that whereas Hastings, Verelst, Shore, or Law had spent decades in administering trade and revenue in different districts of the Company's territories, Francis had come to India carrying a systematically organized package of theoretical ideas drawn from his extensive readings of mercantilist and physiocratic literature in English and French. Later, after his return from India, Francis would become an enthusiastic supporter of the French Revolution. Guha saw in Francis an eloquent proponent of the bourgeois transformation of Bengal's economic order. Francis' plan was clear and robust in its statement of principles, but utterly short on detail. That is where his critics—wizened India hands—tore into him. Cornwallis' act of 1793, while affirming the central tenet of a permanent settlement with zamindars, was forced to incorporate

[2] Reprinted in Guha, *Chirasthayi*, pp. 23–132.

much of the accumulated knowledge from the field which, by its acknowledgement of actual institutions and practices on the ground, necessarily compromised the project of bourgeois transformation.

Guha was indeed saying that the historical mission of bourgeois property was unrealizable in Indian society in the late eighteenth century. But even in the 1956–7 version, when the signs of Marxist orthodoxy were quite clearly visible in Guha's work, he did not use the archival material merely to corroborate a commonplace Marxist formula. He went to the archive to discover, in its specific unfolding, the manner in which a law promulgating the rule of bourgeois property paradoxically resulted in a stagnant neo-feudal agrarian order. In retrospect, Guha has characterized his *Parichay* series as accurate in its perception of the paradox but insufficiently developed as a theoretically grounded problem. That had to wait until the writing of *A Rule of Property* in 1960–2. Reading the two versions side by side, the insufficiency of the earlier work is made starker by the fact that it is incomplete: the complex story of the formulation of a policy does not lead to any conclusion.

There are at least three reasons why *A Rule of Property* may have appeared so unfamiliar to its readers in the field of South Asian history that they did not quite know how to read it. First, while it announced itself as 'an essay on the idea of the Permanent Settlement', it was not by any means a standard exercise in the history of ideas, a genre of historiography that was well established, indeed fashionable, in the mid-twentieth century. Guha's book was a study of ideas as revealed through the making of administrative policy. As a result, it fell between two disciplinary stools: it was neither an intellectual history of late-eighteenth-century Britain nor a contribution to the history of the East India Company—on which there was already a divergence between the conventional British scholarship on imperial policy and an emerging Indian nationalist historiography on colonial economic exploitation. *A Rule of Property* consciously located itself at the interface between theoretical ideas and policy making. To do this, it needed to invent methods of research and exposition that were quite unusual at the time in the field of South Asian historiography.

Thus, Guha carefully traced, strand by strand, the motley assemblage of concepts and arguments of political economy that figured in the policy debates over land revenue in Bengal under the Company back to canonical writers such as Voltaire and Quesnay in France and Steuart, Pattullo, and Smith in Britain. He then made the connection between ideas and policy making by delving into the intellectual and administrative biographies of the key officials involved in the debates over revenue settlement in Bengal in the last three decades of the eighteenth century. He was keen to establish that the economic history of agrarian Bengal could not be reduced merely to an account of faction fights and interest lobbies: modern European colonial rule was also about ideas of the good society grounded in the new theoretical disciplines of knowledge. In defending his novel approach, Guha mobilized in his support a work that had appeared only three years before his. In the preface to the first edition of *A Rule of Property*, he wrote, referring to his *Parichay* series: 'Since then the publication of Professor Eric Stokes' work on the English utilitarian influence in India has made many converts. The author's own humble contribution will have served its purpose if, taken together with Professor Stokes' researches, it helps to some extent at least to redress the one-sided interpretation of British rule in India exclusively in terms of conflicts and coalitions of interests.'

Second, Guha's book was one of the earliest to pose the question of colonial knowledge as a constituent part of the history of the European Enlightenment. He did this by showing, in the specific case of the Permanent Settlement of Bengal, how a plan grounded in the thoroughly anti-feudal economic theories of French physiocracy could have consequences that were the exact opposite of those intended. But the more general implication of the work was to claim that metropolitan and colonial histories had to be written as intertwined parts of the same complex of ideas and practices. The history of British India could be regarded neither as an extended footnote to the history of Britain nor as the continuation of an endogenously generated and self-contained stream called Indian history. *A Rule of Property* was among several new works, authored by scholars such as Bernard

Cohn, Thomas Metcalf, and Burton Stein, that began in the 1960s and 1970s the critical study of the formation of a specifically colonial knowledge. This would form the launching pad for the subsequent work of postcolonial scholarship from the 1980s onward that would claim that modern disciplines of social knowledge such as political economy, liberal political theory, anthropology or international law, and indeed several branches of the natural sciences and even linguistics and comparative literature, were not produced by the internal dynamics of European society but were deeply embedded in the historical experience of Europe's empires in the Americas, Asia, and Africa.

Third, there was an implicit, virtually unstated, argument in the critical study of the idea of the Permanent Settlement of Bengal that would be vigorously pursued by Guha from the 1970s. This had to do with the degree to which colonial knowledge formations were complicit with nationalist ideology and the practices of the postcolonial Indian state. In his preface to the 1982 edition of *A Rule of Property*, Guha spoke of the blunt head of capitalism as opposed to the sharp end of Reason and remarked: 'As the Indian experience shows, the formal termination of colonial rule, taken by itself, does little to end the government of colonialist knowledge. It has been the author's intention in this work to try and grasp some of the initial moments of that thraldom.' This would become the explicit theme of Guha's work on peasant insurgency, the structure of collaboration and resistance during colonial rule, the violence of the postcolonial state, and *Subaltern Studies*.[3]

More than half a century after *A Rule of Property* was first published, it has now become a distant, even if memorable, landmark signalling

[3] Guha, *Elementary Aspects of Peasant Insurgency in Colonial India* (Delhi: Oxford University Press, 1983); Guha, *Dominance without Hegemony: History and Power in Colonial India* (Cambridge, Mass.: Harvard University Press, 1997); Guha, *The Small Voice of History: Collected Essays*, ed. Partha Chatterjee (Ranikhet: Permanent Black, 2009); Ranajit Guha, ed., *Subaltern Studies I–VI* (Delhi: Oxford University Press, 1982–90).

the beginning of a phase in the writing of South Asian history. But the misinterpretations have not ceased. A wave of 'new imperial history' is now discovering a plethora of incoherent projects, ambiguous policies, plural identities, and anxious administrators to claim that there were many imperial futures whose possibilities were rudely cut short by the virulence of anti-colonial nationalist agitation and the ill-considered haste with which metropolitan governments chose to decolonize. In a recent work, Jon Wilson accuses Ranajit Guha of presuming that 'colonial ambitions possessed a degree of coherence they did not have.' Guha had apparently failed to see that 'the forceful and strident language of political debate in London' was very different from 'the vocabulary used in Calcutta.' As an example, Wilson disputes Guha's characterization of Thomas Law as 'the brain behind the permanent settlement' and suggests that, having failed to get his proposals accepted in Calcutta, Law on his return to London managed to portray himself as the true architect of the policy.[4] As it happens, the appellation 'the brain behind the permanent settlement' is not Guha's but that of Law's contemporaries in Britain as well as Bengal, including Cornwallis himself.[5] And Guha did not make the mistake of confusing individual convictions or anxieties with the coherence of state ideology. Indeed, his method was to show how the multiplicity of individual positions, some highly coherent and others not, could produce an institutional policy that was not the sum of the individual inputs and that could have a coherent historical consequence entirely at odds with the original intent of the policy. When reading his historical sources, Guha was far more perceptive, and far less lazy, than his critics.

There is also a huge change in the historiographical context that sometimes contributes to the way this book is now read or misread. Robert Travers, for instance, after acknowledging the merit of Guha's

[4] Jon E. Wilson, *The Domination of Strangers: Modern Governance in Eastern India, 1780–1835* (London: Palgrave Macmillan, 2008), pp. 106–7.

[5] Guha, *A Rule of Property for Bengal* (Durham, NC: Duke University Press, 1996), p. 187.

work, accuses him of having been so enamoured of the modernity of British colonial rule that he could only regard as ornamental, or even disingenuous, the repeated invocation of the 'ancient constitution of India' in the writings of many Company officials, including Francis.[6] There is a major change of perspective here. Guha did indeed discuss in his book the idea of the ancient constitution of Hindostan as understood by Alexander Dow, and through him by Philip Francis. But the problem in the 1960s, especially among historians with Marxist leanings, was to investigate the possibilities of capitalist development in India before and during the period of British rule. The notion of an 'early modern' formation possessing historical possibilities that might constitute a critique of Enlightenment modernity, a trend inaugurated by John Pocock's revival of the idea of the ancient constitution and his identification of a conservative enlightenment, were not on the historiographical horizon when Guha was writing his book.[7] Many in India would argue that the more relevant problem for research is still that of capitalist modernity and not the ancient constitution.

That in itself is good enough reason for republishing this book.

Kolkata
4 April 2016

[6] Robert Travers, *Ideology and Empire in Eighteenth Century India: The British in Bengal* (Cambridge: Cambridge University Press, 2007), pp. 16–17.

[7] J.G.A. Pocock, *The Ancient Constitution and the Feudal Law: A Study of English Historical Thought in the Seventeenth Century* (Cambridge: Cambridge University Press, 1967); *The Machiavellian Moment: Florentine Political Thought and the Atlantic Republican Tradition* (Princeton: Princeton University Press, 1975); *The Enlightenment of Edward Gibbon* (Cambridge: Cambridge University Press, 1999).

A Settlement in Time

RUDRANGSHU MUKHERJEE

I CAN DISTINCTLY RECALL when I first heard of *A Rule of Property for Bengal*. It was in Barun De's office at the Indian Institute of Management, located at the time in Emerald Bower on the Barrackpore Trunk Road. I was then a first year History Honours student at Presidency College. It was September 1970 and the college had been shut *sine die* because of student violence. Barun De had taken on the task of educating me in the reading of history. That morning, among the many books he said I *must* read, was this book by Ranajit Guha. A few weeks later my teacher Ashin Das Gupta, a historian whose approach to the subject and to its teaching was very different from De's, mentioned the book and suggested that I read it. Two such recommendations from two mentors were too much to resist. I asked Barun De where I could get hold of a copy; he lent me his.

Two impressions remain from the first sighting. One was how beautifully it had been produced by Mouton, the reputed academic press based in the Hague: it looked like no other history book I had seen (or have since); and two, the Preface was written in the third person ('In his early youth the author, like many others of his generation in Bengal, grew up in the shadow of the Permanent Settlement.'). The

I am grateful to Semanti Ghosh, Dipesh Chakrabarty, and Neeladri Bhattacharya for their comments on earlier drafts. All errors are mine alone.

subtitle of the book, *An Essay on the Idea of Permanent Settlement*, puzzled me. I knew of the Permanent Settlement as an important, indeed pivotal, chapter of Bengal's agrarian history, an area of learning which brought to my mind books like those written by Irfan Habib and N.K. Sinha. What had ideas got to do with agrarian history? Lay claim as much as I might to intellectual precocity, the history of ideas was for me – I was all of eighteen at the time – alien territory. I started reading the book with a sense of awe, puzzlement, and trepidation. I was bowled over by it, not because I understood everything in it – let alone comprehending the significance of its arguments – but because of being overwhelmed by how well the book was written, by the sheer elegance and beauty of Ranajit Guha's prose. Re-reading the book to write this Introduction, it strikes me that many of its sentences and turns of phrase have long been embedded in my memory ('. . . made it erratic like a child's first attack on a meccano set'; 'Pioneers seldom make a virtue of patience'; and so on). Could history really be written with such style and grace, I asked myself.

It was the first of many readings. It took me a few years to understand the significance of the historiographical intervention that Guha had made, and to appreciate the originality of his approach. The historiographical context in which the book was written is suggested in the closing sentences of its Introduction:

> The image of 'an ant-heap with the human ants hurrying in long files along their various paths' had come to be fastened upon the East India House long before it was made famous in our time as a description of the political scene during George III's reign. What, however, the practitioners of the gentle art of prosopography have not sufficiently emphasized in their writings on Indian history, is that the 'human ants' were also thinking animals, and that the intellectual climate of the late eighteenth century was vigorous enough to have, under certain circumstances, a positive influence on the form and order of interests, much as a hard-blowing wind would shape the dunes.

The full import of these sentences dawned on me much later, after I became familiar with Lewis Namier's *The Structure of Politics at the Accession of George III* (1929). The telling quotation regarding the ant-heap, not acknowledged by Guha,[1] had been taken from the Preface of Namier's *magnum opus*.

In his analysis of mid-eighteenth-century British politics, Namier had removed the influence of ideas. Those who entered politics, he argued, were driven by self-interest: 'the greatest common good is to be reached by every man pursuing his own individual advantage.'[2] Self-interest occasionally made individuals come together to form groups and factions, and this was the stuff of politics, not ideas or ideals. As he put it in his inimitable way, 'Men went there [Parliament] 'to make a figure', and no more dreamt of a seat in the House in order to benefit humanity than a child dreams of a birthday cake that others may eat it.'[3]

In relation to modern Indian history, the first subject to feel the impact of Namier's approach was the English East India Company, most notably in the work of Lucy Sutherland, one of Namier's principal acolytes. Sutherland – or Dame Lucy, as she was famously known in her time in Oxford – analysed the Company as a 'vast network of interests.'[4] In her magisterial study of the Company in the eighteenth century she demonstrated the way these networks were formed and how they influenced decision-making. Summing up the process that resulted in the passing of the Regulating Act in 1772, she wrote, 'The pressure for action of one section of the ministry; the desire of the king for strong action; the parliamentary adroitness of North and that section of the ministry which stood for compromise and modified reform; the disinterested anger of public opinion and the far from

[1] Possibly an uncharacteristic oversight; more likely because the image, having passed into historical lore, did not seem to Guha to require explicit citation.

[2] Lewis Namier, *The Structure of Politics at the Accession of George III* (1929; reprinted London, 1975), p. 18.

[3] Ibid., p. 2.

[4] Lucy Sutherland, *The East India Company in Eighteenth Century Politics* (Oxford, 1952), p. vi.

disinterested fury of disappointed shareholders and speculators had produced a demand for parliamentary action which a few individuals then toiled to put into a form capable of administrative application.' These factors led to the formulation and the passing of an Act that was, according to Sutherland, nothing short of 'a revolution in policy'.[5] There was, however, not even the whisper of an idea in the making of revolution. Already, by the late 1950s, dissatisfaction had begun creeping in among some historians in relation to looking at politics and policy-making as being bereft of ideas. One of the earliest to analyse the influence of ideas on the making of policies in India had been Eric Stokes, to whose book Guha made reference in his Preface.[6]

Guha's book, as its subtitle indicated, directly confronted the Namierite approach in relation to the Permanent Settlement, a piece of policy-making that had initiated a revolution in agrarian Bengal. Guha showed that the principal advocates of the Permanent Settlement – Alexander Dow, Henry Pattullo, Philip Francis, Thomas Law, and Lord Cornwallis – were brought together neither by common interest nor by belonging to a common faction. Guha noted that Pattullo was not involved in Indian affairs. Dow and Francis were friends and had the support of the same group, but the former was a Mercantilist, and the latter a Physiocrat like Pattullo. Cornwallis and Law were Free Traders and were tied as patron and protégé. Francis and Cornwallis, despite championing the same agrarian policy, hated each other. Law inherited some of Francis' ideas but owed the three key appointments of his career to Francis' enemies – Eyre Coote, Warren Hastings, and Cornwallis. The differences were vast, and yet in the matter of one specific policy their ideas converged. This convergence happened, Guha argued, because their ideas 'lay on the same axis as what was indeed one of the most forward moving trends of the age – the transition from Mercantilism to Free Trade.' The

[5] Ibid., p. 268.

[6] *The English Utilitarians and India* (Oxford, 1959).

movement was from Dow, a Mercantilist, to Pattullo and Francis, both Physiocrats; and finally to the Free Traders, Law and Cornwallis.[7]

The initial impulse to write on the Permanent Settlement came to Guha not as the need for historiographical intervention but to solve for himself a puzzle or a paradox. In the only autobiographical piece he has ever written,[8] Guha says that when reading the economic history of Bengal (as a postgraduate student in the University of Calcutta), he began to realize that Philip Francis had recommended the Permanent Settlement out of eagerness to introduce a form of capitalist farming in Bengal's agriculture. Yet the reality around Guha in the late 1930s and early 1940s, and his reading of the Floud Commission Report (1940), had convinced him that the Permanent Settlement had perpetuated a system of semi-feudal exploitation and culture in rural Bengal. The gap between the original vision and the historical actuality had puzzled the young scholar. His incomplete Bengali essay chased this paradox and *A Rule of Property* resolved it.

It is not surprising therefore that the personality and ideas of Philip Francis occupy an important place in Guha's book. Two central chapters comprise a detailed study of his career and ideology, showing how these influenced the comprehensive plan Francis presented in 1776 for settlement of the revenues of Bengal, Bihar, and Orissa. Guha noted that Francis' policy recommendations were not only inspired by Physiocratic ideas on the importance of agriculture but also by 'the central figure in the English agrarian scene at this time . . . the gentleman farmer; he was the agent of all improvement – it was his capital that was invested in the land, his enterprise that made it productive, and often his inventiveness that provided it with new

[7] Ranajit Guha, *A Rule of Property for Bengal: An Essay on the Idea of Permanent Settlement* (Paris, 1963), pp. 18–19.

[8] Ranajit Guha, 'Kaifiyat' (Explanation), in *Chirosthayi Bandobast er Sutrapat* (Origins of the Permanent Settlement) (Calcutta, 2010). The book was a reprint of the original Bengali essay on which *Rule of Property* came to be based. By way of an introduction, Guha explicated how he came to write that essay and why it remained incomplete.

techniques.' Francis conceived of the Bengal zamindar in the image of the English eighteenth-century gentleman-farmer.[9] The underlying assumption of his recommendations was the belief that the landed aristocracy of Bengal still retained 'great potentialities of leadership'. In spite of being an admirer of the French Revolution, Francis was a great believer in inequality. This was an integral aspect of his Physiocratic intellectual inheritance.[10]

He had arrived in Calcutta in October 1774 and his famous plan was dated January 1776. Most of the intervening fifteen months had been spent in Calcutta; he had little or no first-hand experience of the rural world of Bengal: 'his knowledge of India . . . was bookish and second-hand,' Guha noted.[11] So it is legitimate to ask how he formed his particular image of the Bengal zamindar. Was it purely the product of an imagination coloured by Physiocratic notions and biases? Without underestimating the formative influence of Physiocracy on Francis' economic and social views, Guha then drew attention to what Francis actually learnt about the realities of rural Bengal. The principal informant to Francis was Boughton Rous, who had been appointed to Rajshahi in 1769 under Verelst's plan of supervisorship – officers having been put in place in the late 1760s to keep an eye on land revenue collection and the activities of the zamindars. Rajshahi was a rich and fertile region which was not as badly affected by the famine of 1770 as some other areas of Bengal. Large parts of the district were owned and ruled by an unusually powerful landed family whose estate covered around 13,000 square miles. This was the family of Rani Bhabani who, during Rous' time, 'managed her estate like a queen . . . Her charity had its colossal expression in the building of temples and the digging of sweet water lakes and [this] made her the very symbol of benevolence so often associated with the better type of zamindars in that age.' From Rous, with whom he worked very closely, Francis heard about Rani Bhabani,

[9] Guha, *Rule of Property*, p. 105.
[10] Ibid., p. 109.
[11] Ibid., p. 49.

of her attempts at improvement and welfare, of her resistance to the harassment of the East India Company, and of her stonewalling the farming system and its attendant evils.[12] The work of the Rani had an enduring impact on Francis, contributing much to his envisioning the Bengal zamindar as a dark variant of the improving English capitalist landlord.

Not all the advocates of the Permanent Settlement were, as already noted, Physiocrats; neither were they driven by the ideological passions of Francis. What brought them together in advocating a common policy aimed at the agricultural development of Bengal was their recognition of the harm that the farming system was doing to the agrarian economy, and their 'common veneration of private property".[13] The Bengal countryside would, to use W.W. Hunter's telling phrase, be transformed by 'the magic touch of property'.[14] This was the accepted assumption of all proponents of the Permanent Settlement, overriding their other ideological differences.

His analysis of the ideological trajectory of the idea of the Permanent Settlement did not quite answer the initial question that had set the young Guha off on his intellectual journey. How did a policy intending to improve Bengal's agriculture through capitalist farming end up as a mockery of itself? Why did Francis' improving landlord turn out parasitic? Guha found a clue to his answer in a passage in Pattullo's essay of 1772. Writing about the long-term prospects of the Permanent Settlement, Pattullo says: 'Sensible also of the great advantages of property, however small, with fixed family residences and the conveniences of British furniture and way of living, they (the

[12] Ibid., pp. 56–60.

[13] Ibid., p. 17.

[14] The phrase was used by W.W. Hunter in 'A Dissertation on Landed Property and Land Rights in Bengal at the End of the Eighteenth Century', *Bengal Manuscript Records*, vol. 1 (London, 1874), pp. 82–3, quoted in Asok Sen, 'The Bengal Economy and Rammohun Roy', in V.C. Joshi (ed.), *Rammohun Roy and the Process of Modernization in India* (Delhi, 1975), p. 113.

people of Bengal) will without doubt relish them, and thereby open a new branch to the company, of carrying thither British commodities, while they again will find sufficient returns for all, in the growing produce of their country.'[15] Guha realized that the plan 'of carrying thither British commodities' – in other words the establishment of a colonial market in India – ran counter to the project of initiating capitalist development in agriculture that had inspired Francis.[16] Elaborating the point, Guha wrote:

> Conceived, in its final form, as a policy of capitalist enterprise in agriculture, the Permanent Settlement needed a sovereign home market for its potentialities to mature to their full extent. Under the circumstances, however, this was not feasible. For the progress of the Industrial Revolution in England was at the same time pressing its own demands on India ... In the unequal contest that followed, the weaker capitalism had to yield. During the nineteenth century India gradually emerged as a vast agrarian hinterland of the British Empire. Correspondingly, the Permanent Settlement, too, assumed the character of a pre-capitalist system of landownership, mocking its own original image ...[17]

Guha had thus found an answer to the conundrum that had bothered him as a young man. In the process of arriving at this answer, he had carried out a significant historiographical intervention. Far in advance of his time, he had demonstrated how to study the history of an idea. He had done something more – and this is where the text of *A Rule of Property* transcends its own historiographical context. In his Preface to the second edition of the book (1981), Guha drew his readers' attention to this aspect: 'It [this book] addresses itself to the question of *colonialist knowledge*.'[18] It was Guha's belief that the book, by tracing the intellectual lineage of the Permanent Settlement to Physiocratic thought, had gone back to the very beginnings of political

[15] Guha, *Rule of Property*, p. 149. I have kept the passage as Guha quoted it, though in the original the last word is 'industry' and not 'country'.

[16] Ibid., p. 49.

[17] Ibid., p. 186.

[18] Emphasis in the original.

economy. Physiocracy was a critique of feudalism in France and had thus helped to undermine the *ancien régime*. But when Britain, 'the most advanced capitalist power of that age', had grafted Physiocracy to India, a powerful intellectual current had become its own caricature: 'it became instrumental in building a neo-feudal organization of landed property and in the absorption and reproduction of pre-capitalist elements in a colonial regime.' Guha's reiterated the point that 'a typically bourgeois form of knowledge was bent backwards to adjust itself to the relations of power in a semi-feudal society,' and it was this 'epistemological paradox' that he had attempted to trace and explain through the idea of the Permanent Settlement. There were other bodies of knowledge, as Guha noted, which had been imported to India during British rule – knowledge that the bourgeoisie in the West had used in its struggle against feudalism. But in India under colonial rule those bodies of knowledge 'suffered a sea change' as alien rulers sought to find a social base for their power.

Through these words, written at the beginning of the 1980s, Guha was alerting his readers to his new intellectual concerns. These were to be manifest in his second book, *Elementary Aspects of Peasant Insurgency in Colonial India* (1983), and in the first six volumes of Subaltern Studies.[19] One crucial aspect of *Elementary Aspects* and the Subaltern Studies project had been an analysis of the relations of power in colonial India. The study of power and dominance in the rural world carried, for Guha, resonances from his childhood. In the autobiographical fragment referred to he had remembered groups of people around him and his family, and including some of his playmates, who were invariably referred to as *praja* (subjects); and the latter referred to Guha's family (including the child Ranajit) as *manib* (master). The word *praja* had become an integral part of Guha's memory – a sign of the power and dominance that zamindars, products one and all of the Permanent Settlement, had enjoyed and

[19] Amartya Sen, in his Foreword to a 1996 Duke University Press reprint of *A Rule of Property*, had drawn attention to the links between the book and Guha's later work.

exercised in the rural world of Bengal. When he studied the idea of the Permanent Settlement, Guha saw for himself the contrast between the original vision of the improving capitalist landlord and the reality of the parasitic zamindar who exercised dominance in Bengal. Guha's work on peasant insurgency and the politics of the subaltern classes would have such dominance as its context, even perhaps as its *raison d'être.* The dominance of ruling elites generally, as well as of the Indian elite in particular, became a major theme of Guha's work. Elites in India found hegemony to be perpetually elusive because 'Capitalism which had built up its hegemony in Europe by using the sharp end of Reason found it convenient to subjugate the peoples of the East by wielding the blunt head.'[20] *A Rule of Property* captures most tellingly and memorably the initial moment in that process of distortion.

It is good to have one of the best books on modern Indian history available again in print.

February 2016

[20] Guha, Preface to the Second Edition of *A Rule of Property* (1981), p. 7.

1

Introduction

THE PERMANENT SETTLEMENT OF Bengal had a very long lease of life which, like that of the Indian elephant, was matched by an exceptionally prolonged gestation. It remained in force for about one hundred and sixty years as an act of law, and the ideas which had gone into its making took over twenty years to assume the form in which they were finally incorporated in Lord Cornwallis's proclamation of 22 March 1793. The first three articles of this proclamation were as follows:

> Article I. In the original regulations for the decennial settlement of the public revenues of Bengal, Bahar and Orissa . . . it was notified to the proprietors of land with or on behalf of whom a settlement might be concluded, that the jumma assessed upon the lands, under those regulations, would be continued after the expiration of the ten years, and remain unalterable for ever; provided such continuance should meet with the approbation of the honourable court of directors for the affairs of the East Indian Company, and not otherwise.
>
> Article II. The Marquis Cornwallis, knight of the most noble order of the garter, governor general in council, now notifies to all zemindars, independent talookdars, and other actual proprietors of land, in the provinces of Bengal, Bahar and Orissa, that he has been empowered by the honourable court of directors for the affairs of the East India Company, to declare the jumma, which has been or may be assessed upon their lands under the regulations above-mentioned, fixed for ever.

> Article III. The governor general in council accordingly declares to the zemindars, independent talookdars and other actual proprietors of land, with or on behalf of whom a settlement has been concluded under the regulations above-mentioned, that at the expiration of the term of the settlement, no alteration will be made in the assessment which they have respectively engaged to pay, but that they and their heirs and lawful successors will be allowed to hold their estates at such assessment for ever.[1]

The central theme of this policy, 'assessment for ever', had already been vaguely anticipated by some of the junior officials in the East India Company's service during the period separating the assumption of Diwani from the appointment of Warren Hastings to the governorship of Bengal. It was first formulated as a policy recommendation by Alexander Dow in 1770. It was the thesis of Henry Pattullo's *Essay* published two years later. In 1776 Philip Francis made it the very basis of his famous revenue plan, and he went on arguing for its acceptance during the rest of his term in office until 1781. The idea was incorporated, at least in its essence, in both Fox's bill which did not pass and in Pitt's which received Parliament's assent as the India Act of 1784. During the second half of the decade it was adopted by Thomas Law for his mukarari experiments in Bihar, given legal sanction by Cornwallis in his rules for a decennial settlement issued in the winter of 1789–90, and finally entered into the statute book as Regulation I of 1793. Dow, Pattullo, Francis, Law and Cornwallis were thus its leading champions in the eighteenth century. In spite of all their doctrinal differences they had between them some common area of agreement in two respects: first, in conceiving of the Permanent Settlement as a clean break with what was the basic agrarian policy of the Company's government in Bengal up to 1785; and secondly, in justifying their alternative as an indispensable measure to ensure the right of private property in land.

[1] *Fifth Report*, Firminger (ed.), vol. I, pp. 35–6.

To turn first to the negative view taken by all of them of the early revenue policies. This followed from the notion then held by most critics of the East India Company that the conduct of its affairs in Bengal was singularly lacking in consistency and orientation. The piecemeal and haphazard growth of power for nearly thirty years after Plassey created a lag between conquest and sovereignty, between the formal accession to power and the decision to execute it, and this, in its turn, seriously weakened the control of policies and made it erratic like a child's first attack on a meccano set. Clive and his colleagues of the Select Committee confessed to this weakness when they wrote in 1767:

> When we embraced the political System now established it was with diffidence: when we entered upon the correction of abuses, and the punishment of misconduct it was with Reluctance . . .[2]

It was the intention of the Select Committee to suggest by these remarks that the situation had radically improved since they took command. In reality, however, the regime of 'diffidence and reluctance' continued for long afterwards. Philip Francis was on very strong grounds when, about a decade later, he condemned the 'short-lived fluctuating administrations' which cared only 'to provide for the demands of the day.'[3] And a much more level-headed person, John Shore, had exactly the same complaint to make and in stronger terms as late as 1789. 'Our administration has heretofore been fluctuating and uncertain,' he said; 'an idea of improvement has been hastily adopted, unsteadily pursued, afterwards abandoned from a supposed defect in principle; new measures have been substituted, followed and relinquished, with the same facility; and the natives, from these variations, with every succession of men expect a change of system.'[4]

[2] *Fort William – India House Correspondence*, vol. V, p. 276.
[3] *Sir Philip Francis's Minutes*, pp. 36–7.
[4] Firminger, vol. II, p. 60.

What this meant in terms of policy is perhaps best illustrated by the early Bengal regulations. The way these go on repeating, amending, overlapping, cancelling each other from season to season and year to year, the ingenuity with which their makers continue to miss the wood for the trees, their lack of consistency and often of purpose, the signatures they bear of widely divergent views and interests – all this makes up a perfect picture of a rudderless boat blown by every wind and turned by every tide. There is no commentary on early British rule more devastating than Colebrooke's *Digest*.

Where empiricism and short-sightedness hurt most was the new sector of the economy – the revenues of Bengal. The Company had come to acquire this in successive stages during the eight years since the conquest, beginning first with the revenues of a single district and eventually extending it to cover the entire Presidency as a result of the grant of Diwani. This was an immense addition to income, but proved to be an equally great embarrassment to those who were entitled to it. They knew nothing about the agrarian system of India. For most of the English officers sent out to the districts to manage the collection of revenues, it was a journey into the unknown in more than one sense. At every step they came up against quasi-feudal rights and obligations which defied any attempt at interpretation in familiar western terms. The hieroglyphics of Persian estate accounts baffled them. It was only a part of the difficulty that they could not easily master the languages in which the ancient and medieval texts relating to the laws of property were written; for tradition recorded only in memory and customs embedded in a variety of local usages wielded an authority equal to that of any written code. It is therefore easy to understand why at this very early stage of its rule the Company did not succeed in evolving a coherent and uniform revenue policy for Bengal.

Firminger joins issue with Macaulay in trying to set straight the record of revenue administration for the period before Hastings's rule. He emphasizes the value of the experience gained by the English in the districts placed under their charge before 1765 and subsequently in the Diwani portion of the country during the seven years after that date.[5] He has in fact sufficiently established that a good deal of hard thinking and honest effort went into the local administration of this period. It has not been proved, however, that these experiments had any appreciable influence on the making of policy at the centre of power.

For, in the first place, three of the four pre-Diwani districts, that is, all except Burdwan, were special cases: the zamindari of Twenty-four Parganas because of its proximity to Calcutta and dependence on the life of the garrison town; Chittagong because of its situation as a border district far from Calcutta and Murshidabad; and Midnapur because of the military operations still in progress there. The experiences acquired in these districts were not typical and therefore, could hardly serve as a guide to administration elsewhere.

Secondly, there was the very serious problem of communication limiting the influence of local experience on the formulation of policy. Firminger's estimate of the validity of early administrative experience is based on the assumption that it percolated through the proper channels to reach the higher level of authority and was there distilled and integrated into the general conduct of government. In reality nothing of the sort happened, for between the base and the summit the process was subject to disturbances all along the line.

The tenure of the Company's local officers was often far too short to permit experience to accumulate to a point where it could serve any useful purpose. Midnapur was placed under the charge of six Residents following each other in quick succession during a period of five years between 1761 and 1765. Among the officers of the pre-Diwani period Verelst alone was fortunate enough to be left in charge of a single district, Chittagong, for an uninterrupted term of five years. He was thus given time to assimilate and sort out what he had learnt and no wonder that he promptly and decisively put it to use during his next assignment in Burdwan.

[5] Firminger, vol. I, pp. cxviii–cxix, clxvi.

There was, no doubt, a definite improvement in this respect after Diwani. But then for the entire period up to 1772 there were two kinds of conflict hindering communication: first, the want of co-operation between the English revenue officer and their native assistants; and secondly, the disputes between the Council and the Select Committee. In everything except purely military operations the Englishmen in the district had to depend on the native amils – on their local contacts, their familiarity with the language, their expertise in matters concerning the land revenue and agricultural practice. These, however, were a precious monopoly which the amils were not keen to share with others. At a time when the landlords were as wary of the Supervisors and Collectors as some tend to be today of the Income Tax Officer, a knowledge of the *subhankari* system of computation and of the esoteric science of estate accounting could easily be sold for a good price. Complaints against the amils, about their frauds, prevarications and downright villainy, poured into the offices of the Resident at Durbar and Controlling Council of Revenue at Murshidabad. The Supervisors were powerless against such abuse, because the state of diarchy always made it possible for the amils to seek shelter behind the authority of the Naib Diwan, Muhammad Reza Khan. It did not make matters any easier that Richard Becher, the Resident, often ranged himself on the side of the alleged culprits. The records of the period are full of masses of information collected by the district officers and faithfully compiled by them in their letters to the higher authorities at Murshidabad, but as a result of the division of authority which reached down to the lowest level of the administration little was done to process it all into the stuff of policy.

Equally unhelpful was the dispute between the highest organs of the Company's government in Bengal – the Council and the Select Committee.[6] The latter had been created as a sort of emergency device to assist Clive who had judiciously demarcated the respective areas of

[6] *Fort William – India House Correspondence*, vol. V, pp. 25–6, 67–8, 278.

responsibility of the two bodies. The Council was entrusted with the management of commercial affairs and the revenue of the pre-Diwani territories and the Select Committee with the conduct of foreign affairs and the administration of the Diwani portion of the country. The seed of discord was sown by the Court of Directors when after Clive's departure they took it upon themselves to continue the Select Committee and restate its functions *vis-à-vis* the Council. All that they achieved by this was to confound the jurisdictions of the two bodies and thus give the government the unhappy appearance of the bird described in a Sanskrit fable as having two heads, each intensely jealous of the other. Verelst, who managed to escape trouble by retiring just in time, nevertheless saw that it was coming. 'The Court of Directors themselves,' he wrote the week before laying down office, 'are at a loss where the precise line of each is drawn, sometimes attributing to the Council what belongs to the Committee and again transferring from one to the other without rule or distinction.'[7] His successor was left to face the consequences: while the country lay writhing in the grip of a famine and crying out for prompt and radical measures of relief, the two highest councils of government kept themselves busy denouncing each other.

Thus during the seven years following the grant of Diwani contradictions within the administrative apparatus itself made the emergence of a unified policy almost impossible. Their effect was, at the base, to inhibit contact between the English officials and native functionaries; at the intermediate level, to hinder the process of digesting whatever experience was gathered; and at the top, to cut off the perspective for broad and far-sighted decisions. They created bottlenecks which frustrated even the best of intentions. Harry Verelst's plan of supervisorships was one of the worst victims of such circumstances. It was an ambitious programme in which the author had packed all his great understanding of the problems of

[7] Verelst, *View of the Rise, Progress and Present State of the English Government in Bengal etc.*, Appendix, p. 124.

rural Bengal. But it was a little too ambitious. The long list of tasks assigned to the Supervisors was, indeed, a very good index of how little had been done so far, but it was in any case beyond the power of any single body of men, as inexperienced as the Supervisors were, to carry them out within a reasonable time even if they were allowed to work under much better conditions. What, however, condemned this project to remain on record more as a monumental promise than an achievement was again another characteristic breakdown in the channel of authority.[8] The plan was adopted by the Council on 16 August 1769. But just as the Supervisors were getting ready to proceed to the districts, the Resident at Durbar, Richard Becher, advised that they should not do so until the end of the current fiscal year. Otherwise, he feared, there might be difficulties with the amils and consequently in the collection of revenues. This was in October. Two months later the Council was still explaining to the Directors why the plan could not be put into operation until the following summer. Eventually when the officers reached their stations it was about a year to fourteen months after their appointment. The difficulty they had now to contend with was much more formidable than the dark intrigues of the amils. It was the Great Bengal Famine itself which had just begun to stalk the countryside, reducing the validity of Verelst's elaborate directives to that of an exercise. Had they been allowed to take up their duties earlier as originally proposed, they would have been better equipped to cope with the calamity and perhaps avoid some of the costly mistakes into which they blundered out of sheer inexperience.

The memory of the famine of 1770 was still fresh when Dow and Pattullo wrote. It was in fact at its worst when Dow's *Hindustan* appeared. Pattullo, on his part, might have learnt about it from the massive details of death pouring into the press on both sides of the Channel from writers as well known as the Abbé Raynal and as

[8] *Fort William – India House Correspondence*, vol. V, pp. 616–17, Firminger, vol. I, pp. cxc–cxcvi.

undistinguished as 'J.C.' who contributed a lengthy account to the *Gentleman's Magazine* of 1771. The first two advocates of Permanent Settlement both regarded the famine as the most conclusive evidence of the worthlessness of the existing economic policies and the best reason that could be there for seeking an alternative in terms of a more stable and comprehensive land settlement. But the argument had to shift to another plane when Warren Hastings took over from Cartier. For whatever else might be said of Hastings's rule, he could by no means be accused of lacking a sense of direction. He was indeed the first English governor in Bengal to succeed in working out a unified policy of rural administration. Only he did it on the basis of what turned out to be an utterly disastrous principle. This was to auction the estates at the end of each term of settlement and farm them out to the highest bidders for leases not extending beyond five years. To contemporaries this was known as the 'farming system'.

The theory of Permanent Settlement, in the hands of its later champions, had its edge sharply turned against the farming system. It is not that the mistakes of the period between the assumption of Diwani and the outbreak of the famine were spared criticism. It was described in Francis's plan as 'that period of delirium', and in a paper found among his manuscripts as 'the period of Darkness'.[9] But on the whole the concentration of attack was on the policies of Warren Hastings who, according to his critics, was guilty of extending legal sanction to an abuse he should have used his authority to end at once. The settlement made by the Committee of Circuit which inaugurated the farming system for the greater part of Bengal, was Francis's *bête noire*, and innumerable folio pages are devoted to its condemnation in his minutes. His plan for Bengal was in every respect a total and deliberate contradiction of all that the mode of revenue-farming stood for. Later on, Thomas Law was to work out a method of representing the opposition between the two systems in a graphic form. His

[9] *Sir Philip Francis's Minutes*, p. 36. 'Hints on the Revenue', *Francis MSS* 74 (3) 53.

letters to Shore on this subject were, on each page, divided into two columns – 'farming' and 'mukarari', and went on to state, paragraph by paragraph, how for everything that the former could do, the other could do better.

In the light of this criticism, the charge of inconstancy in policies assumed a new and deeper meaning. The objection was no longer to 'fluctuations' in the old sense, for Warren Hastings was a man of strong determination and made it a point to stick to his principles. The argument now was that a lack of permanence was inherent in the farming system itself. The farmers had no abiding interest in the lands settled with them; their leases were far too short to permit this; and all that was achieved in this process was the expropriation of zamindars of long standing. In short, the consequence of revenue farming was the subversion of property and there could be no form of instability more dangerous than this. By contrast, it was claimed by the advocates of Permanent Settlement that they had a policy which was based on what they called 'the principle of property'.

What brought these men together and united them in one school of thought was thus not merely a common aversion to the existing policies, but also a common veneration of private property. They all shared the belief that a sound administration must have the security of landownership as its basis, and nothing but a permanent settlement could ensure this. In other words, Bengali society was to be fashioned after the image of Whig England. Francis did in fact often speak of the Company's territories as an 'estate.'[10] 'We had an estate in Bengal,' he said, 'the greatest, the most improveable, and the most secure, that ever belonged to any state.' But it was ruined by the rapacity of imprudent farmers: 'the Company's servants must be supposed to have considered Bengal as an estate, to which the Company had no

[10] *Sir Philip Francis's Minutes*, pp. i, vii, 21.

good title, which they had no hopes of possessing long, and which it was their interest to exhaust and make the most of, while they had it in their power.' Only Permanent Settlement could rehabilitate it now: 'Considering the country as our estate, there is no other way to make it productive.' England was thus required to assume the responsibilities of an improving landlord in Bengal. The distance between the two countries and the inadvisability of colonization made it necessary that the property should be entrusted to the care of a class of native entrepreneurs who had solid interests in the land and were politically reliable. This alone could establish 'the permanence of dominion'.

But the recognition of property as the basic principle of government was only the greatest common measure of their agreement. About the uses of property the champions of Permanent Settlement held widely divergent views. In what way was the establishment of permanent proprietary rights in land going to help? They believed, and the history of British rule in India has eminently confirmed them, that this would make it possible for the raj to strike its roots deeply into the loyalty of its beneficiaries, the new landowning class. But the social and economic considerations in terms of which this political perspective was worked out proved little identity of outlook. Dow wanted private property to be made secure because this, he thought, would strengthen the pillars of society. Francis also shared this social attitude, but, like Pattullo, he regarded property primarily as a stimulus to agriculture. Cornwallis, going further, visualized it as the spring of all economic improvement. For Law, it was important above all as the most effective method of creating a land-market.

These cannot be dismissed just as minor differences in emphasis. They proceeded, in fact, from divergent, and even opposing, intellectual affiliations. Dow was a mercantilist; Pattullo and Francis were physiocrats; Law, and to a lesser degree Cornwallis, free traders. If in spite of these differences their ideas came to converge on one common and irresistible solution for Indian policy, it was because they lay on the same axis as what was indeed one of the most forward-moving trends in that age – the transition from mercantilism to free trade, a movement which had reached its final phase in the last quarter of the eighteenth century. The stress of the change is clearly visible in Dow and Francis. The former, with his anti-monopolistic bias and emphasis on agriculture, approximated the physiocratic position as closely as could be done without giving up mercantilism altogether. The latter, with all the cobwebs of bullionism still clinging to him, manages to emerge on firm physiocratic grounds. The departure is complete when the last two of the group join in and continue to move towards the other end of the process. Thus the idea of Permanent Settlement, relayed from stage to stage during two decades, passed through the whole gamut of contemporary economic thought, but never lost its direction. It was this that gave it a driving force which was expressed in its extreme form by Francis in terms of what read like a dogma, and by Cornwallis in terms of what looked like overbearing authority. Pioneers seldom make a virtue of patience.

It would have been satisfying perhaps if it could be proved that the pattern of ideas characterizing the school of Permanent Settlement conformed to a pattern of common interests. But this cannot be done. The intellectual sympathies uniting the five leading architects of this policy cut across their partisan alliances in other respects. In terms of interests they fall into three distinct classes. One of them, Henry Pattullo, was in no way involved in Indian affairs. Dow and Francis were friends and enjoyed the support of closely allied groups. Cornwallis and Law stood in the relation of patron and protégé. Again, the two among them who could be best described as politicians, that is, Francis and Cornwallis, hated each other. The incompatibility between doctrinal and personal affiliations is perhaps best illustrated in the case of Thomas Law, who inherited from Francis the essentials of the theory underlying his mukarari system but owed all the three key appointments of his career to Francis's enemies: to Sir Eyre Coote who recommended him for the Company's service;[11] to Hastings

[11] *Gentleman's Magazine*, New Series, vol. II, p. 437.

who put him in charge of Gaya where he first made his name as an officer of great reforming zeal and initiative;[12] and to Cornwallis who promoted him to the Board of Revenue and thus made it possible for him to apply his Bihar experiences to the formulation of policies for the entire Presidency. The image of 'an ant-heap with the human ants hurrying in long files along their various paths' had come to be fastened upon the East India House long before it was to be made famous in our time as a description of the political scene during George's reign. What, however, the practitioners of the gentle art of prosopography have not sufficiently emphasized in their writings on Indian history is that the 'human ants' were also thinking animals, and that the intellectual climate of the late eighteenth century was vigorous enough to have, under certain circumstances, a positive influence on the form and order of interests, much as a hard-blowing wind would shape the dunes.

[12] *Law*, An Answer to Mr Princeps's Observations on the Mocurrery System, p. 62.

2

Early Departures, 1769–1772

Rumours about abuses in the East India Company's administration in Bengal had been current in London society ever since 1765. But it was not until 1772 that the stuff for scandal crystallized into public opinion. The impact of the famine on popular imagination, the financial difficulties of the Company, the threat of a French invasion of India, the venom of Bolts's pen, the rise of groups representing the interests of the Company's servants returned from the East, and the realignment of opposition forces inside Parliament – all contributed to make the East India question into a major political issue.[1] Out of the welter of motives and pressures which were now brought to display, there emerged the focus of a common problem – the problem of reform which, in the opinion of many of the Company's critics, could be best solved by some kind of parliamentary intervention. The speech from the throne at the opening session of Parliament in January 1772 both reflected and reinforced this sentiment when it listed the affairs of the Company among 'the Concerns of this Country', and described them as being 'so peculiarly liable to Abuses and exposed to Danger that the Interposition of the Legislature for their Protection may become

[1] Sutherland, *The East India Company in Eighteenth-Century Politics*, ch. VIII.

necessary.'[2] The mounting literary assault on the East India Company could find no better encouragement than in such pronouncements issuing from the highest seat of power, and the first five years following the Regulating Act were indeed remarkable for the very large output of political writings on this subject.

This literature on East India affairs may be broadly classified into two categories, although no individual publication of one kind can be said to have been altogether free from the characteristics of the other. There were, in the first place, the polemics like those by Bolts and Verelst, which were written with the purpose of attacking or defending a given act of policy. Like all other forms of political statement of this period, these two contained much that was often abstract and speculative; but, on the whole, the 'philosophical observations' were strictly geared to the consideration of the specific administrative questions under discussion. The other class of East India tracts and pamphlets is perhaps best described as the literature of plans. They, too, are on the whole concerned with judging actual policies and have a polemical edge. But they go a step further and attempt to lay down rules for the conduct of government in the light of some 'general system'. The importance of this body of writings for the early history of British rule in India has not been fully studied yet, but there is some contemporary evidence to show that they were a significant influence on policy-making. The existence of an elaborate summary of some of these plans among the Pitt Papers may be taken to indicate the use made of them in formulating the Act of 1784.[3] It was still felt in 1793 that 'the review of these plans seems to be the proper foundation upon which to rest a system for the future government

[2] *The Journals of the House of Commons*, vol. XXXIII, p. 410. I have relied on Auber's interpretation that these remarks in the speech from the throne referred to East India affairs. Auber, *Rise and Progress of the British Power in India*, vol. I, p. 337.

[3] 'Abstract of the Several Plans transmitted relative to the future Government of Bengal and the other British Settlements in India'. John Rylands Library, Eng. MSS, 215 and 235. Also see Appendix below.

of our Asiatic dominions and trade to the East Indies'.[4] But they are valuable above all as the record of a series of experiments with political ideas. For many of the authors of these plans the conquest of Indian territory had posed 'the greatest question in commercial and political economy, that has occurred in the annals of civil society'.[5] In formulating their recommendations therefore they often borrowed profusely from the repertoire of contemporary thought. No understanding of the eighteenth-century imagination can be complete without an appreciation of these attempts to find for the sprawling Spirit of the Laws a Procrustean bed in Bengal. Philip Francis's minute of January 1776 on the administration of revenues in the eastern provinces is in many respects the most outstanding specimen of this literature of plans, but as Firminger has already noted, he comes only after Alexander Dow and Henry Pattullo in building models for the Permanent Settlement of Bengal.

1. Alexander Dow: Philosopher and Mercantilist

Alexander Dow was born in Scotland, educated at Creif and trained for the career of a merchant.[6] In spite of his sojourns in the East and his career of about twenty years in the Bengal Army he apparently succeeded in maintaining his connections with Scotland throughout his life. The two visits to England in 1768 and 1774 must have helped him to keep in touch with the intellectual climate of the north – in 1772 David Hume found him a good enough correspondent with whom to discuss history[7] – while the existence of more solid contacts is indicated by the interest Lord Mansfield was known to have taken in his affairs.[8] As in the case of another and much more celebrated

[4] *Historical View of Plans for the Government of British India etc.*, p. 44.

[5] *Ibid.*, p. 44.

[6] Baker, *Biographia Dramatica*, pp. 195–6. Hodson, *Officers of the Bengal Army*, vol. II, pp. 78–9. *Dictionary of National Biography*.

[7] Greig (ed.), *The Letters of David Hume*, vol. II, p. 267.

[8] Clavering's letter to Lord North, 25 August 1775. Weitzman, *Warren Hastings and Philip Francis*, p. 254.

native of Perthshire, Adam Ferguson, the Scottish background had considerably to do with Dow's view of oriental society in general and of India in particular.

Scotland, to generalize Smollett's description of Edinburgh, was a 'hotbed of genius' during the middle decades of the eighteenth century. The concurrent progress of industries and of ideas at this time has, not unnaturally, induced many writers to describe this development as a veritable renaissance. The contribution of Scottish men of letters to philosophy, history, political economy and natural sciences was so distinguished and prolific in this period as to make Edinburgh almost a rival of Paris as the intellectual centre of Europe.[9] The spiritual affinity between the two capitals was the result of a two-way traffic in ideas that had been going on ever since the time of the Stuart exile. But it was not until the eighteenth century that the reciprocal influence came to produce its most creative impact in either country. How true this was of Scotland is most easily understood by taking into account the numerous translations of the French philosophers published in Edinburgh during this period and the great use made of them in the contemporary reform movement.[10] But it was by no means the agitators alone who sought their ammunition in French thought. The emphasis on political economy in the proceedings of the Select Society and the inept imitation of Montesquieu in Ferguson's best-seller, *Essay on the History of Civil Society*, are only two examples among many that might be quoted to show how the Scottish literati were all drawing upon the same source for inspiration.

France and England were, according to Hume, 'so intermix'd in all Transactions since the Revolution' that 'the History of one Country must throw Light upon the other'.[11] This observation applies equally to political and intellectual history, and particularly in relation to Scotland which came to reflect the influences from across the Channel much more than any other part of the British isles. Small wonder then

[9] Meikle, *Scotland and the French Revolution*, p. xvi.

[10] *Ibid.*, pp. 15–16.

[11] *Letters*, vol. I, p. 491.

that Scottish thought under the full impact of the Enlightenment should have overflowed and spilt into areas far out in the world wherever Scots with ideas happened to travel. Scotland thus directly contributed to the intellectual expansion of France very much in the manner of a daughter colony planting her own settlements abroad. Among her natives there were those who, like Alexander Dow, did some pioneering experiment with political and economic concepts of European origin in Eastern conditions. There were others who, like Quintin Craufurd completed in space as well as in ideas the full circuit of this strange odyssey: he left Scotland at the age of eighteen, served for nearly forty years in India and in Manila, and returned to Europe in 1780 to live for the rest of his life in France and there produce a work which, apart from its interest as an early essay in comparative religion, was in its view of India strongly reminiscent of Voltaire.[12] These merchants, travellers and adventurers from Scotland had between them succeeded in popularizing in the West an interpretation of oriental societies and cultures which was indeed characteristic of the French *philosophes* of this age.

In his work on India, Craufurd speaks in glowing terms about the 'mighty empire . . . which, in extent, riches, and the number of its inhabitants, has not yet been equalled by any one nation in the globe'. He then goes on to say how this empire was 'over-run by a fierce race of men', the 'Mahommedans, who, in the beginning of their furious conquests, endeavoured . . . to subdue the minds of the Hindoos . . . till, at length . . . they were constrained to let a religion and customs subsist, which they found it impossible to destroy.'[13]

[12] See Francisque-Michel, *Les Écossais en France: Les Français en Écosse*, vol. II, pp. 458–65, for some biographical details about Craufurd. His work, *Sketches chiefly relating to the History, Religion, Learning and Manners of the Hindoos*, was first published in London in 1790 and translated the following year into French. The *Sketches* must not be confused with his other work, *Researches concerning the Laws, Theology, Learning, Commerce, etc. of Ancient and Modern India* (2 vols), published in 1817, two years after his death.

[13] *Sketches*, vol. II, pp. 105–16.

This admiration for the ancient civilization of the East, the one-sided emphasis on the destructive aspect of Islamic conquests by ignoring altogether their highly creative effects, the overestimation of the resistance put up by the indigenous culture, and the error of representing as capitulation of the new to the old what was in fact a complex process of synthesis, are all notions very similar to those displayed in Voltaire's oriental pieces. In his *Fragments sur l'Inde* Voltaire speaks of the eventual Indianization of the Mahommedan invaders.[14] His play, *L'Orphelin de la Chine*, is built on a similar theme for China. The central thesis here is that the Tartars, although they had conquered China, were forced to submit to what he calls the 'natural superiority' of Chinese culture. This is how he puts it in the dedicatory statement introducing the play:

> Voilà un grand exemple de la supériorité naturelle que donnent la raison et le génie sur la force aveugle et barbare; et les Tartares ont deux fois donné cet exemple: car lorsqu'ils ont conquis encore ce grand empire, au commencement du siècle passé, ils se sont soumis une seconde fois à la sagesse des vaincus; et les deux peuples n'ont formé qu'une nation, gouvernée par les plus anciennes lois du monde.

In the play itself the conqueror Gengis-Kan represents the blind and barbaric forces; the mandarin Zamti – the wisdom of China; and Idamé his wife – the Spirit of the East. Gengis tries to break the resistance of the people by terror, but cannot conceal his admiration for them:

> Si j'arrête une vue attentive
> Sur cette nation désolée et captive
> Malgré moi je l'admire en lui donnant des fers:
> Je vois que ses travaux ont instruit l'univers;
> Je vois un peuple antique, industrieux, immense.
> Ses rois sur la sagesse ont fondé leur puissance,
> De leurs voisins soumis heureux législateurs,
> Gouvernant sans conquête, et régnant par les moeurs.
>
> (Acte IV, Scène II)

[14] Voltaire, *Fragments*, p. 48.

Eventually it is the conqueror who yields to the system he had been trying to destroy. The people remain loyal to their ancient institutions and refuse to co-operate; the wise mandarin seeks courage in tradition to defy the threat of torture and death; and the rude but simple-hearted barbarian, passionately in love with the beautiful Idamé, is resolutely spurned by the latter: her fidelity to her husband is also a part of the granite tradition. Overcome thus, Gengis bows to the mandarin and asks him to govern the country according to its own laws:

> Soyez ici des lois l'interprète suprême;
> Rendez leur ministère aussi saint que vous-même;
> Enseignez la raison, la justice, et les moeurs.
> Que les peuples vaincus gouvernent les vainqueurs,
> Que la sagesse règne et préside au courage;
> Triomphez de la force, elle vous doit hommage;
> J'en donnerai l'exemple, et votre souverain
> Se soumet à vos lois les armes à la main.
>
> (Acte V, Scène VI)

What brought about Gengis-Kan's capitulation was not merely the awe and respect inspired by a superior system, but love which transformed a conqueror into a king: 'Je fus un conquérant, vous m'avez fait un roi.'

Served straight as by Craufurd or packed in allegory as by Voltaire, this faith in the *supériorité naturelle* of Eastern civilizations was an important ideological feature of the Enlightenment. The thesis underlying the story of Gengis-Kan in China was adopted by many Englishmen as a guide to their interpretation of Indian history as well as to the formulation of Indian policies. Thus, it was William Bolts's idea that the Portuguese had lost their power because they tried to 'abolish the customs' of the Hindus and force Christianity on them, so that 'as soon as the natives had found protection and toleration in any new-established European settlements, all the trade in the neighbouring Portuguese ports dwindled away to nothing'.[15]

[15] Bolts, *Considerations*, p. 67.

Even for the men who governed Bengal for the East India Company, loyalty to the native institutions was an article of faith from which no deviation could be allowed without harming the interests of the regime itself. C.W.B. Rous, the philosophically minded Supervisor of Rajshahi, took it upon himself to advise his superiors that 'some Degree of Tenderness' must be shown to the prejudices of the Bengalis, 'an indolent and superstitious People,' in order 'to attach them to the Government of Foreigners of different Customs and Religion.'[16] Again, to take into account the attitudes which went into policy-making, one of the charges from Philip Francis to which Warren Hastings was most susceptible and which he took great pains to refute, was that his administration had undermined the native institutions.[17]

This notion about the superior oriental way of life had the effect of popularizing in Europe a fascinating view of the East seen through philosophers' lenses. The distorted image of eastern societies, peoples, laws and even of landscapes, thus obtained, was reproduced in a thousand variations in many works of imagination and scholarship of this period. Strange fruits and flowers, and animals more grotesque than any described in the mediaeval bestiaries came to embellish contemporary works of art. Brahmins, mandarins, sultans and slaves crowded into plays and novels. A shipwreck in the torrid zones not unlike those occurring in the tales of Sindbad and leading up to no less marvellous discoveries – *des pays qui faisaient honte à l'Europe*[18] – was a cue commonly used in the new genre of fiction which came to be known as *le voyage imaginaire*. In France these oriental utopias provided for their writers some kind of an escape from the ugly realities of the *ancien régime*, and on both sides of the Channel they constituted an inverted form of social criticism.

The other important consequence of this attitude was to develop oriental research with a political slant. In England, in particular, it

[16] Rous to Becher, 18 November 1770. *Proceedings of the Controlling Council of Revenue at Murshidabad*, vol. II, p. 158.

[17] See p. 197 below.

[18] Hazard, *La Pensée Européenne au XVIIIème Siècle*, t. I, p. 8.

almost became a matter of convention for a writer on East India affairs to preface his remarks about the English government in Bengal by a dissertation on the 'ancient constitution' of the country, or conversely, if the work was intended to be of scholarly rather than political interest, to conclude an essay of remote and antiquarian learning with observations on the existing state of the Company's administration there. We owe the beginnings of Indological studies to this body of literature which, with all its curious mixture of the erudite and the polemical, must be recognized as being among the first intellectual attempts in modern times to explore the East.

To explore the East was above all to study the nature of oriental despotism. Such at least was the idea of many of the political writers of the period. In English the search for a new vocabulary of politics, corresponding to attitudes related to the new problems of power, had already in the seventeenth century led to the revival of the word 'despot' in its pejorative, Aristotelian sense, which had not been in use for two thousand years.[19] It was in this sense that Milton had used the word when he spoke of the prelates trying 'to thrust the Laitie under the despotical rule of the Monarch',[20] and Locke when he defined 'Despotical Power' as 'an absolute, arbitrary Power one Man has over another'.[21] In France, too, it was at about this time that the neology *despotisme* with its abusive ring came to be introduced in political writings. It had already firmly established itself during the last years of Louis XIV's reign, and on the publication of the *Esprit des Lois* three decades later came to acquire the status of a fundamental political concept. Montesquieu enshrined it in his well-known formula: 'Il y a trois especes de gouvernements: LE REPUBLICAIN, LE MONARCHIQUE, ET LE DESPOTIQUE',[22] and from that moment it became an indispensable

[19] Koebner, 'Despot and Despotism: Vicissitudes of a Political Term'. *Journal of the Warburg and Courtauld Institutes*, 1951, vol. XIV, nos 3–4, pp. 275–302.

[20] Milton, *Of Reformation Touching Church-Discipline in England* (1641), in *Works*, vol. III, part I, p. 59.

[21] Locke, *Two Treatises of Government*, p. 209.

[22] Montesquieu, *Oeuvres Complètes*, t. I, p. 10.

part of the sociologist's tool-bag both in France and in England. Particularly after the French Revolution there was an increasing tendency to use the word as a description of all authoritarian regimes in Europe – those of the tsars and the *empereurs* everywhere. This, however, was a development beyond Montesquieu, geographically if not logically. For him despotism was almost exclusively an oriental phenomenon, the strange fruit which grew only in the fertile soil of the East and matured only in its burning sun. The constitution and characteristics of despotism were illustrated by him from the histories of a wide range of countries from Peking to Persia. The 'laws' of despotic government, as defined by him, were regarded by almost all subsequent writers of the century as providing a master model universally valid for all historical interpretation of the East. The end product of it all was the making of a Western myth about an undifferentiated Orient characterized by the rectilinear simplicity of its social structure, the immutability of its laws and customs, the primitive innocence of its people: a myth taken over from the *philosophes* and imaginatively enriched by the nineteenth-century romantics, and uncritically absorbed into much of later oriental research in the form of nostalgic nonsense about the glory that was. Alexander Dow's *Dissertation on the Origin and Nature of Despotism in Hindostan*[23] is a highly representative specimen of such orientalism. It

[23] Alexander Dow's publications include the following works: *Tales translated from the Persian of Inatulla of Delhi* (1768); *The History of Hindostan from the Earliest Account of Time to the Death of Akbar, translated from the Persian of Mahummud Casim Ferishta of Delhi together with a Dissertation Concerning the Religion and Philosophy of the Brahmins, with An Appendix containing the History of the Mogul Empire, from its Decline in the Reign of Mahummud Shaw, to the present Times*, 2 vols (1768); *Zingis, A Tragedy* (1769); *The History of Hindostan from the Death of Akbar to the Complete Settlement of the Empire under Aurungzebe*: to which are prefixed, *I. A Dissertation on the Origin and Nature of Despotism in Hindostan. II. An Enquiry into the State of Bengal, with a Plan for restoring that Kingdom to its former Prosperity and Splendour* (1772); *Sethona, A Tragedy* (1774). In the present essay the *History of Hindostan* is referred to simply by the author's name followed by a Roman numerical to indicate the volume, the continuation of the work

opens with the dictum: 'Government derives its form from accident; its spirit and genius from the inherent manners of the people.'[24] But these 'inherent manners' were themselves determined by factors quite independent of human nature. As Montesquieu pointed out, 'le caractère de l'esprit et les passions du coeur', and consequently the laws governing human societies, tended to vary from country to country, depending on differences in their geographical conditions. This massive generalization, which occupies a very important place in the *Esprit des Lois*,[25] was, characteristically enough, founded on a rather narrow plinth of geographical concepts.[26] The factors which, according to its author, wield the most formative influence on man's

---

published in 1772 being regarded as the third volume of the series. Baker in *Biographia Dramatica* (pp. 195–6) doubts whether Dow was really the author of the works which appeared under his name. The *Dictionary of National Biography* repeats the doubt. Neither of the statements is supported by any real evidence. A careful student will, however, find that the notions about the Orient as expressed in the plays are similar to those developed in the dissertations; that the Preface to the first volume of the *History* discusses the problems of translation and of Persian literary style in very much the same manner, and in fact sometimes in the same words, as the Translator's Preface to the *Tales*; and that there is a certain stylistic unity to suggest that all this was the work of one man. John Shore, who knew Persian well enough and was Dow's contemporary in Bengal, wrote thus to the Rev. Professor Ford from Calcutta on 17 September 1783: 'The Tales of Inatullah are very common: they are written in a very pleasant style, though rather inflated. Dow has not translated one-third of them: indeed I might affirm, he has not translated any; for the English version is too vague to be called a translation. I compared part of them some years ago, and endeavoured to make use of the translation for my own advantage, but without success. His character as a Persian scholar was far from being high in Bengal; and I should suppose that he took the substance of the original as read and explained to him by his Moonshee or Interpreter, and published it as a translation. His version of Ferishta is more correct, and in some parts exact.' Teignmouth, *Memoir*, vol. I, pp. 105–6.

[24] Dow, III, p. vii.

[25] The thesis is treated in detail in Livres XIV–XVII, and observations based on it appear throughout the work.

[26] Febvre, *La Terre et l'Evolution Humaine*, pp. 108–11.

social and political behaviour are only two in number: climate and soil. Even these are not broken down into their constituent elements and related to the full diversity of the human situation. The result is an oversimplified picture of the physical world drawn in sharp blacks and whites, where climate is either hot or cold, terrain hilly or plain, and soil barren or fertile. This schema, in spite of all its superficiality, was adopted as an instrument of historical analysis by some of the best contemporary writers. When Adam Ferguson put into his *Essay* a whole chapter entitled 'Of the Influences of Climate and Situation', he was perhaps consciously imitating Montesquieu. But when Voltaire, unaware that he was almost paraphrasing the opening statement of the third chapter of Book XIV of the *Esprit des Lois*, attributes the unwarlike character of the Indians to 'leurbeau climat',[27] or when he speaks of the assimilative faculty of Indian culture as being due to the climate of the subcontinent,[28] it shows how deeply the idea of geographical determinism had cut into eighteenth-century thought. Dow, too, was very much the child of his age when he sought to explain the course of Indian history in terms of the two factors mentioned by Montesquieu. The fertility of the soil, he said, was a source of misfortune for the natives. It made them so prosperous that 'they became objects of depredation to the fierce nations of northern Asia'. What made conquests easy was the 'peaceable and harmless' nature of the people, and this itself was a product of climatic conditions. It was Montesquieu's opinion – since similar results must follow from similar causes – that Europeans born in India tended to become as timid as the natives. Ferguson spoke of the Dutch, so industrious at home, becoming 'more languid and slothful in India'. Dow, too, expressed himself in contemporary idiom in ascribing the 'phlegmatic sentiments' of the natives, their 'indolence and ease' to 'the languor occasioned by the hot climate of India'. This, combined with the fact that they could find subsistence without much toil and had, therefore, little use for property, made them 'submit without

[27] *Fragments sur l'Inde*, p. 48.

[28] *Essay sur l'Histoire Générale* (Paris, 1756), t. III, p. 301.

resistance to violations of right which may hurt but cannot destroy them'. The political consequence of such an attitude was that the Indians considered 'the evils of despotism less severe than the labour of being free', and this was not very different from what Adam Ferguson said about the sun 'which ripens the pine-apple and the tamarind' having the effect of inspiring 'a degree of mildness that can even assuage the rigours of despotical government'.[29]

Another factor which, apart from climate and soil, had promoted the development of Indian despotism was, according to Dow, religion. The causal relation between the two had already been forcefully discussed by Nicolas-Antoine Boulanger,[30] a writer of the Holbach group, in a notorious pamphlet published about a decade before Dow's *Dissertation*. Boulanger's essay is described on the title page of its English version as 'an Introduction and Key to Montesquieu's Spirit of Laws', but actually it opens with a straightforward rejection of geographical determinism. He doubted whether it was at all valid to explain the origins of authoritarianism in Asia only in terms of soil and climate, ignoring the numerous moral and political influences which contributed to it.[31] This most pertinent criticism of the monistic view of history did not, however, prevent the author himself from

[29] Montesquieu, *Esprit des Lois*, liv. XIV, ch. III. Ferguson, *Essay*, pp. 185, 198. Dow, III, pp. vii–ix.

[30] Nicolas-Antoine Boulanger's work was published posthumously in Amsterdam in 1766 as *L'Antiquité de voilée par ses usages, ou examen critique des principales opinions, cérémonies et institutions religieuses et politiques des différens peuples de la terre, par feu M. Boulanger*. The last chapter of this work had been issued separately five years earlier as *Recherches sur l'origine du despotisme oriental*. The edition of *Recherches* used in the present text is dated 1762 and described on its title-page as the 'ouvrage posthume de Mr B.I.D.P.E.C.', the initials standing for Boulanger, ingenieur des ponts et chaussées. This edition was 'privately printed at the press of the celebrated John Wilkes in his house in George Street, Westminster'. A rather inaccurate English translation was published by Wilkes in 1764 under the title *The Origin and Progress of Despotism in the Oriental and other Empires of Africa, Europe and America*. For a recent assessment of Boulanger's ideas, see Frank E. Manuel, *The Eighteenth Century Confronts the Gods*, pp. 210–27.

[31] Boulanger, *Recherches*, p. 8.

carving his own thesis out of one single block. In his opinion it was the exercise of power by a sacerdotal class which alone made an oriental government despotic: 'Quoique Dieu fût l'unique Roi de la Société, comme il n'y a aucune pacte ni aucune convention à faire avec un Dieu, la Théocratie dès son institution and par sa nature fut un Gouvernment Despotique, dont le grand Juge étoit le Sultan invisible, et dont les Prétres étoient les Vizirs et les Ministres, c'est-à-dire, les Despotes réels.' That is, despotism, as defined by him, was a form of 'théocratie payenne'.[32]

Alexander Dow's understanding of the political institutions of the East combined the two opposing interpretations of Montesquieu and Boulanger into a historical view which, whatever its ultimate validity, was at least more balanced than either. The physical and moral aspects, he suggested, fed on each other to give rise to despotism. 'The seeds of despotism, which the nature of the climate and fertility of the soil had sown in India, were . . . reared to perfect growth by the Mahommedan faith.'[33] It was, according to him, in the very nature of the religion of Islam to encourage authoritarianism: the circumstances of its origin and expansion, its laws for the family and for the state, even the code of personal conduct it prescribes, all contribute to the growth of tyranny.[34] 'The faith of Mahommed', he observed, 'is peculiarly calculated for despotism; and it is one of the greatest causes which must fix for ever the duration of that species of government in the East.' This rather one-sided view of Islam was complementary to Dow's idea of Hinduism. The latter is, according to him, 'productive, from its principles, of the greatest degree of subordination to authority', and thereby 'prepares mankind for the government of foreign lords.'[35] Thus ground between the upper and the nether millstones of their two principal religions, the Indians remained the most perfect prey of despotism.

[32] *Ibid.*, pp. 137, 233.
[33] Dow, III, pp. xx–xxi.
[34] *Ibid.*, pp. xiii–xxi.
[35] *Ibid.*, p. cxxviii.

But despotism in India was not quite the same thing as elsewhere in Asia. 'Though despotism governs Asia, it appears in different countries under various forms.'[36] This, in Dow's opinion, could be best illustrated by the different ways in which absolute power was exercised in India itself by two groups of invaders who successively came to rule the country. The Turco-Afghans were born rude and wild in a severe climate. Consequently, 'the despotism which the Pathans established in their conquests, partook of the violence of their national character'. Their rule was 'oppressive through pride and tyrannical from passion.'[37] But the Mughal conquest of India was the outcome of an entirely different set of circumstances. Their conquest, unlike that by their predecessors, 'proceeded from the abilities of one man and not from the effort of a nation.' As a result, the personality of the conqueror, Babar, had so completely influenced the conduct of government that his benevolence was preserved as a legacy and cultivated as a code by all succeeding emperors of the same dynasty from Humayun to Aurangzib.[38] The religion of Islam, otherwise so favourable to the growth of tyranny, actually helped in this case to keep it under control by a code of laws 'which circumscribed the will of the prince.'[39] Hence, 'the despotism of Hindostan . . . was never a government of caprice and whim.' On the contrary, it was 'mild', benevolent', 'humane' and even 'engaging' – adjectives which frequently occur in Dow's text. He surveys Mughal rule as an unbroken succession of wise and virtuous kings each of whom handed down to the next monarch the scales of justice together with the sceptre of authority. He wrote:

> The uncommon abilities of most of the princes, with mild and humane character of all, rendered Hindostan the most flourishing empire in the world during two complete centuries. The manly and generous

[36] *Ibid.*, p. ix.
[37] *Ibid.*, pp. xi–xii.
[38] *Ibid.*, p. xii.
[39] *Ibid.*, p. iii.

> temper of Baber permitted not oppression to attend the victories of his sword . . . Humaioon, though not equal in abilities to his father, carried all his mild virtues into the throne . . . Akbar was possessed of Baber's intrepidity in war, of Humaioon's mildness in peace . . . Jehangire . . . was the invariable protector of the people against the rapacity and tyranny of his own officers . . . His son, Shaw Jehân . . . rendered his people happy by the gravity, justice and solemnity of his decisions . . . Aurangzêbe . . . kept the great machine of government in motion through all its members: his penetrating eye followed oppression to its most secret retreats, and his stern justice established tranquillity, and secured property over all his extensive dominions.[40]

Thus throughout a period of two hundred years a Confucian pageant of noble patriarchs each of whom was as distinguished as that other oriental despot whom Gibbon so admired. It was the latter's opinion that 'in the long competition between Chosroes and Justinian the advantage, both of merit and fortune, is almost always on the side of the barbarian'. For though the Persian emperor 'would merit, in our feelings, the appellation of a tyrant', he did, in fact, deserve 'the appellation of *just*'.[41] Underlying this paradox there is the assumption, characteristic of much of contemporary political philosophy, that there is 'one great law' which, in the East, converts the tiger of absolute power into the white lamb of virtue. As Dow puts it: 'The despotic form of government is not . . . so terrible in its nature as men born in free countries are apt to imagine. Though no civil regulation can bind the prince, there is one great law, the ideas of mankind with regard to right and wrong, by which he is bound.'[42] This is clearly that *politique naturelle* enunciated by his hero, Zingis, who in summoning all his subject princes and vassals to a council ('not that we require/ Advice, but proofs of their allegiance due,/And prompt obedience to the will of Zingis'), declares:

[40] *Ibid.*, pp. xxiii–xxviii.

[41] Gibbon, *The History of the Decline and Fall of the Roman Empire*, vol. IV, pp. 359–61.

[42] Dow, III, p. xxii.

We mean to publish laws to rule mankind –
To bind the nations in one general chain
Of policy – to mark, with strict regard,
The bounds of justice between man and man.[43]

This rule of justice, we are told, was not interrupted by the break-up of the Mughal empire after Aurangzib's death. For the independent Nawabs of Bengal, though they usurped imperial authority, still emulated 'the mild despotism of the house of Timur' in their own administration. They understood their own interests well enough to recognize that their power depended on the prosperity of their subjects. As a result, 'commerce, manufactures, and agriculture, were encouraged; for it was not then the maxim to take away the honey by destroying the swarm'.[44]

Dow does not seek the germs of Bengal's decline in the disintegration of Mughal power. 'The miseries of Bengal', he darkly observes, 'were reserved for other times.' It was the sharp historic chasm of 1765 which divided past eminence from present degradation. 'We may date the commencement of the decline', he categorically states, 'from the day on which Bengal fell under the dominion of foreigners; who were more anxious to improve the present moment to their own emolument, than, by providing against waste, to secure a permanent advantage to the British nation.'[45] This idea of a millennium coming abruptly to an end with the advent of British power is a gift of the Age of Enlightenment which continues to influence historical judgment down to the present day. The political use made of this thesis by writers with a nationalist bias has often provided an escape from the difficult task of investigating the source of Bengal's malaise in the slow decomposition of the Mughal economy, and produced, in its own turn, an equal and opposite reaction in the form of naive attempts to justify the entire record of East India Company rule in India. But not all of those who have been tempted to join on either side of

[43] Dow, *Zingis: A Tragedy*, p. 34.
[44] Dow, III, pp. lxvii–lxviii.
[45] *Ibid.*, p. lxxvii.

this academic ping-pong seem to be aware that this notion is much older than Digby and Dutt, and is rooted, in fact, in the tradition of eighteenth-century European thought itself.

After the battle of Plassey, says Dow, 'an ample field lay open before us, but we have appropriated revolution and war to history'. He speaks bitterly of the revolutions engineered by the conquerors after Sirajuddowla's death, but reserves the full weight of his indictment for 'the system, which advances still with hasty strides, to the complete ruin of that once opulent province'.[46] This was the 'system' which came into force with the assumption of the Diwani in 1765. He defines it as a 'double government' characterized by a quick succession of *rois fainéants*, the wickedness of a native prime minister and the expensive luxury of the office of an English Resident at Durbar.[47]

The consequence of diarchy was to bring about a new despotism in which the native officials, the Company's servants and the revenue-farmers all combined to ruin the country. The abilities of even the best among the English administrators could do little to help in this situation. Dow throws a passing bouquet at Verelst for the good work he did in Burdwan, but adds acutely that 'even Burdwan owed part of its prosperity to the misery and distress of the surrounding districts'. The government itself ran into difficulties: a huge fiscal arrear piled up which it had little hope of ever being able to clear. In the end, Dow asks, 'what mighty advantages have the Company derived from their great acquisitions in Bengal?'[48]

The political solution he puts forward is that the East India Company should assume full sovereign powers without further delay. He is not tormented by any legalistic doubts about its right to do so. His concept of power, in striking contrast to the prevarications of the Court of Directors on the same subject, has the healthy directness of the buccaneer's confidence in his sword. 'The provinces of Bengal and Behar', he says, 'are possessed by the British East India

[46] *Ibid.*, pp. lxx–lxxii.
[47] *Ibid.*, pp. lxxxix–xcii, xciv, cxli.
[48] *Ibid.*, p. cv.

Company, in reality, by the right of arms, though, in appearance, by a grant from the present emperor.'[49] In view of this a new political arrangement should be made to replace the treaty of Diwani. The proposed reorganization is stated all in the imperative mood: 'Give the province of Allahabad to Suja-ul-Dowla, the territories of Bulwant Singh to the emperor, recall your troops into your own dominions, make Patna or Mongeer the residence of the representative of Timur, degrade the wretched Mubarick from his nominal Nabobship, and let Mahommed Riza RESIGN.' These pawn movements would require no constitutional justification, 'no address', for the simple reason that 'the persons mentioned were the creatures and they still continue the slaves of your power.'[50] In their finality and want of common sense these measures are comparable only to those invented four centuries ago by the mad genius of Muhammad bin Tughluq. But Dow's emphasis on the 'right of arms' indicates how by 1772 there had already emerged a new school of thought trying to resolve the knotty question of the Company's status in the light of a powerful political concept inherited from Hobbes – that is, of sovereignty acquired by force.[51] In the same year, too, Warren Hastings characterized 'the sword which gave us the dominion of Bengal' as a 'natural charter'.[52]

Alexander Dow's diagnosis of the economic infirmities of Bengal and the remedies he had to suggest reflect many shades of mercantilist thought. Bengal before the Company's assumption of power, he said, 'was always remarkable for its commerce'. Both physical and natural conditions contributed to make it so: the fertile land, the abundant rivers and the bay opening up to the highways of the sea, the skill of the people and their characteristic aversion to luxury – a virtue

[49] *Ibid.*, p. cxvii.

[50] *Ibid.*, p. cxvii.

[51] Hobbes, *Leviathan*, pp. 129–30.

[52] Hastings's Minute, 12 October 1772, quoted in *Cambridge History of India*, vol. V, p. 597.

imposed on the natives by necessity but much admired by contemporary European observers. Its prosperity consisted of a favourable balance of trade, so favourable indeed as to make up for the loss of great quantities of wealth from the depreciation and recoinage of its metallic currency, from hoarding and the use of the precious metals in handicrafts as well as from fiscal remittances to Delhi (which, as we know on the good authority of Orme and Grant, had never really been made since the days of Alivardi Khan). In fact, 'the balance of trade . . . was against all nations, in favour of Bengal; and it was the sink where gold and silver disappeared, without the least prospect of return.' The English, the Dutch, the French, the Danes and the Portuguese and the various nations of eastern and western Asia taken together poured into this bottomless pit a total volume of trade worth, at a conservative estimate, about one million and nine hundred thousand pounds.[53] Bengal, in the imagery of its own folk tale, was the temptress with whom all adventurers would irresistibly stop to try their luck at dice and inevitably lose.

The ruin of this commercial paradise began with the establishment of British power in the country. Taking together the total annual 'investments' of the various East India Companies minus the annual value of bullion imports into Bengal, Dow estimated that 'she loses . . . yearly to Europe £1,477,500.' There was nothing to compensate for this loss in what had once been its Asian market now broken up and scattered by revolutions and civil wars. This sum constituted 'the savings of the Company on the revenue, the value of British exports, the private fortunes of individuals, which center in this kingdom.' This was, in other words, the annual drain of wealth from Bengal. 'With a peculiar want of foresight', he wrote in the familiar idiom of mercantilist literature, 'they began to drain the reservoir without turning into it any stream to prevent it from being exhausted.'[54]

[53] Dow, III, pp. lxii–lxiv.
[54] *Ibid.*, pp. lxxvii–lxxxi.

This idea of a 'drain' of Indian wealth to Britain figures very prominently indeed in Dow's writings – and for that matter in much of the East India literature of the period. It is therefore difficult to appreciate the suggestion postdating this historical concept by over a hundred years and attributing its invention to Romesh Dutt who allegedly was 'preoccupied with the idea that India was being systematically looted by the invaders from the West'. In what may be regarded as a seminal statement on the subject, Professor Holden Furber observes, 'Nearly all Indian and many British writers who have dealt with the first half-century of British rule in India have followed Romesh Chundra Dutt in believing that the most important consequence of European expansion in India was what they have chosen to call the "drain" of Indian wealth to Britain.'[55] The fact however is that long before Dutt and Digby the phrase 'drain of wealth' had come into common use – to the extent of turning into a cliché – by writers who found in it a most convenient figure of speech for their theory of international trade.

For wealth according to mercantilist opinion (that is, to take into account the consensus and not the brilliant asides) consisted of precious metals, in bullion and in specie, and it was only through a favourable balance of trade that a nation could build up and go on adding to its stock of gold and silver. It was the influx or outflow of this particular form of wealth which made a country rich or poor. That Dow like all other minor adherents of this school adopted this 'pure Midas-like view of the precious metals'[56] is quite evident from the manner in which he sought to express the problem of export surplus in terms of bullion. In the days of the Mughals, he said, 'the balance of trade for which Bengal received bullion' was £1,687,500 which excluding 'the annual revenue sent in specie to Delhi' amounted to a yearly acquisition in money' of £437,500. But the 'decrease in the specie of Bengal since the accession of the company to the dominion

[55] Furber, *John Company at Work*, pp. 304, 310.

[56] Heckscher, *Mercantilism*, vol. II, p. 188.

of that kingdom' amounted to £5,212,500. Thus within a matter of seven years only the 'balance of bullion', on which the economy of the country had been based under the previous regime, collapsed and 'the decrease of her specie' brought about her present degradation.[57] The complete identification of wealth and money in statements of this kind was a very good reason why Adam Smith found it both convenient and necessary to ignore the intelligent discrimination of some of the moderate mercantilist writers[58] and concentrate his attack on the crude and still popular misconceptions characteristic of that school.

Thus it was the scarcity of money that had led to the decline of Bengal. The English mercantilists never tired of complaining about this particular evil in relation to their own economy.[59] But Dow was no dialectician like Lionel Cranfield to argue that it was not the want of money which was ruining trade, but 'the want of money is because trade is sick.'[60] He believed the other way round in the more conventional juxtaposition of cause and effect. 'The kingdom of Bengal, it appears', he said, 'has not in the midst of her misfortunes, fallen off greatly from her former exports of manufactures . . . But let us suppose that her whole currency amounted to fifteen millions; the entire loss of a third part of that sum must have inevitably distressed her; and an annual decrease of near half a million must, if not prevented, in a few years, totally ruin the little commerce that still remains. The prospect is gloomy.' Then in a remarkable passage 'to illustrate the argument by comparison' he goes on to define in terms of the mercantilist doctrine the nexus connecting money with trade, prices and interest.

> Were the paper-currency of Great Britain totally suppressed, and her gold and silver currency, which is estimated at seven millions, left for the purpose of trade and taxation, it is evident, that ruinous consequences

[57] Dow, III, pp. lxxxiii–lxxxv.

[58] Viner, *Studies in the Theory of International Trade*, pp. 19–21.

[59] *Ibid.*, p. 87.

[60] Tawney, *Business and Politics under James I*, p. 192.

> must ensue; but none will pretend to affirm, that the nation, by such a measure, would become one farthing poorer than before: Trade, however, from the want of a sufficient quantity of the signs of wealth and property, would be cramped in all its veins. The interest of money, inspite of laws, would rise to an enormous pitch. The same want of currency would at the same time become such a check upon luxury, that the price of labour, and especially of provisions, would fall, unless the latter were kept up by rigorously inforcing the present taxes without abatement. The price of provisions, in that case, would rise every day, and the poor would daily become less able to purchase . . . Bengal, from the decrease of her specie, feels, in fact, the miseries which we have in speculation just described.'[61]

It would appear from passages like this that in pleading for an increase in the supply of money he drew freely upon both the so-called quantity and circulation theories without being aware, like Potter and Asgill, of any contradiction between the two views.[62] His idea of the quantity of money being inversely related to its value is as old as Malynes and Mun, and is amply illustrated by his statements on price and interest. But he was certainly not one of those mercantilists who were so admired by Keynes for having been 'aware of the fallacy of cheapness'.[63] On the contrary the bogey of high prices haunts all his nightmare visions of an economy starved of money, and the reforms he has to suggest are all aimed at bringing down the price level by increasing the quantity of money.[64] Pursuing further the notion of identity of money and capital, he represented the rate of interest as a function of the quantity of money. In Bengal, he said, 'ten per centum is the present interest, not so much owing to insecurity as to the want of credit', and 'the immediate fall of the exorbitant interest' would be, according to him, one of the first effects of an increased supply of money.[65]

[61] Dow, III, pp. lxxxiv–lxxxv.
[62] Viner, op. cit., pp. 42–4.
[63] Keynes, *General Theory*, p. 345.
[64] Dow, III, pp. xcvii, cxii, cxxvi.
[65] *Ibid.*, pp. cxxiv, cxlvii.

Side by side with this inflationary theme there occurs throughout the text and sometimes embedded in the same passage, as in the one quoted above, a constant emphasis on the need for greater circulation in order to ensure a genuine physical increase in trade or capital. The analogy between the circulation of blood and that of money, popularized by Hobbes but known even before Harvey,[66] is often used. He speaks, for instance, of the court of the Nawab of Bengal in the days before the British conquest as 'the heart, which only received the various currents of wealth, to throw it with vigour, through every vein of the kingdom'; or of a large sum of money, economized as a result of political readjustments, which 'thrown at once into the circulation would animate the languid pulse of commerce'; and so on.[67]

The cure suggested by Dow of Bengal's malady was taken straight out of the pharmacopoeia of the circulation school: that is, the introduction of paper money. 'The want of a sufficient quantity of specie for the purposes of trade and the common intercourses among mankind', he says, 'is one of the greatest evils under which Bengal at present labours. Let, therefore, a paper currency be introduced.' He also advocates the establishment of a bank for the use of the Europeans, and this would, he hopes, 'by becoming familiar to the natives, prepare them for a more general paper currency.'[68]

This recommendation is central to Dow's thesis on Bengal. It is the magic formula of what he would call his 'science of finance'[69] emerging from all his laboured analysis of the history and economy of the country. He expected all sorts of benefits to follow from this panacea. 'Were every man enabled, by a paper currency, to bring his whole property to the market, monopoly, in spite of oppression, would be at an end, and trade extend itself through a thousand channels not known now in speculation.'[70] Above all – and here we come back to

[66] Heckscher, op. cit., p. 217. Viner, op. cit., p. 37.

[67] Dow, III, pp. lxxvi–lxxvii, cxlvi–cxlvii.

[68] *Ibid.*, p. cxxiii.

[69] *Ibid.*, p. cxxi.

[70] *Ibid.*, p. cxxiv.

the point which had set off the entire train of argument – the balance of trade would be redressed in favour of Bengal. Paper money, he thought, would not drive bullion out of the country, but on the contrary 'Bengal would draw great quantities of money from all regions of Asia.'[71] Of the two schools of paper-money enthusiasts mentioned by Viner, that is, those who had intelligently enough got rid of the notion of balance of trade and those who had not, Dow apparently belonged to the latter, no doubt 'because of blind acceptance of traditional doctrine.'[72] In fairness to him, however, it should be mentioned that he had vaguely sensed the dilemma involved – the dilemma of robbing Peter to pay Paul, for he adds, a little uneasily perhaps, that 'the Author of the Enquiry means not that specie should be drawn from the East, but it might center in Bengal'.[73] It would have been more convincing had he said with the simple and ruthless logic of Sir James Steuart: 'When one nation is growing richer, others must be growing poorer; this is an example of a favourable balance of trade.'[74]

It is only in the context of this programme for the commercial recovery of Bengal that Dow's recommendations regarding lands and agriculture assume their true significance. These are as follows:[75]

1. The Company should 'be impowered by an act of Parliament, to dispose of all the lands in Bengal and Behâr, in perpetuity, at an annual sum not less than the present rents.'
2. Only a quarter of the total amount of lands should be sold in each successive year. The sales when completed ought to yield, according to Dow's calculation, a total price of ten million pounds.

[71] *Ibid.*, p. cxxv.
[72] Viner, op. cit., pp. 39–40.
[73] Dow, III, p. cxxv.
[74] Quoted in Viner, op. cit., p. 10.
[75] Dow, III, pp. cxix, cxxi–cxxii.

3. Apart from this profit from the sale of lands, the Company will have an annual income of four million pounds from the revenues of the lands thus settled 'when properly paid'. But he shrewdly anticipates much later development as he remarks that 'should this sum appear too small for perpetuity, many ways and means of encreasing the taxes, without raising the rents, wilt present themselves'. In order to achieve this, he says, 'the British nation' ought to transfer to the banks of the Ganges, a part of that science of finance, which has so much distinguished their councils at home.' We, however, know that for the greater part of a century after these recommendations had, in their essence, been given the force of law by Lord Cornwallis, the 'science of finance', far from umpiring the unequal race between rents and taxes, watched on helplessly from the gallery and was even caught sometimes applauding the wrong side.
4. Dow believed like many of his contemporaries that larger estates 'are productive of pernicious consequences in all countries'. He, therefore, asks for preventive legislation (a) to impose a ceiling on the size of individual holdings, and (b) to resist any possible development of the laws of inheritance in the direction of primogeniture. 'Let the purchasers be confined', he says, 'to a certain quantity of land not exceeding, upon any account, fifty thousand roupees a year. To prevent the accumulation of landed property, let the spirit of the laws of a commonwealth be adopted, and the lands divided equally among all the male issue of the proprietor.'

It is in these proposals that Firminger found an anticipation of Philip Francis's plan of 1776. A similarity between the two schemes is further suggested by the fact that the same political string is attached to both of them. They both aimed at achieving in India a 'permanence of dominion', a phrase which occurs frequently in Francis's minutes. The security of landed property, it was thought, would create a climate of loyalty helping the British raj to thrive. 'Men of speculation may suppose', says Dow, 'that the security of property to the natives might infuse a spirit of freedom, dangerous to our power, into our Indian subjects . . . To give them property would only bind them with stronger ties to our interest: and make them more our subjects; or, if the British nation prefers the name – more our slaves.'[76] It is well known that the Permanent Settlement of 1793, the end product of all these earlier exercises in planning, was itself justified by Lord Cornwallis in similar though somewhat more sophisticated terms.

But apart from this political orientation there is little that is common between Dow and Francis. In fact their agrarian programmes are drawn from two completely different economic premises. Francis in the true physiocratic manner considered agricultural prosperity as the essential condition of economic development in Bengal. In Dow's plan, on the other hand, the recommendations regarding land are inserted only as a tail-piece to sustain the effect of his primary argument about trade and money. Agriculture is envisaged as a mere auxiliary of commerce, as means to the mercantilist end of achieving a favourable balance of trade. The sale of lands, said Dow, would cause an 'influx of specie and inhabitants'[77] into Bengal. 'The deficiency in the currency would be restored, commerce would diffuse itself through every vein, and manufactures would flourish to a degree before unknown.'[78] The profits from this transaction and the rise in the value of land would also permit the government to introduce a project symbolizing in English economic thought the perfect marriage of landed and commercial interests;[79] that is, to create a land-bank 'for the purpose of lending out sums of money, not exceeding three years purchase on landed security to the proprietors', which would reduce the existing rate of interest by half, increase the annual income of the Company by seven hundred thousand pounds, and by using up the money otherwise destined to lie idle, ensure an even circulation, for 'the treasury . . . ought not to be too rich,

[76] *Ibid.*, p. cxx.
[77] *Ibid.*, p. cxlvii.
[78] *Ibid.*, p. cxx.
[79] Schumpeter, *History of Economic Analysis*, pp. 295–6.

lest circulation should deaden in the kingdom'.[80] And not the least in order of importance, 'larger investments might be made by the Company, the consumption would encrease, and the profits rise'.[81] In setting forth these unmistakably mercantilist objectives, Dow does not appear to acknowledge at all the independence of agriculture as a primary factor of production. He is concerned mainly with the institutional importance of landed property rather than with the economics of agriculture. The causal relation is clearly defined when he says that 'cultivation would be the consequence of security'.[82]

It is in search of this security, then, that Dow proceeds to recommends Permanent Settlement of the lands of Bengal. 'An established idea of property', he says in one of his sweeping generalizations, 'is the source of all industry among individuals, and, of course, the foundation of public prosperity.'[83] The sense of property, he thought, had not developed in India, because under the Mahommedan dynasties all land belonged to the Crown.[84] Like most of his contemporaries he had inherited this notion from Bernier. However, he knew his history well enough to recognize that 'time . . . wrought a change in things', and that 'the posterity of Baber alienated, for particular services, estates from the crown in perpetuity' which became hereditary and transferable by sale. But he hastens to point out that this process never really triumphed, and was kept in restraint by 'the violence of the crown', it being necessary for the king occasionally to resume many such estates in order to keep up the revenue.[85] He, therefore, rejects the suggestion that these grants, known as jagirs, were in any way comparable to feudal property in Europe. 'This species of grant', he says, 'was for no term of years. It was given through favour, and recoverable at pleasure . . . No conditions of service, none for the

[80] Dow, III, pp cliii–cliv.
[81] *Ibid.*, p. cxii.
[82] *Ibid.*, p. cxix.
[83] *Ibid.*, p. cxviii.
[84] *Ibid.*, p. xxvii. Dow, I, p. xiv.
[85] Dow, III, pp. xxvii–xxviii.

maintenance of troops, was annexed to this grant. These are the fables of men who carried the feudal ideas of Europe into their relation of the state of India.'[86] On the whole, Dow maintains that 'during the domination of the house of Timur, there was no transferable landed property in Hindostan'.

The benevolence of the Mughal despots, however, fully compensated the people for the absence of property. The 'great farmers' – a term often used by Dow interchangeably with 'zamindar' to mean farmers of revenue – were prevented by the government from rack-renting the peasants. It was not the tenant but the zamindar whom the administration took to task for any failure in the payment of revenue dues. 'In the Imperial officers of the revenue, the poor had friends, and the Zemindar spies upon his conduct' – a view confirmed by the solicitude expressed in Aurangzib's directives to his officers, but judged in terms of reality, somewhat larger than life. Finally, what was no doubt one of the virtues of the old zamindari system, the 'general farmers' were encouraged by the government to spend a part of their income 'for the purpose of building houses for the husbandmen, for furnishing them with implements of agriculture, for embanking to prevent inundations, for making reservoirs of water for the dry season; and, in general, for all expences attending the improvement and cultivation of lands'.[88]

All this was in strange and painful contrast to the ruin of rural Bengal since the acquisition of Diwani by the East India Company. In his catalogue of the iniquities of the fiscal system Dow has place for all the items mentioned by Holwell and Bolts: the tyranny of the revenue collectors such as 'the Gomâstas, or agents, Dellols, Pikes, Pikars, Burkândaz, and other vermin'; the violence of the Company's troops in the countryside; fines and levies arbitrarily imposed on tenants by officials and landlords alike; the monopolies enjoyed by the Company's servants in internal trade; the duplicity of Reza

[86] *Ibid.*, p. xlix.
[87] *Ibid.*, p. 1.
[88] *Ibid.*, pp. xlvi–xlvii.

Khan, and so on.[89] But the source of it all was 'the ruinous policy of farming out the lands annually'. In words almost similar to those used by later critics of the farming system under Warren Hastings, Dow speaks of its consequences during Reza Khan's administration: 'The farmers having no certainty of holding lands beyond the year, made no improvements. Their profit must be immediate, to satisfy the hand of Avarice, which was suspended over their heads. Impressed with the uncertainty of their situation, they raised the rents, to the last farthing, on the wretched tenants; who, unwilling to forsake their ancient habitations and household gods, submitted to impositions which they could not pay.'[90]

The sense of property was thus undermined by insecurity and oppression. Dow, therefore, describes his remedial measures as a 'Proposal for establishing landed Property'. For property had to be *established* where none existed so far. His recommendation has in it the thrill of perfect invention; and the suggestion that all the lands should be sold and then settled on a permanent basis comes easily and unhesitatingly to him. It does not occur to him that putting up the lands for sale in this manner might involve a certain degree of violation of existing proprietary rights; for he is satisfied that no such rights exist. Calmly he proceeds to fill the imaginary vacuum.

The difference between Dow's plan for a permanent settlement and that of Francis is most emphasized in this historical view of Indian property. The latter took it for granted that private property in land had already been in existence on a significant scale when the country was conquered by the Mahommedans. The proprietary right of the zamindars was a fact to which the government of the East India Company had only to extend legal recognition to make it permanent. In other words, there was no question of *establishing* landed property, but only of rehabilitating and reinforcing it. Dow's definition of the zamindars as temporary officials and his idea of putting up all properties to sale were, therefore, an outrage that was

[89] *Ibid.*, pp. xcvi–xcix, c, civ and *passim.*
[90] *Ibid.*, pp. xcv, xcii–xcix.

bound to provoke criticism. Twenty years after his thesis was first published, it came under fire from one of the ablest exponents of the Francis doctrine, C.W.B. Rous, who wrote at a time when the pilot scheme of the Permanent Settlement was well under way:

> . . . there is one, whose representations once carried considerable weight in this country, and therefore must not pass unnoticed. I mean Colonel Dowe. This gentleman, whilst he was inveighing against the tyrannical measures of the Company's administration, might, one should expect, have felt as much tenderness even for the prescriptive title of the Zemindars as would have restrained him from proposing to raise ten millions sterling by a general sale of all the lands of Bengal: – I will venture to say, a scheme as wild and arbitrary, as the operation would be delusive and impracticable . . . Colonel Dowe, as if something were wanting to heighten the injustice and absurdity of such a proposal, and expose his own incompetency to advice upon the subject; speaks continually of Zemindars as temporary possessors of the land, admitted, and removed at pleasure, which never happened; and at last produces, as a Zemindary Sunnud, that is the tenure which he proposes to confiscate and sell, a grant of rent-free land, given in perpetuity, for a religious endowment.[91]

To trace the ancestry of Francis's plan in the recommendations of Alexander Dow would, therefore, be to ignore the very important differences in economic and historical outlook underlying the two schemes of Permanent Settlement. There is a much greater justification for Henry Pattullo's claim as a forerunner of Philip Francis, for they were both adherents of the physiocratic school.

2. Henry Pattullo: A French Lesson for Bengal

The late Venerable W.K. Firminger, whose keen eye missed nothing that was relevant to his magnificent survey of the early English administration in Bengal, mentions Pattullo as one of the first advocates of Permanent Settlement. However, in referring to the pamphlet,

[91] C.W.B. Rouse, *Dissertation Concerning the Landed Property of Bengal*, pp. 107–8.

An Essay upon the Cultivation of the Lands, and Improvements of the Revenues of Bengal, he encloses the author's name within inverted commas as if to imply a pseudonym.[92] The name Pattullo does sound un-English, but thanks to Black's researches in Scottish surnames we are now in a position to trace its origin in the place-name Pittilloch in Fife or in Perthshire. The French connections of the family go back to the fifteenth century. 'Robert Pittiloch, a Dundee man of humble rank', says Black, 'raised recruits for the French service in the neighbourhood of Dundee in 1423–4. He accompanied them to France, entered the French service becoming commander of the *Hommes d'armes à la grant paye.* In 1452 he obtained letters of naturalization, was made lord of Sauveterre, and was known as *le petit roi de Gascoyne.* As Robert Pettillo de Clermont he was one of the ambassadors accredited by James II to the kings of France and Castille, and in records relating to the Scots Guards in France he appears as Robin Petit Lo.'[93] Three centuries later we find our author Henry Pattullo following the example of his illustrious ancestor in acquiring for himself in France both a home and high official recognition. In his famous essay on agronomy, published in Paris in 1758, he speaks of his residence in France for over ten years and the royal favours he received there. He was then looking forward, it seems, to spending the rest of his life in that country,[94] and a friendly critic refers to him as 'un étranger devenu François . . . qui regarde son asyle comme sa veritable patrie'.[95]

[92] Firminger, *Fifth Report,* vol. I, p. cccix. The name is written as 'H. Patallo'.

[93] George F. Black, 'The Surnames of Scotland. Their Origin, Meaning and History', in *Bulletin of the New York Public Library,* vol. 50, no. 2 (February 1946), p. 153. The four variations of the surname mentioned by Black are Patillo, Pattillo, Patullo, Pattullo. The last two of these occur interchangeably in French references to our author but the pamphlet in English was signed 'Henry Pattullo'. This is how he will be referred to throughout the present work.

[94] Henry Pattullo, *Essai sur l'Amélioration des Terres,* p. 1.

[95] *Journal de Commerce* (Fevrier 1759), p. 77.

It was to prove himself useful to the country of his adoption that Pattullo wrote his tract on agriculture,[96] and this did in fact establish him at once as a most important authority on the subject. Even before him some of the Jacobite émigrés in France had carried much agricultural lore across the Channel. But with the possible exception of Lord Ogilvy there was none among the Scots who made a more lasting impression on the French agronomes than Pattullo.[97] This was to a large extent due to his talent as a keen observer of agricultural practices and to the wide range of experience he had acquired in 'the renting and culture of lands both in Britain and in foreign countries'.[98] But his influence is to be explained more than anything else by the fact that he had imbibed and represented in his *Essai* the dynamism of an agricultural renaissance. In the middle years of the eighteenth century rural Scotland suddenly rose from its ancient torpor, caught up with the technical progress of the South, and helped by the capital and inventive genius of a generation of enlightened gentry, began to add its own new techniques and processes to a repertoire already enriched, for the rest of England, by Townshend and Tull.[99] Learned societies like the Edinburgh Society for Encouraging Arts, Sciences, Manufactures and Agriculture joined hands with the gentlemen farmers in further promoting this development,[100] and a large crop of agronomic literature written in the form of popular catechisms, practical handbooks and regular scientific treatises circulated the results of experiment and innovation throughout the countryside.[101]

[96] *Essai*, p. 1.

[97] André J. Bourde, *The Influence of England on the French Agronomes, 1750–1789*, p. 182.

[98] *Essay*, p. 1. Also see autobiographical reference in *Essai*, p. 2.

[99] For an excellent survey of the stagnation in Scottish agriculture until 1750 and its sudden leap forward after that date, see Graham, *The Social Life of Scotland in the Eighteenth Century*, vol. I, chs V and VI.

[100] Francis Home's famous essay, *The Principles of Agriculture and Vegetation* (Edinburgh, 1757) was written to compete for a gold medal offered by this Society for the best dissertation on vegetation and the principles of agriculture. Home won the prize. Handley, *Scottish Farming in the Eighteenth Century*, p. 129.

[101] *Ibid.*, ch. VI, esp. pp. 127–43.

Henry Pattullo in his *Essai sur l'Amélioration des Terres* communicated the experience of this upsurge to France: he analysed the English techniques for French farmers, advised the latter on how concretely to use these under French conditions, and improved on the existing theory of rotation by introducing an entirely original and important method of combining the cultivation of grain with that of artificial fodder. Many of the significant changes which occurred in French agriculture during the rest of the century in favour of a conscious adoption of English techniques followed directly from Pattullo's work. 'Its influence', writes Bourde in the only study in the English language doing justice to this great agronomist, 'was to be very great and Patullo was to be quoted throughout the rest of the century as one of the famous agriculturists of his time, and the founder of a definite agricultural system. Besides expounding the theory of rotation, the *Essai* is a handbook of English farming for the use of the French.'[102]

The political economy of Pattullo's *Essai* is unmistakably physiocratic. The technical changes recommended by him followed directly from the experience of the new capitalist enterprise in land in England and Scotland, and could not, in fact, be given effect without it. Some of the first French companies to undertake *défrichements* during the 1760s were, indeed, noted to have been functioning 'according to the best principles of Patullo'.[103] No wonder then that with all his empiricism[104] he, like many other agronomists of that period, allied himself closely with the new school of speculative thinkers who, led by Quesnay, were for the first time working out the economics of capitalist development in land. Pattullo's *Essai* appeared shortly after the publication of Quesnay's *Fermiers* (January 1756) and

[102] Bourde, op. cit., p. 78.

[103] *Ibid.* 'What the agronomes desired', says Bourde, 'was the creation of an aristocracy of money, of an agricultural capitalism, which would not only help the peasants by providing the necessary advances, but also take up model farming and act as an example', p. 201.

[104] For the purely empirical nature of progress in eighteenth-century agriculture, see A. Wolf, *A History of Science, Technology and Philosophy in the Eighteenth Century*, pp. 501–2.

Grains (November 1757), and contains many admiring references to these articles. He reproduced almost literally (though without acknowledgment) large extracts from Quesnay's *Hommes*, which the great doctor had written for the *Encyclopédie* in 1757 but, for political reasons, held back from publication, so that it was not printed until long after his death.[105] This, to my mind, is very good evidence not only of a doctrmal agreement between the two men, but of personal association too. It indicates that Pattullo must have been very close to the inner circle of the sect to have access to a document which Quesnay thought might incur royal disfavour. Above all, there is in the *Essai* all the internal evidence one needs to show how its argument is based entirely on physiocratic theories. To quote only a passage from the address dedicating the work to the patroness of the *école*, Madame de Pompadour, where Pattullo outlines his general thesis:

> Que nem'est-il permis, Madame, de développer à vos yeux ces idées élémentaires de l'œconomie politique! Vous verriez les produits de la terre se diviser dans les mains du laboureur en (rais de culture et en revenus; les frais se distribuer aux habitants de la campagne; les revenus se répandre, par les dépenses des propriétaires, dans toutes les classes de l'Etat. Vous verriez ces mêmes richesses, après avoir animé le commerce, la population, l'industrie, retourner dans les mains du cultivateur, pour être employées à la reproduction. Vous reconnoîtriez que c'est à la plentitude de ce reflus périodique des revenus de l'Etat vers leur source, qu'on doit attribuer leur renouvellement perpétuel, que c'est à cette circulation ralentie, interrompue ou détournée, qu'on doit attribuer leur épuisement.[106]

As an example of the miraculous effects of agriculture on the economy of a country the author cites, towards the end of his *Essai*, the case of the English colonies in America. Here, according to him, was a

[105] For this reference to Pattullo's plagiarism I am indebted to the Institut National d'Etudes Démographiques (ed.), *François Quesnay etla Physiocratie*, t. I, p. 374. The passages reproduced by Pattullo from the article 'Hommes' are those which occur in *ibid.*, t. II, pp. 529–34. For a historical note on the publication of this article, see *ibid.*, t. II, p. 511n.

[106] *Essai*, pp. vii–ix.

wilderness transformed by the settlers into an agricultural paradise by their labour on the land: 'dès instants où les nouveaux colons se sont donnés à l'agriculture, l'abondance, les richesses, l'extrême population l'ont bientôt suivie, et se sont mutuellement soutenues.'[107] Fourteen years later he took it upon himself to write about another part of the British empire; but then it was to deal with a case in reverse: that is, the decline of the agricultural paradise of Bengal since the advent of the English – 'the intire desolation and ruin of these fertile and very improvable lands'.[108]

When Pattullo's essay on Bengal appeared in London in 1772 it at once won the acclaim of his admirers on the other side of the Channel. The *Journal de Physique* recommended it for translation into all the languages of Europe.[109] Its attraction for the French lay obviously in the ample use the author made of his knowledge of France in analysing the conditions of Bengal. The economy of this eastern Presidency under the Company could not but suggest to a physiocrat a close parallel to that of the *ancien régime*. The grinding burden of taxes on the peasantry, their lack of initiative following from the insecurity of property, the evils of the system of annual letting of lands, the large tracts of waste land crying for the application of labour – all these provide for Pattullo, on almost every page of his essay, the theme for an elaborate analogy between the two countries.[110] The economic conditions of France, it has been said,[111] served in this epoch as an ideal ground for the growth of the Physiocratic movement: in very much the same sense, for an English adherent of that school, Bengal served as an excellent laboratory for testing out its theories. For in both cases the most essential condition of economic recovery was the rehabilitation of agriculture.

[107] *Ibid.*, p. 244.

[108] *Essay*, p. 1.

[109] *Journal de Physique*, t. I, p. 243. For all its enthusiasm for Pattullo, referred to as 'ce grand agriculteur', the review was the merest short notice.

[110] *Essay*, pp. 2, 5, 8, 13, 15,18, 19, 20 and passim.

[111] Marx, *Theories of Surplus Value*, pp. 50–1.

The *Essay* is packed with high speculation in a way characteristic of this genre of economic writing. All those Pekin-to-Peru type of generalizations are there. 'The minds of mankind we find are much the same in all countries, and actuated by the same views and desires', and therefore, says the author by way of a straightforward deduction, 'there can be no doubt that the acquisition of property will be as desirable to Asiatics as it is to Europeans.'[112] That he had not much use either for facts or for figures is evident from his 'political arithmetic': his statistical assumptions about the rate of rent, the amount of the Company's land revenue, the acreage of cultivated and waste land – all fit neatly into his model, but quoted without chapter and verse, they had nothing to do with the actual conditions of Bengal.[113] The detached tone of the pamphlet does, indeed, convey the impression that it was written, as the author claims, 'solely to satisfy private curiosity',[114] in other words, for the sheer delight of an intellectual exercise.

But no reflection on the state of the East India Company's affairs during that anxious and eventful decade could be completely divorced from public opinion. Pattullo had, apparently, read Bolts with great care, and no wonder that the *Essay* contains many an allusion to 'prospects of spoil' and 'robberies and rapines to the amount of millions'; to 'the inhuman masters of these infortunate Asiatics'; and speaking of the transactions of the Court of Directors, to 'the mask of mystery', 'the gropings in delusive darkness', and 'dark designs'.[115] Like Dow, he, too, recalls 'the fate of some of the Roman provinces, which were abandoned, at a distance, to the direction of Generals, Governors, and Praetors, whose rapacity robbed those provinces of

[112] *Essay*, p. 8.

[113] See, for instance, how from the assumption that Bengal, including Bihar, was of the same size as France, he goes on to conclude that the proportions of cultivated, fallow and waste lands were the same in both countries. *Essay*, p. 2.

[114] *Ibid.*, p. 1.

[115] *Ibid.*, pp. 27–33.

their wealth and circulation', and finds that 'the case, it is too true, has hitherto been precisely parallel in Bengal, or worse'.[116] He urges on the Directors to come out with 'satisfactory solutions of these problems' and to formulate a programme, for 'something . . . must be done, and some plan of proceeding must be formed'.[117] Thus a vein of agitation throbs under the placid academic surface of his dissertation, and gives it a quick, nervous quality reminiscent of the writings of many of those physiocrats who liked their universal and timeless abstractions with just a shot of contemporary anxiety.

Pattullo's recommendation for Bengal is the same as Dow's: that is, a settlement of the lands in perpetuity. Unlike Boughton Rous, he raises no historical objection about the Company's right to dispose of all the lands of Bengal. But the way he interprets the measure gives it an economic significance altogether different from what was conceived by Dow. The latter, as a mercantilist, considers agriculture as subsidiary to commerce. Pattullo, on the contrary, believes in the primacy of agriculture, and states the physiocratic position very clearly thus:

> Lands and agriculture are the subsistence of all ranks, and the source of all revenues. Their produce are the only real riches. Without their regular reproduction, all other riches can be of no value. Banks and bankers might shut up or even might lye open. Their treasures can neither feed nor clothe. The rarest jewels would appear bubbles of folly; high and low would be brought upon a level, and the world would soon be at an end.[118]

This is an emphatic reversal of the relative order of importance ascribed by Dow to commerce and agriculture. In Pattullo's *Essay* the pride of place goes to agriculture which according to his school of thought produces 'the only real riches', and all problems relating to circulation – commerce, money, banking – are treated as foil to this

[116] *Ibid.*, pp. 34–5.
[117] *Ibid.*, pp. 30–2.
[118] *Ibid.*, p. 24.

central issue. In this context, his concern for the security of landed property has an implication far exceeding the limits of mercantilist economics.

Agriculture, he observes, cannot thrive if the people 'are debarred the acquisition and enjoyment of property'. The peasants under such conditions have no incentive to productive labour and, therefore, tend to resign themselves to misery and despair 'as the peasants in some of the interior provinces of France now actually do'. A government which fails to give its subjects security of property is as unwise as those who, he says after Montesquieu, cut down the tree to eat the fruit, 'which to the reproach of Britain, has been too much the case in Bengal ever since the British arms made the conquest'.[119] The author joins all other critics of the East India Company in condemning the 'destructive measures' of annual farming of lands and short-term leases. In this respect, too, he finds a notorious similarity between this system and the prevailing one in France. 'The great oppressions which are at present practised there', he says about Bengal, 'with the imprudent way of letting the lands annually, have already had their natural effect, in laying many of the cultivated lands so soon waste and desolate; that the residing labourers have abandoned them, and that there is now a necessity of letting them much under their value to vagrants . . . The like measures have had the like effects in many of the interior provinces of France, where all the former residentary farmers have been ruined, and none can now be found in these parts, but such as present themselves with no other funds than scarcely cloaths to cover them . . . Such, and worse if possible, will soon be the infallible consequences, over all the provinces of Bengal, of the present destructive measures.'[120]

Pattullo's analysis of the causes of the agricultural decline of Bengal is thus the same as Dow's, and so also is the remedy he suggests – that is, a permanent settlement of rights in land. But as a physiocrat he

[119] *Ibid.*, pp. 8–9.
[120] *Ibid.*, p. 20.

goes far beyond Dow in ascribing to property an economic function in terms of capitalist development in agriculture. It was his opinion that the security of proprietary rights would induce a large amount of investment in land.[121] It did so even in Europe where the price of land was much higher than in India. In France the *lods et vente* sometimes amounted to anything between a third and a fifth of the agreed price while the price itself could be as high as the equivalent of six years' rent of the estate. Yet this 'never discourages people from purchasing, as preferring property to all other means of placing money'. In England, too, a long lease would cost a farmer a fine amounting to two to five years' rent, but 'they soon draw the returns by doubling their industry from a certainty of long possession.' In Bengal the price of land was relatively more moderate. 'So in this case, there can be no doubt that all who possess money in India, will with pleasure pay in fine for a perpetual property, confirmed by the British legislature, and supported by the laws and power of Britain, as much at least as purchasers in France pay a fine to the superior, and farmers in Britain for a long lease.' He was quite certain that under such circumstances the more prosperous among the natives 'would hasten to employ' their money in land 'even to emulation'.

Pattullo's vision of a resurgence of Indian agriculture on these lines is remarkable for its fine blending of intellectual convictions of French origin with the experience of contemporary developments in the Scottish countryside. Like Thomas Somerville, he, too, must have witnessed a large number of the nabobs coming back home with fortunes made in India and descending on the Lowlands to set up as country gentlemen.[122] Why then could not the wealthy

[121] *Ibid.*, pp. 8–10.

[122] 'There can be no doubt', wrote Somerville in his autobiography, 'that the rise in the price of land is also in part attributable to the increased competition for this kind of property, owing to the great number of Scotchmen who have recently returned to this country from the British colonies with large fortunes, and with a natural desire to invest them in the purchase of Scotch estates . . . The fortune . . . brought from the East Indies alone in

Indians themselves make a similar use of their money in their own country? Given permanent proprietary rights and a buyers' market in land, there was no reason why Bengal should not be blessed with the capital and initiative of its own indigenous entrepreneurs. Speaking of the far-reaching possibilities of his plan for Permanent Settlement, he says:

> Sensible also of the great advantages of property, however small, with fixed family residences and the conveniences of British furniture and way of living, they (the people of Bengal) will without doubt relish them, and thereby open a new branch to the Company, of carrying thither British commodities, while they again will find sufficient returns for all, in the growing produce of their country[123]

Pattullo could not, of course, see so far into the future as to realize that one part of his economic prediction for Bengal would in course of time be frustrated by the other coming true. It was precisely the plan 'of carrying thither British commodities' which was eventually to turn his physiocratic utopia into the quasi-feudal settlement of Lord Cornwallis. For a capitalist development in Indian agriculture at that stage could not coexist with the more powerful urge of establishing a colonial market there. In history, as in life, it is not always possible both to have the cake and eat it.

3. The Supervisors and the Rejection of the 'Farming System'

A theory of Permanent Settlement had thus already taken shape by 1772. In these earlier versions, however, it was significant only as an

---

the course of the last fifty years, have been so large, and have been so generally applied to the purchase of estates, that the property thus acquired now bears a great proportion to the whole landed property in Scotland. This is remarkably illustrated in my own neighbourhood. Not fewer than eight estates of considerable value have, in my recollection, been bought in Roxburghshire by gentlemen who have returned from the East Indies.' My *Own Life and Times*, 1741–1814, pp. 359–60.

[123] *Essay*, p. 28.

exercise in the contemporary hobby of model-building. It was the mission of Philip Francis to convert speculation into policy. For this he needed authority as well as experience. Authority came to him by virtue of his appointment to the Supreme Council of Bengal, but of administrative experience he possessed very little indeed. As a clerk and political writer he had never before been called upon to act as a captain of men handling complex responsibilities within ill-defined jurisdictions. His knowledge of India too was bookish and second-hand. His critics played up this deficiency in order to establish the relative superiority of his rival, Warren Hastings, in this respect and to suggest that the want of realism in his policies was a necessary product of inexperience. Consequently, the fact has often been ignored that Francis sought in a most sensible way to make up for his initial lack of direct personal acquaintance with the Indian situation by drawing upon the experience of others. It would be difficult to argue that he was less informed about the country than, for instance, Lord Cornwallis,[124] or for that matter, than some of the other very able Governor-Generals of a subsequent period, when they first took up their appointments. Cornwallis learnt from Shore, Malet and Anderson,[125] the later Governor-Generals, from the best men of the Indian Civil Service. In the same way Francis, too, profited from the advice and collaboration of some of the most efficient and knowledgeable officials serving then in Bengal.

[124] Charles Ross, the official editor of Lord Cornwallis's correspondence, wrote: 'Lord Cornwallis did not arrive at Calcutta till the beginning of September, 1786. He had of course no previous knowledge of the mighty empire over which he was about to rule, and he was necessarily ignorant of the manners, usages, and language of the country. For information, therefore, he was obliged to rely on his Council and his subordinate officers' (*Correspondence of Charles, First Marquis Cornwallis*, vol. I, p. 223). The advantage of this comparison is, indeed, on Francis's side, because before his departure for Calcutta he had at least equipped himself with whatever he could learn about Bengal from a large amount of documentation and personal advice provided by Clive.

[125] *Ibid.*, p. 224.

From the very outset Francis himself was quite clear about the need for assistance from younger people. As early as 1774 he had already laid it down as a principle for his own guidance that he ought 'to encourage the Resort of young people to me, from whom I may learn the current opinions with respect to persons and Things'.[126] Two years later, that is, long before Joseph Price was to come out in public accusing him of plagiarism, he made it known to his friends that he had been working with a team trying to incorporate his ideas into official statements. '*All* these Minutes', he wrote at that time, 'are not of my Composition. Some of them are so plainly underwritten that I hope they will not be attributed to me. This Observation goes merely to the Form; for as to the Substance, I must be content to answer for whatever I have once set my Name to. The Labour we have all gone thro' is truly incredible.'[127] On his plan of Permanent Settlement he sought and received the opinions of some of the ablest officials of that period including Richard Goodlad, David Anderson, William Young, Richard Becher, John Shore, William Harwood, C.W. Boughton Rous and George Ducarel.[128] There is not much evidence to suggest that his collaboration with the first four of them was of any long standing, while Shore, the most famous of them all, was far too independent and far too removed from either of the leading factions to be counted as a member of any inner circle.[129] Harwood, who had served in Rajmahal, Bhagalpur and Dinajpur, was personally close to Francis and had imbibed many of the latter's ideas.[130] It is quite evident that he was actively associated with anti-Hastings intrigues both in India and in England: he travelled by the same boat as Francis on his way

[126] 'Hints for my own Conduct' (1774). *Francis MSS* 65 (51) 2.

[127] To H. Strachey (20 March 1776), *ibid.*, 47 (36) 86.

[128] *Ibid.*, 77 (31) 7, 77 (31) 9, 51 (41) 41, 49 (38) 98, 77 (31) 6, 53 (49) 26.

[129] For Shore's independence, see Teignmouth, *Memoir of the Life and Correspondence of John Lord Teignmouth*, vol. I, pp. 52–3; for his impartiality and a refutation of Price's charge that Francis picked his brains, Weitzman, *Warren Hastings and Philip Francis*, p. 75n.

[130] Harwood to Francis (23 January 1777). *Francis MSS* 49 (38) 70.

back home, and there is just a touch of complicity in Burke's letter to Francis saying that Harwood should be briefed before being examined by the Select Committee in 1783.[131] But apart from this and Price's insinuating statement that Francis *could have used* the other's talents to edit his memoranda to the Select Committee if he wanted to do so, there is nothing very definite to prove his indebtedness to Harwood in the same way as to Ducarel and Rous.

What Francis owed to the administrators will be best judged by the record of his association with these two officers. G.G. Ducarel was very much of a personal friend who, as Francis himself acknowledges in one of his letters, was his adviser on matters concerning the land revenue.[132] While the collaboration with Ducarel dates from the earliest days of Francis's Indian career, that with Rous belongs mainly to the period following the completion of his plan for the Permanent Settlement of Bengal. He had already been in touch with Rous on a routine administrative matter as early as February 1775,[133] but judging from the correspondence preserved among the Francis papers, it was only by the middle of the next year that they began earnestly to exchange ideas on economic and political questions.[134] Here we find Francis discussing with his junior colleague the two important themes of agrarian and monetary reform in which he was so interested, receiving from him an elaborate note on revenue administration,[135] defending his own plan in two letters both written on the same day and welcoming Rous's comments on it with a most unusual gesture of humility to say, 'A simple Approbation, however

131 P. & M., II, p. 217.

132 To C.W.B. Rous (21 October 1776). *Francis MSS* 49 (38) 61.

133 To same (14 February 1775), *ibid.*, 48 (37) 47.

134 To same (21 October and 8 November 1776), *ibid.*, 49 (38) 61 and 62.

135 'Hints on the Revenue' (n.d.), *ibid.*, 74 (3) 53. The nature of the argument as well as Francis's reference to 'the Hint, contained in your Letter of the 13th Instant etc.' in his private letter to Rous mentioned in the note below, are the grounds on which I am inclined to ascribe the authorship of this document to Rous.

strongly expressed, would not have satisfied me, if it had not come, as yours does, supported by Argument and accompanied with Objections.'[136] From the tone of all these letters, not the least from the way in which he begs Rous to continue to write to him,[137] it is obvious that Francis found in his correspondent a mind he could respect. The highly complimentary reference to Francis in Rous's *Dissertation* published many years later shows that the admiration was mutual. The assistance Francis received from both Ducarel and Rous in all the intrigues leading to the impeachment of Warren Hastings proves that their co-operation was not limited to matters of strictly intellectual interest alone.[138]

What made their services so valuable to Francis was the knowledge they had of the intricate agrarian system of the eastern provinces. Among the first Englishmen to receive appointment in 1769 under Verelst's plan of supervisorship, Ducarel and Rous were placed in charge of the districts of Puria and Rajshahi respectively. These two districts were among the largest fiscal units the Company had undertaken to manage under the Diwani and represented, each in its very different way, a most important type of rural economy prevailing in Bengal in the late eighteenth century. Purnia, once the pleasure ground of the Nawabs, but left in shambles after the pageantry had passed, was distinguished by a small and impoverished peasant population, vast tracts of waste land, miserable smallholdings and lack of estates of any considerable size.[139] Rajshahi on the other hand, was fertile and prosperous, with one of the most powerful landed families

[136] To Rous (22) June 1776), *ibid.*, 77 (31) 8. This letter is marked 'Private', and as such should be differentiated from another letter to Rous bearing the same date and preserved *ibid.*, 53 (49) 26. Both the letters are valuable for the comments Francis has to make on his own revenue plan submitted to the Council earlier that year.

[137] To same (11 August 1777), *ibid.*, 48 (37) 104.

[138] Weitzman, op. cit., pp. 145–6.

[139] *Proceedings of the Committee of Circuit at Krishnagar and Kasimbazar*, part 3, p. 109.

owning the greater part of the district as what according to Grant was 'the largest Zemindary in Hindostan'.[140] Between them they posed two very contrary aspects of the task facing the early British administration in Bengal. In one case it was the problem of filling a vacuum created by the decay of Mughal power in an outlying part of the empire; in the other, of breaking down a whole structure of living authority vested in the zamindar. The two Supervisors may thus be said to have complemented each other in acquiring for themselves and providing for Francis the entire range of typical administrative experience available to local officers at that time.

To a certain extent the association between these three men might have been the product of common frustration. For like Francis these officers themselves had set out on their respective careers in the districts with the zeal of true reformers only to find their initiative curbed by their superiors. The heady mixture of generalities and good intentions in Verelst's famous mandate to the Supervisors was strong enough to make any young officer, gifted with imagination and courage, read it as a manifesto rather than as a departmental circular. Ducarel and Rous, too, took up their posts with their minds already made up about the many-sided improvements they thought it would be their duty to introduce. Consequently, some of their earliest policy statements, recorded in their letters to the Resident and the Council at Murshidabad, have the impatience and sweep of a benevolent dictator's first decrees broadcast within an hour of the coup.

The point of departure for both of them was the conviction that the economy of Bengal had been on the decline ever since the assumption of Diwani by the East India Company. Boughton Rous had not been a week in Bhushna, a part of the district under his charge, nor even learnt to read the native revenue accounts properly, before he sent a report about its all-round deterioration – about its

[140] Grant, *An Inquiry into the Nature of Zemindary Tenures in the Landed Property of Bengal*, p. 33. The extent of this estate owned by Rani Bhabani's family was, according to Grant, 13,000 square miles and it comprised 16,000 villages. See also Hunter, *Statistical Account of Bengal*, vol. VIII, p. 20.

agriculture having been ruined by the farming system and 'that flourishing Commerce which was formerly carried on thro' this Province' having 'greatly suffer'd as a natural Consequence of the Declension of agriculture'.[141]

Ducarel's conclusion about the state of Purnia was no less categorical. It contained the same elegiac notes on what Verelst had ironically called the 'golden age' of Mughal rule[142] and a very similar explanation of the recent economic changes. 'The country has been less flourishing since our Time than heretofore', he said. The prosperity of the district depended mostly on the sale and export of grains. So long as Murshidabad was the seat of government there was a ready and easily accessible market for its agricultural products in the northern districts. Besides, the Nawabs did not extract from Purnia more than an annual revenue of four to five lakhs of rupees. Above all 'what was collected here was spent here, besides the Trade being in Favour – and altho' the Government was bad and property insecure (money) only changed Hands, the province was not thereby impoverished (nor) Cultivation lessened'. But when the Company took over the management of the revenues, the district was 'too highly rated', paying as it did about twelve lakhs of rupees as revenue every year, that is, thrice the amount paid under the former regime. Consequently, 'the wealth of the Country has flown since the Company's time'. The transfer of the capital from Murshidabad to Calcutta ruined Purnia's grain trade and there was no influx of money to compensate for this loss. 'It appeared to me', he wrote, 'that the Imports of Treasure were no wise equal to these Remittances.' In other words, the drain of wealth – to use the vocabulary of the economic theory underlying

[141] *Letter Copy Book of the Supervisor of Rajshahi at Nator*, p. 12. About eight months after this report Rous was still complaining about the native accounts being 'so extremely perplexed from their grant (*sic*) Want of Method' – *Proceedings of the Controlling Council of Revenue at Murshidabad*, vol. II, pp. 155–6.

[142] Verelst, *View of the Rise, Progress and Present State of the English Government in Bengal*, p. 64.

these observations – had resulted in an unfavourable balance of trade. Here within the scale of a single district we have the microcosm of that happy commercial empire of the House of Timur described by Dow. The same striking contrast of colours is used in both cases to distinguish former glory from subsequent decline, and even the details of the analysis agree so closely as to suggest a parallelism between the loss of Purnia's market in the upper provinces and that of India's export trade in the Middle East and South-East Asia, as described by Dow.[143]

Francis, too, shared this view of the economic consequences of the Diwani, but another and even more powerful inducement to his collaboration with Ducarel and Rous was their common disapproval of the official policy of short-term revenue-farming. The controversy about its merits was nearly as old as the earliest English experiments with the land settlements of Bengal, a fact which easily escapes notice in the noise of the disputes it provoked at a later date. More than a decade before the great debate was launched in the Calcutta Council, John Johnston had introduced and Harry Verelst reversed the policy in the ceded district of Burdwan, each using on his part arguments very similar to those put forward by the rival spokesmen of 1775–6.[144] The adoption, or rather the continuation, of the farming system as the basic land policy of the government made it possible for the district officials to gather a first-hand knowledge of its abuses during the early years of the Diwani. Their letters to the Resident at Murshidabad contain the record of many unhappy experiences. But it was not until the economy of rural Bengal had been shattered by the famine of 1770 and the problem of recovery had put all policies to test that the inadequacies of this method began to engage serious official attention. Ducarel and Rous both found the policy unworkable

[143] This summary of Ducarel's economic ideas is based on his correspondence published in *Proceedings of the Controlling Council of Revenue at Murshidabad*, vol. II, pp. 62–3, 68, and vol. V, pp. 109, 110; and *Proceedings of the Committee of Circuit at Krishnagar and Kasimbazar*, part 3, pp. 108–9.

[144] Firminger, *Fifth Report*, Introduction, vol. I, pp. cxli, cxlv–cxlvi.

in the two difficult regions of the Presidency placed under their charge during and after the famine.

Purnia was ravaged by the famine which, according to Ducarel's estimate, 'swept away nearly half the People, the Number of whom, not the quantity of Lands is acknowledged to constitute the Wealth and real Value of every Country'.[145] It had also upset his three-year plan for the recovery of this region from the state of decay that had set in there since 1765.[146] Under the changed circumstances he came out with a new scheme for settling the lands of the district:

> In the ensuing Year (that is the fiscal year 1771–2) the plan I would recommend for the Bundibust is as follows – such of the Purgunnahs as are either Khas or in the hands of people not sufficiently answerable for the ensuing Year's Revenue, I would propose to form an exact Hustabood of (*sic*) on the Spot from the Measurement and Jummabundy of the present year and upon that Hustabood which is the most accurate Valuation that can be formed with a due Consideration of local Circumstances let out the Lands in small Etmams of 2, 3 or 4 Villages mostly to the principal Gyrhests or husbandmen of the pergunnahs. These people can take small farms with Security and I have found by Experience are the most proper for the management of the Land here and from knowing best how to make advantage for themselves can afford to take them on the most favourable Terms for the Company. I have already mentioned to you . . . that from the great want of people of sufficient property it (this mode of settlement) was much to be preferred to large Farms or letting the purgunnah entire as the Company will thereby receive almost the whole produce of the land with very little Danger of Ballances from the small Sum each Man engages for at the same time that this Method will always lay before you the clearest state of the Mofussil and be the most improveable for the Country in general.[147]

The originality and realism of this proposal cannot be overestimated. I do not know of any other plan dating from this period which suggests

[145] *Proceedings of the Controlling Council of Revenue at Murshidabad*, vol. VI, p. 454.

[146] *Ibid.*, vol. II, p. 65.

[147] *Ibid.*, vol. V, pp. 59–60.

a settlement with smallholders, and in a district distinguished by the absence of large estates one would imagine a policy of this sort to be the best way of encouraging agricultural enterprise. The Controlling Council of Revenue, however, had a very different opinion about it, and Ducarel soon ran into trouble. His recommendations were referred to Muhammad Reza Khan, the Naib Diwan, for his opinion, and the most important criticism offered by the latter was that 'as the Settlement is concluded with petty Farmers Ryotts and Talockdars there can be no Dependance on its being fully realized and whatever falls short in the Collection may be deem'd a Loss to the Government'. The Council accordingly condemned Ducarel for 'the adoption of a diffusive Plan' which they thought 'leaves the Government without any collateral Security for the payment of their Revenues'. When the charge was repeated in another resolution of the Council a few months later, Ducarel was moved to write a lengthy reply in defence of his own policy and the authorities were eventually forced to admit that he had been on the whole justified.[148] But the wisdom of the plan for a settlement with smallholders becomes clear in retrospect when a year later, early in 1773, we find the Committee of Circuit at Purnia looking in vain for local men to come forward with offers for farming backed by sufficient security. That the quinquennial settlement there was ultimately made with notorious speculators like Huzurimal, Madan Datta and 'other substantial persons of Calcutta', and even this was achieved 'after much Difficulty and Discussion', merely shows that the government, deeply committed as it was by this time to Hastings's farming system, had learnt nothing from the experience of one of its most acute and knowledgeable district officers.[149]

While Ducarel was thus busy vindicating his deviation from the general line of revenue-farming, Boughton Rous was at the same time engaged in questioning the system in another part of the country. Rajshahi was less affected by the famine than Purnia, but not

[148] *Ibid.*, vol. VI, pp. 96–9, 232, 452–9, 460.

[149] *Proceedings of the Committee of Circuit at Krishnagar and Kasimbazar*, part 3, pp. 105–6.

altogether spared. In fact, one of the first letters Rous wrote from the district in the summer of 1770 mentions a drought killing the crops and the consequent distress of the people. As the correspondence proceeds the shadow of the famine grows longer, and by winter many of the parganas were reported to be in such a state of desolation as to find it difficult to pay even five per cent of their revenues. A flood followed and completed the ruin.[150] Under these circumstances to farm out the lands to the highest bidder in order to keep up the revenue to the exaggerated amount assessed for the previous year[151] was a policy which Rous found it hard to justify in principle and realize in practice.

From one of his earliest recorded impressions about the economy of the district it would appear that he had begun his career there full of doubts about the principle of revenue farming. Agriculture was on the decline, he thought, 'by reason of the undue influence which many of them (the revenue-farmers) have assumed, and which has enabled them to displace the Zemindar's establish'd officers, and thus to remove the Chief Controll which stood between them and the Ryots'.[152] The theoretical concept underlying this view is that of an ideal society connected between its apex and base by an intermediate class of landed proprietors. This notion, which was widely shared by many eighteenth-century writers, was one of the most important points of agreement between Francis and Rous in their defence of the zamindari system. Writing twenty years after he had packed in that bit of bold sociology with his report from Bhushna, the latter, armed now with the authority of Mirabeau the Elder, made vigorous use of the idea in his *Dissertation Concerning the Landed Property of Bengal*. 'The good government of a nation, and the energy of its

[150] *Letter Copy Book of the Supervisor of Rajshahi at Nator*, pp. 15–16; *Proceedings of the Controlling Council of Revenue at Murshidabad*, vol. II, pp. 157, 165, 167–8; *ibid.*, vol. V, pp. 252–3.

[151] For an official admission that Rajshahi was overassessed during the fiscal year 1768–9, see *The Letter Copy Books of the Resident at the Durbar at Murshidabad, 1769–70*, pp. xv–xvi.

[152] *Letter Copy Book of the Supervisor of Rajshahi at Nator*, p. 11.

exertions, foreign and internal,' he wrote, 'depend more upon the train of discipline and authority, carried down from the sovereign to the lower orders of the people by the agency of intermediate ranks, than by the wisest laws issued by the imperial cabinet.'[153] Indian society, he argued, had 'its best, if not its only cement' in the zamindar class.[154] Consequently, 'if the old Zemindars were removed, we should have the peasants and cultivators without any superior to look up to, between themselves and the sovereign power, no patron to mediate for them, and compose their little differences; expecting to be harassed by the inquisitorial officers of revenue, or temporary farmers sharing in no common interest with them'.[155]

Of the harassment caused by the temporary farmers Boughton Rous himself was both a witness and a victim. Only a few weeks before his appointment the Resident's office had received reports about the tyranny of Pran Bose, an ijaradar of Rajshahi.[156] In the year of famine and flood two parganas of the district were ruined by an agent of Dulal Roy who had taken them in farm and fleeced the peasantry.[157] In the course of a single year, following the famine, the ryots in another area were forced by their newly appointed farmer, Hutoo Roy, to pay seventy thousand rupees in addition to rents.[158] Apart from being oppressive, the farmers were often so 'extremely remiss in their Payments' that on one occasion the Supervisor had to remove many of them in the interest of the government itself and in order to fulfil his own quota of revenue collections.[159] Firmness of this sort must have been an expensive luxury for a district officer

[153] Dissertation, p. 193.

[154] *Ibid.*, p. 192.

[155] *Ibid.*, p. 187.

[156] *The Letter Copy Books of the Resident at the Durbar at Murshidabad, 1769–1770*, p. xv.

[157] *Proceedings of the Controlling Council of Revenue at Murshidabad*, vol. V, p. 253.

[158] *Proceedings of the Committee of Circuit at Krishnagar and Kasimbazar*, part 1, p. 110.

[159] *Proceedings of the Controlling Council of Revenue at Murshidabad*, vols VI–VIII, p. 214.

of moderate income, for we find Boughton Rous complaining to his superiors that an agent of the farmer of Ameerabad 'had the insolence to offer me a Present of a thousand Rupees on Accot. of his Master I suppose by Way of Atonement'.[160]

The contrast between this foul band of fortune-hunting, pettifogging farmers of revenue and the solid, solvent and awe-inspiring local zamindar might have had a formative influence on the Supervisor's estimate of the relative merits of the two rival systems of land settlement. Rani Bhabani, the dowager, managed her estate like a queen. The size and value of her property in what was one of the most fertile districts of Bengal gave her a place at the very top of the landed aristocracy. Her charity had its colossal expression in the building of temples and digging of sweet water lakes and thus made her the very symbol of benevolence so often associated with the better type of zamindars in that age. The most visible proof of her authority was the immense estate sprawling all over northern Bengal. But the harassment caused to her by the East India Company and her manoeuvres to defy the fiscal pressure in a manner many other zamindars would not dare, were the stuff out of which popular imagination easily fashioned a legend of resistance and martyrdom. The fact of her being a woman made it convenient to fix upon her the image of the Mother, abused and insulted by foreigners and their lackeys, the *nouveaux riches*, and for a people unreconciled to British rule her suffering was charged with a dark, disturbing message. The band of vagrant raiders from the northern provinces known as the Sannyasis and the Fakirs who descended on the plains of Bengal in this epoch sought in her recalcitrance abetment, if not actual aid, for their plundering forays.[161] These huns with no local roots terrorized

[160] *Ibid.*, vol. II, p. 156.

[161] For a letter addressed by Majnu Shah, the leader of the Fakir raiders, to Rani Bhabani in 1772, see Jamini Mohan Ghosh, *Sannyasi and Fakir Raiders in Bengal*, p. 47. The letter complains about the Fakirs being oppressed by the English and ends thus: 'You are the ruler of the country. We are Fakirs who pray always for your welfare. We are full of hopes.'

the countryside as much as did the Maratha horsemen in the troubled years of Alivardi's rule and were no more friends of the peasantry than the armed levies of the revenue-farmers themselves. Thanks, however, to Bankimchandra's powerful invention in *Anandamath*[162] nationalist imagination at a later date invested them with the mantle of peasant-resisters. In much the same way, out of the shifts and equivocations of Rani Bhabani's attempt to evade the farming system Bengali patriotism in search of a hero abstracted the material for a lofty image of defiance – the image of a brave, lone Boadicea defending the last outpost of independence.[163]

In reality the Rani, like thousands of other zamindars at that time, was only trying by supplication and subterfuge to keep her estate safe from the auctioneer's hammer. But exceeding even the fear of loss of property was the fear of social disgrace. For land was still regarded as the highest status symbol. To suffer ancestral acres to pass into the hands of moneyed upstarts was a public admission of indigence and therefore dishonourable. The Rani's young son told Boughton Rous with bitterness and pride that 'it would be less disgraceful to relinquish their Lands than to farm them at a public Sale'.[164] In any case to transfer the management of such an ancient zamindari to other hands was bound to do very great harm. The Rani herself warns the authorities that 'the farming out the Districts to other

[162] A novel by the nineteenth-century Bengali writer, Bankimchandra Chattopadhyaya. The action of the story takes place during the years immediately before and after the famine of 1770. The picture which the author drew here of a highly disciplined, educated, patriotic and idealistic band of Sannyasi robbers, taking away from the rich and aiding the poor, and above all resisting the troops of the East India Company in several armed encounters, had a great influence on the nationalist movement in both its individual-terroristic and mass-civil variations.

[163] For a highly unhistorical portraiture of Rani Bhabani as a leader of the anti-British aristocrats opposing Mir Jafar's betrayal at Plassey, see Nabinchandra Sen's famous poem, *Palasir Yuddha*.

[164] *Proceedings of the Controlling Council of Revenue at Murshidabad*, vol. VI, p, 140.

People, will increase their present calamities and impoverished State, the Realization of the Revenue will hereafter be an Impossibility, and the Complaints of the Ryots will daily be more and more'.[165] But words like these could at most help in postponing the doom. From what was happening all over the Presidency to other proprietors the Rani had the astuteness to realize that it was inevitable. One of the last desperate ways in which she tried to escape the consequences of farming was to allow parts of the zamindari to be leased out nominally to her son and other relatives, while retaining the actual control herself.[166] This method of holding estates *benami* (literally, without using the name of the actual owner) was already known in the later period of Mughal rule.[167] But the very large number of cases of benami holdings under Warren Hastings's regime clearly indicates how the farming system helped in popularizing this particular form of fraud in Bengal. It recorded the reaction of the old propertied classes to the increasing mobility of the land-market, and as with the progress of the century land began to assume more and more the character of a commodity subject to all the vicissitudes of exchange, the practice came to be recognized as one of the best ways of evading the law. In this respect the Rani of Rajshahi anticipated by over two decades another powerful zamindar, Raja Tejchand of Burdwan, who also sought by the same ruse to keep his estate from falling to pieces after the Permanent Settlement.[168]

Much more than artifice, however, it was passive resistance that slowed down the progress of farming in Rajshahi. Already in the summer of 1771 Boughton Rous had expressed his fear that in spite of ample advertisement 'the Influence of the Zemindar [referring in this

[165] *Proceedings of the Committee of Circuit at Krishnagar and Kasimbazar*, Part 1, p. 88.

[166] *Proceedings of the Controlling Council of Revenue at Murshidabad*, vol. IV, p. 144.

[167] For a seventeenth century example, see R. Guha, 'Report on an Investigation of the Gauripur Raj Estate Archives', in *Report of the Regional Records Survey Committee for West Bengal, 1955–56*.

[168] *Bengal District Records: Burdwan Letters Issued, 1788–1800*, Introduction, p. lxxiii.

case to the Rani's son] may be the means of preventing the Inhabitants of the District from offering to farm any of the Purgunnahs now in his Hands'.[169] The report he sent to the Council four months afterwards shows how right he had been in his prediction.

> In Pursuance of Your Orders . . . after having circulated Letters of Advice to every Pergunnah in the District, and made repeated Publications by Beat of Tomtom at Nattore, I have endeavoured to procure Farmers for the Rany's Talooks and other Lands by Means of a public Sale. The Talooks of different Pergunnahs both in Bhettooreah and Bhoosnah were exposed to Sale; but no Bidders appeared for any. I then gave the public Notice, that any Person was at Liberty to mention such particular Village as he was inclined to farm, and offer his Terms of Increase. But this Plan was as ineffectual as the former. I do not apprehend this Backwardness gives any Grounds for Belief, that the Value of those Lands is exaggerated; but that it arises principally from the Attachment and Subserviency generally shewn by the Inhabitants of the District to the Station and Honour of the Zemindar, and very probably to the Influence employed by the Dependents of the Rany to discourage People from renting her Lands.[170]

By winter as the harvesting season drew near, panic turned into despair. 'I must really confess,' he wrote, 'it is my Opinion, Gentlemen, that there is very little Prospect of my being able to let these Lands in any advantageous Manner. The Inhabitants of the District, if Men of any Reputation, are totally averse to the Renting either of the Rany's or Diaram Roy's [her manager] Lands by which they must incur such a general Odium and, the Farmers of the Pergunnahs where these Lands are situated, whom I have pressed upon the Subject, seem equally unwilling to engage.'[171]

The procedure of farming was thus stonewalled by the authority of the zamindar. It was the kind of authority which demanded recognition not only from those among the ryots who could be bullied

[169] *Proceedings of the Controlling Council of Revenue at Murshidabad*, vol. V, p. 238.

[170] *Ibid.*, vol. VI, pp. 139–40.

[171] *Ibid.*, p. 253.

by the Rani's retainers, but even from more substantial people including the farmers. This was a most impressive tribute paid by all sections of a village society to the old zamindari system in the hour of its crisis. From the manner in which Rous presents the problem in his correspondence it is evident that the experience of this early encounter inspired in him a genuine respect for 'the Station and Honour of the Zemindar' and in general, for the institution of permanent and hereditary proprietorship itself. The conclusion which the young Supervisor derived for himself from this trial of strength between the two systems was hardly affected by the insistence of his superiors that 'at all Events the Lands held by the Zemindar must be let to farm.'[172] His failure to do so drew from the Council what he felt was unmerited censure,[173] and this bitterness might have gone a long way in forming in a proud and young mind a firm focus of resistance to all policies and groups based on support for revenue-farming. Philip Francis, with his instinct for both dissent and dogma, was quick to locate this keg of explosives and lay a friendly fuse to it. Having drawn Rous into a discussion of his revenue plan he went on to follow it up by marking out the measure of their common agreement on theoretical grounds[174] and eventually setting himself up as his patron and protector.[175]

[172] *Proceedings of the Controlling Council of Revenue at Murshidabad*, vol. V, p. 160.

[173] *Ibid.*, pp. 118, 157–8.

[174] To Rous (22 June 1776). *Francis MSS* 53 (49) 26.

[175] Francis's 'private' letter to Rous of 22 June 1776 concludes thus with an emphasis on the identity of their interests: 'If ever the Time I speak of comes, I shall request your Permission to name you for a Share in the Execution of this great and important Trust [that is, in connection with the Permanent Settlement of Bengal]. I am not quite disinterested in making this Request. I wish to lessen the Hazard of my own Credit as much as possible, by uniting it with that of Men whose Characters are generally respected and esteemed' – *ibid.*, 77 (31) 8. By early next year Francis was already writing about Rous as if the latter were his protege and consequently victimized by Warren Hastings. – To Lord Barringron (9 January and 13 February 1777), *ibid.*, 49 (38) 67 and 73.

3

The Personality and Politics of Philip Francis

THE VIEWS OF ALEXANDER DOW and Henry Pattullo on the necessity of Permanent Settlement were important as a germinal idea rather than as an aid to policy. It was left to Philip Francis to build up this idea into a comprehensive system and press for its acceptance as a formula of government. Unfortunately, however, this contribution has not been properly assessed so far in the literature on this period except in a negative sense, that is, only for what it was worth as an impediment to the policies represented by Warren Hastings.

1. Verdicts on Francis

To contemporaries Francis's reputation was slightly higher than that of Warren Hastings: but later historians reversed the scales. During the greater part of his career he was involved in issues of English politics which had very little to do with India; yet the manuals preserve only the memory of his Indian intrigues. The records of the period contain much evidence of his powerful and original ideas relating to the economy of Bengal; in the standard histories, however, his influence on Cornwallis's land laws is either not mentioned at all or passed over with only an incidental bow. How could it so happen?

The answer is that Francis has been the victim of second thoughts about Warren Hastings. All the luminous adjectives which are commonly applied to Hastings's Indian record are in fact a nineteenth-century invention. During the 1780s opinion about him was at least divided, and in the balance, would perhaps be found to have been mostly critical. There were, of course, those who with the cartoonist Sayers imagined Edmund Burke in the role of a showman with a magic lantern treating the crowd to a highly magnified spectacle of the Governor-General's misdeeds. But there were others who with the rival artist Gillray suspected Hastings's friends of trying to induce the public to look at his Himalayan crimes through the peephole of a camera obscura reducing the images of elephants, hills and whales to the respective dimensions of fleas, warts and weasels.[1] Indicative also of a quick hardening of attitudes during the trial was Gillray's abrupt changeover from an enthusiastic defence of the 'Saviour of India' to his downright condemnation as a plunderer wading through a sea of blood.[2] The verdict of acquittal had little immediate effect on the

[1] For these contradictory interpretations, see M. Dorothy George, *English Political Caricature*, v. I, p. 194. Sayers's cartoon *Galante Show* and Gillray's Camera-Obscuraare reproduced in that volume as Plates No. 80 and No. 81 respectively.

[2] *Ibid.*, Plates No. 78 and No. 79. The first of these two caricatures by Gillray appeared in 1786 under the caption, *The Political-Banditti assailing the Saviour of India*; the other, *Blood and Thunder Fording the Red Sea*, in 1788. They are thus described by Dorothy George: 'In *The Political-Banditti assailing the Saviour* of *India* . . . Hastings, in oriental dress, rides a camel, which like its rider looks down with proud contempt at the antics of Burke, Fox, and North who wear armour. Burke, like a malignant insect or a burlesqued Don Quixote, carrying a wallet of "charges", fires a blunderbuss at the "Shield of Honour" on Hastings's arm, Fox, frenzied with rage, lifts a conspiratorial dagger. North grabs at one of the money-bags on the camel – "Rupees added to the Revenue"; his damaged (but sheathed) sabre is inscribed "American Subjugation"': (p. 190). 'Excitement seethed and bubbled in 1788 . . . The prints are predominantly anti-Hastings . . . The most savage attack was Gillray's, *Blood and Thunder Fording the Red Sea* . . . Thurlow, scowling, wades waist-deep in a sea of blood in which float the mutilated corpses of Indian

judgment of the ale-houses and the yellow press. It was not until his eightieth year that Hastings received what he could consider as 'the most convincing and affecting proofs of my having outlived all the prejudices which have, during so many past years, prevailed against me'.[3] England had then just emerged victorious from her long contest with France and begun to rediscover her heroes. The time had come for the statues to be taken out from forgotten cupboards and to be set up in sacred niches reserved for the family idols. Hastings, in his turn, was called up from retirement in the country, and in the course of the two crowded summers of 1813 and 1814 the Court, Parliament, the University of Oxford and the East India nabobs – the four pillars of the Establishment – vied with one another to press honours upon him. All this was marked by the haste and heartlessness of a package deal, or to use an Eastern image, by the pathetic grandeur of a despot trying to make amends for a miscarriage of justice by showering largesse on the victim. Nothing, however, was done to follow up this loud display of affection by the kind of material aid Hastings so badly needed at that time. What, in the first flush, had looked like a sudden improvement in his fortune, turned out in the end to be only a minor ritual in a complex, impersonal and growing cult. For the idea of Empire was already fast outstripping in importance the individual records of its architects and as an abstraction, assuming the independence of a firm's goodwill with respect to the personality of its founder. As with the progress of the nineteenth century this idea continued to gather strength the father figure too acquired a corresponding increase in stature. It was part of an irresistible process which could not be stopped either by the censures of Mill and

---

victims. On his shoulders sits Hastings, serenely content, with a huge money-bag marked £4,000,000 crooked in each arm' (pp. 192–3). Commenting on these two cartoons Miss George asks: 'Was one, or both, commissioned? Or is the contradiction Gillray's ironic contempt (which he shows repeatedly) for the extremes of propaganda? Or had he simply changed his opinion?' A change of opinion seems to be the most likely explanation.

[3] Gleig, *Memoirs of the Life of Warren Hastings*, vol. 3, p. 460.

Macaulay, or by the cool discrimination of Sir John Malcolm who refused to mix up the question of the Governor's personal integrity with what he believed to have been the abuses of his government,[4] or by the sophistications of Harriet Martineau who wrote that it was impossible 'to esteem him' and at the same time 'not to admire him'.[5] In any case, all such reserve was soon swamped by the cult which received a powerful political impetus from the passions of 1857 and intellectual justification from the researches of Sir James Stephen and Sir John Strachey. By the end of the century an entirely new and flawless image of Warren Hastings emerged from the pages of Anglo-Indian history, portraying him at the same time as the darling of his Indian subjects, as a great organizer of the internal administration of the country, and as a far-sighted pioneer who had set the pace for all the subsequent Caesars – Wellesley, Dalhousie and Napier – in short, as an archetype combining all the necessary virtues of benevolence, efficiency and toughness which an Englishman must possess in order to maintain and enlarge a spreading empire.[6]

[4] Malcolm, *The Political History of India from 1784 to 1823*. vol. I, pp. 34–5.

[5] Martineau, *British Rule in India*, p. 135.

[6] Professor Keith Felling alone among the historians has noted how the search for new political ideals towards the end of the Napoleonic wars led to the restoration of Warren Hastings. 'Greater causes', he writes, 'a whole world changing, brought new light and warmth to shine upon him. War and revolution demolished the party which had denounced him, put in the ascendant the qualities that defy danger and the men who used the strong medicine of power, and immersed British India in the epoch of Napoleon. Those who saved the State did not disdain the praise of a tested man of action. In 1801 he wrote to Nelson of "the love and veneration of your country", to which the admiral answered he could value no man's praise more highly, "you that have been the chief of an Empire nearly as large as Europe must be a fair judge of merit". The triumph of Wellesley over Tippu, his drastic handling of Oudh and the Carnatic, seemed to vindicate Hastings' claim for British supremacy, and justify his short-cuts to great ends. The memorable band of his political officers obeyed Hastings' vision of Britain as an Oriental power.' *Warren Hastings*, p. 385.

While Hastings thus went on gaining in stature, the balance of historical judgment was corrected, logically enough, by a proportionate devaluation of his adversary, Philip Francis. By the intensity of his hatreds and loyalties the latter had succeeded even in his lifetime in making many enemies. But as Brougham pointed out, even his worst critics regarded him with a kind of grudging respect. He was known for the angularities of his character; feared for the asperity of his opinions; and towards the end of his life, treated in whig circles as perhaps a misfit and a failure. But it was conceded everywhere that he combined a fine intellect with two very rare virtues for a politician of that age – that is, incorruptibility and consistency. As for intrigues, he was simply playing the game of power which in the reign of George III recognized no rules of penalty for fouling. However, as the lights of glory and immortality were turned on the memory of his rival, a shadow fell on his own reputation. The image of the hero found its inevitable complement in the image of the villain, and there was enough material lying ready for use – not the least in Francis's own correspondence, journals, minutes, and speeches – to permit such a reconstruction of his character. The preconceived notions about Warren Hastings which he carried with him to Bengal; his ruthlessness in singling out his enemy and pursuing him from day to day and year to year throughout his Indian career and back home during the long period of impeachment; the organization of a wide network of agents, accomplices and correspondents, complete with a code of ciphers which he had set up in order to maintain his pressure on his enemy;[7] the servile tone of his address to his own patrons; and his desperate attempt to get himself appointed to the governorship

[7] Francis's letter of 21 August 1776 to John Bourke shows how he set about buying the services of informers. 'If you could find out some clever Fellow', he wrote from Calcutta, 'who would undertake to send me constant Accounts of what is going forward in Leaden Hall Street, I would be very glad to make him a Compensation' – *Francis MSS* 47 (36) 111. Many of his unpublished letters are in parts written in cipher. For some specimens, see P. & M., II, pp. 214–16.

of Bengal which he believed to be 'the first situation attainable by a subject'[8] – all this is ammunition enough to blow up any claim to respectability.

There is, indeed, some kind of poetic justice in this great inquisitor being himself burnt at the stake by the admirers of his victim. However, as the scales were tipped more and more heavily in favour of moral retribution, did there develop among nineteenth-century historians a tendency to bypass or underestimate the grounds of principle on which Francis took his stand against Hastings. The critics worked out in great detail the patterns of his malevolence, but took no notice of the mass of evidence that is there of a highly original mind. They threw out the baby with the bathwater.

2. A Young Alcibiades

These observations are not intended to imply that the personality of Philip Francis is irrelevant to his politics. On the contrary, it is to be regretted that no one has yet written his biography with a little more penetration than is to be found in the Victorian narrative of Parkes and Merivale. In this work the authors have sacrificed insight for respect, and as a result, none of the twisted strands of Francis's early life has been woven into his public figure.

Plutarch's description of Alcibiades as a spoilt and ambitious youth would perfectly fit Francis. 'Among many strong passions of his real character', wrote Plutarch, 'the one most prevailing was his ambition and desire of superiority which appears in several anecdotes told of his sayings whilst he was a child. Once being hard pressed in wrestling, and fearing to be thrown, he got the hand of his antagonist to his mouth and bit it with all his force; and when the other loosed his hold presently, and said, "You bite, Alcibiades, like a woman". "No" replied he, "like a lion."'[9] It was not only in his precocity,

[8] To Godfrey (4 February 1778). *The Francis Letters*, vol. I, p. 306.
[9] Plutarch, *Lives*, vol. I, p. 291.

drive and desire for superiority that Francis resembled this brilliant Athenian bully, but also in his self-righteousness and arrogance. This resulted from those influences which at a very early stage in his life set the course for an independent and oblique development of his character. He lost his mother when he was still very young and found no substitute for it in the affection of any elder female relative.[10] During the formative years of childhood between six and twelve he was separated from his father by all the distance between Dublin and London. He went to school at thirteen and when he left it three years later, he was considered grown up enough to start his career as a junior clerk in the Secretary of State's Office. This is the picture of a child who never knew a home, and it is not surprising that in the letters the elder Francis wrote to his son, then only in his first year at school, there is already a sufficient recognition of mutual independence – and of estrangement.[11] As a gifted but emotionally deprived child, Philip sought compensation in the usual form of a highly developed competitive urge. The register of St Paul's School at Mercer's Hall contains a record of his phenomenal progress from the bottom of the class to its very top in two clear jumps in the course of the three years he was there.[12] What sense of power he derived from such success, we do not know, but the following extract from Dr Francis's letter to his son warning him against the urge to overreach himself when at the top of his form may have a story to tell:

> I rejoice with you at being so long head of your class, and I hope you will enjoy your superiority over your class-fellows by condescension, compliance, and if they desire it, by assisting them. Genius and abilities are in general very happy possessions; yet an injudicious use of them makes the possessor odious and sometimes even contemptible . . . Be it your lot, my dear boy, to be amiable rather than admired, envied and hated. When you come into the world, you must hide whatever superiority you possess,

[10] P. & M., I, p. 4.

[11] For an example of the calculated cordiality with which the father wrote to his son, see *ibid.*, p. 8.

[12] *Ibid.*, p. 5.

> if you would turn it to advantage Few people, very few, will forgive an insult to the generality of mankind; it really lowers them, and they will take exceeding care it shall not exalt you . . . As to moving into a higher form, I could not wish you to press Mr Thicknesse [headmaster of the school] by showing any impatience in your desire . . . In life, as in plays, we cannot all play principal characters.[13]

Young Philip had apparently not much use for such advice, for in life, as at school, he continued to try playing the head boy.

This 'desire for superiority', however, cannot have been due entirely to the peculiar conditions of his childhood. For in terms of emotional insecurity and early achievement there was a good deal that was common between him and the orphan of Daylesford who also grew up to be a very bright pupil at Westminster. The divergence in their development was due, in the first place, to the contrary effects of discipline and freedom on their respective characters. Hastings was saved by the cruel decision of a rich uncle's legatee – that Mr Creswicke must be regarded as a genuine tool of history – to get rid of him. He was taken away from school at the age of fifteen and put through the mill learning arithmetic and book-keeping at a commercial academy in London and superintending the export of saltpetre and textiles in successive warehouses at Calcutta and Kasimbazar. For the first twelve years of his career he had his abilities harnessed to cold and unexciting tasks in which success was measurable only in terms of tons, bales and sterling. The drudgery of duties not very dissimilar to these had at one stage turned Clive with all his toughness into a misanthrope and maniac. Hastings, however, had the subtle adaptability of a born executive. He absorbed all the minutiae of the Company's administration while serving at the lower rungs, so that he was in a position to make effective use of this knowledge when called upon to serve at the summit.

Francis, on the contrary, had never had his mind thus framed by protracted application to the details of a single given responsibility.

[13] *Ibid.*, pp. 8–9.

'I am quite jaded with writing despatches', he complained from his secretarial office in Lisbon.[14] This characteristic hatred of routine was largely the result of the diversity of his early appointments: junior clerk in the Secretary of State's Office, 1756–7; out serving with the expedition to Cherbourg, 1757–8; back to his clerical post, 1758–9; off again to Portugal as secretary to Lord Kinnoul's embassy for a few months in 1760; amanuensis to Lord Chatham, 1761–2; appointed first clerk in the War Office, December 1762; and after that date until his departure for India taken up more and more with what was to develop into his major occupation, that is, political journalism. It is not that the duty of a clerk performed in the 'intervals for gossip with fellow-clerks and intermittent reading of newspapers'[15] was not quite the best apprenticeship one could have for a career at the head of a government. Only he was diverted far too often from his office to learn how an administration works even in its humblest sector. It is not surprising therefore that on every issue which came under discussion in the Bengal Council, the advantage of a more concrete knowledge of the situation and a better command of facts proved to be on the side of his rival.

Francis grew up differently from Warren Hastings in still another sense. The latter was not called upon to exercise political authority on any considerable scale until the eleventh year of his service in Bengal, that is, until he was twenty-nine, and even then not as the leader of the government but only as one of the five members of Vansittart's Council. Power in a real sense did not come to him until ten years later when in 1771 he was appointed Governor of Bengal and getting on to be forty.

Francis, on the other hand, left school to walk straight into the free air of politics. He owed the very first appointment of his career to the political patronage of Henry Fox, the first Lord Holland. His assignments with the expedition to Cherbourg and the embassy at

[14] *Ibid.*, p. 35.
[15] *Ibid.*, p. 17.

Lisbon helped him to acquire, very early in life, both political interest and political judgment. From his correspondence with his father during this period he clearly emerges as a youth who was learning to make up his mind with confidence. 'Pray undeceive people', he wrote after the fall of Cherbourg, pointing out that the Commodore was receiving more than his due share of credit for that military exploit.[16] The letters from Portugal already indicate the facility, so characteristic of his later writings, with which he would generalize about men and societies. Only, an attitude of humility, rarely found in his adult statements, would sometimes interpose thus to amend a hasty youthful conclusion: 'The character I gave you of this nation, in my last, was perhaps too harsh; to speak more favourably of them I ought to say etc.'[17] It was also at this embassy that he learnt for the first time to view the power of England in terms of the trade and politics of another country. 'I do not think my time absolutely lost', he wrote to his father, 'as this country, though it makes so mean a figure in Europe, is closely connected by trade and politics with England.'[18]

Here, too, he acquired the knowledge of certain techniques which were to prove highly useful later on. First, the art of writing political letters, reports and statements. It has been suggested that 'almost all Lord Kinnoul's despatches are written not only in the hand, but also in the palpable style of Francis',[19] and it is not unlikely that the ambassador, a man of mediocre abilities himself, permitted the secretary more than his legitimate share of initiative in drawing up his papers. Secondly, the uses of secrecy. Francis, as we know, set very great value on 'the firmess of keeping a secret against every trial or temptation'. He used an elaborate code of ciphers in his correspondence with his partisans in England during his Indian period. Secrecy, he wrote in 1774, 'is of the highest importance in the commerce of the world; and I am convinced it may be acquired . . . if boys

[16] *Ibid.*, p. 22.
[17] *Ibid.*, p. 35.
[18] *Ibid.*, p. 43.
[19] *Ibid.*, p. 28.

are accustomed, early in life, to be trusted with little secrets, under the condition of not revealing them'. This was part of his instruction on the education of his son.[20] He himself learnt his first lessons in the language of political secrecy in Lisbon. 'The Kinnoul embassy', write his biographers, 'used a particular cipher, and Francis thus became versed in that diplomatic art, and in the various clandestine modes of obtaining secret foreign papers then common to all courts. Many of the Kinnoul despatches to Pitt are headed, private, 'confidential', 'secret', 'most secret', 'a copy of a letter from a spy'; &c. &c.'[21]

Above all, it was the experience of these few months in his twentieth year that set Francis decisively on the path of his eventual development as a politician. He hated every bit of the drudgery of his secretarial function. 'My Lord Kinnoul works me to death', he would grumble.[22] But at the same time he was conscious both of the advantages of his position and its importance. The many references to servants, silks and wines in his Lisbon letters indicate how he relished the good life that went with a diplomatic career. But much more significant is the pride he takes in handling the small fund of authority attached to his office. There is yet no evidence of an articulate urge for power, but only a naive awareness occasionally breaking through otherwise impersonal accounts of official duties and entertainments thus:

> Our time has hitherto been employed in making and receiving visits of ceremony, in which the secretary bears a principal and very laborious part. I have been sent to the several ministers, ambassadors, &c., to announce His Excellency's arrival.
>
> I am perfectly well, and live in great state and am highly considered as an appendix to his Excellency.
>
> . . . my title of secretary acquired no small addition of importance by my receiving and communicating such authentic intelligence (about Lord George's trial) from England.[23]

[20] *Ibid.*, p. 408.
[21] *Ibid.*, p. 46.
[22] *Ibid.*, p. 36.
[23] *Ibid.*, pp. 33, 34–5, 36.

But in spite of such gratification Philip hated the unexciting provincial life of Lisbon. It was 'certainly the dullest and most stupid place . . . except Portsmouth', in a real sense 'the tag end of the world'.[24] Nothing ever happened there. His appetite for politics whetted by his initial contact with power, he longed to get back to the shuffle and din of London's public life. He had been in touch with it even before his departure for Portugal. It was not until many years later that he was himself admitted to that 'modified, socialized arena for battle, drive and dominion' – the House of Commons.[25] But even as a very young man just out of school he came to know many of its leading contestants. His father, a well-connected if anonymous pamphleteer himself, had obtained access for his son to the world of journalism and parliamentary activity, the two professions which in the eighteenth century not merely sustained each other as they do even now, but together dominated the field of English politics. Francis was, therefore, wanting in neither the determination nor the necessary contacts to make a beginning for himself in this field when he returned home in the winter of 1760. He was twenty at the time. During the next fourteen years he lived an intensely political life by writing on political questions, getting involved in political intrigues, making political enemies and winning political friends. It was as a politician too that in 1774 he took up his Indian appointment, a fact that explains a good deal of his conduct in Bengal and many of his differences with Warren Hastings. Unlike his rival he had not grown up with the Company's administration, nor was it possible for him at that late age of thirty-four to acquire the instinct of a confirmed bureaucrat ready to adjust his attitudes to the interests he serves. He felt bound by no ties of loyalty to Leadenhall Street, but belonging as he did to the mainstream of English politics, regarded the Indian scene as a part of the broad perspective viewed from Westminster. To the last day of his office in Bengal, therefore, he remained an outsider, 'an external critic'.

[24] *Ibid.*, pp. 36, 44.
[25] Namier, *The Structure of Politics at the Accession of George III*, p. 1.

3. The Search for 'Public Virtue'

In politics Francis was known for his rigid intellectual attitudes. How he came to acquire these is indicated, however retrospectively, by his views on the education of his son. 'I think', he wrote, 'his moral and political sentiments of much more consequence than what is commonly called his learning.' Having thus defined the aim of education he went on to discuss its methods. Political knowledge, as such, was not to be introduced in the lessons until the child was ten years old, but 'in the meantime' the tutor would be well advised to 'give him general notions of liberty and property, and inspire him with zeal to defend them'. The examples of 'great and good men' – 'Brutus, Cato, Harry the Fourth of France, and our Algernon Sydney' are mentioned – should be quoted in order to inspire patriotism and public virtue. Above all it was important to initiate the child to the study of history – Greek and Roman as well as English: 'I would have his first reading directed, as far as his years will admit of it, to history.'[26]

An education which was thus oriented towards politics and promoted through the study of history was evidently modelled on Francis's own intellectual development. His political ideas were powerfully influenced by his understanding of history. In his view the purpose of history was to uphold public virtue. A society wanting in such virtue could never produce a great historical work. 'Why have we no classics in history? Because there is no commonwealth, of course no interest, but to plunder and divide; because our historians breathe no public spirit, and inspire no virtue.'[27] Nor, according to Francis, was it possible for a historian to produce a noble work on a theme of political degeneration. He had, therefore, no use for Gibbon. 'Gibbon's narrative', he said, 'is a journey over a desert, endless *in transitu*, and immediately forgotten. No power of writing could have sustained such a detail of obscure and odious characters, religious disputes and holy massacres, insignificant events, and senseless

[26] Letter from Francis to M. Ribouville on the education of his son. P. & M., I, pp. 406–9.

[27] *Ibid.*, II, p. 494.

tyrants . . . In one sense his book and his subject are identified. The author and the empire slowly fall together into oblivion, without exciting one natural feeling or leaving a rational impression, but sorrow for the loss of so much time, and some regret that the foolish empire and the tedious story should have lasted so long. No power of words can preserve the perishable subject from gradual decay and final putrefaction.'[28]

Tacitus, not Gibbon, was the historian for him. It is true that the authority of Tacitus has sometimes been quoted in support of quite contradictory political principles.[29] This is well illustrated by the attitudes of the two great eighteenth-century translators, Gordon and Murphy: the former interpreted the *Annals* as a textbook of republicanism and even succeeded in drawing from it a precedent for the whig justification of resistance to tyranny; the latter found in it a warning against anarchy as grave as Burke's condemnation of the French Revolution.[30] In the balance, however, it would appear that Tacitus served to nourish primarily the republican trend in English politics. His authority was highly suspect under the Stuarts. A history lecturer was dismissed from Cambridge in 1627 for the crime of giving lessons on Tacitus with emphasis on republicanism.[31] After the Revolution the partisanship associated with his name is indicated by the frequent use Milton makes of his works in political arguments. In his *Defensio Prima*, for instance, he quotes the Roman historian to show how it was customary for Nero and other emperors to do public homage to the people and how the Germans had the right to reject the opinion of their kings. Tacitus, he says, 'is an approved

[28] *Ibid.*, pp. 495–6. Francis's observations on Gibbon illustrate both his view of history and his characteristic malice. Thus after having fully denounced Gibbon's work he gently adds: 'Yet Gibbon had faculties, industry, and as much of ancient Greek learning as could be obtained from translations.'

[29] Michael Grant in Tacitus, *The Annals of Imperial Rome*, p. 10.

[30] Gordon (tr.), *The Works of Tacitus*, vol. I: 'Political Discourses', pp. 52–4 *et passim.* Murphy (tr.), *The Works of Cornelius Tacitus, vol. I: 'Dedication to the Right Honourable Edmund Burke'*, pp. vi–vii.

[31] Christopher Hill, *Puritanism and Revolution*, p. 64.

writer and the greatest possible enemy to tyrants.'[32] In the Age of Enlightenment, too, he was made to side with the angels. D'Alembert and Rousseau both translated him in part and he was in the former's opinion 'un des meilleurs Maîtres de morale, par la triste, mais utile connoissance des hommes'.[33] Francis's own translation of the first book of the *Annals* when he was not yet twenty-three is an early sign of his political inclination. For, if it is true, as Butterfield observes, that 'there is a tendency for all history to veer over into whig history',[34] a young Englishman in the third quarter of the eighteenth century could receive no better encouragement in favour of whiggism than from reading Tacitus. He had to take only a few steps along the beaten tracks of contemporary thought to discover for himself the foundation of two very important whig ideas of history in Tacitus. The first of these was that politics is the essence of history. This followed from the notion admirably summed up by Francis in one of his parliamentary speeches: 'History, in effect, is prophecy.'[35] It was a favourite device of both the French *philosophes* and the English whigs to extrapolate the past in a manner as to yield directives for the future.[36] Lord Acton has in our own day formulated the idea in his famous imagery representing the relation between history and politics as that between the stream and the grains of gold deposited by it in the riverbed. Did not Tacitus himself deplore how historical truth suffered in the hands of writers ignorant of politics?[37] Secondly, there

[32] Milton, *Works*, vol. VII, pp. 185, 317–18, 334–5, 365. Milton uses the authority of Tacitus on a large number of points in his *History of Britain* (*ibid.*, vol. X) and in a letter to Henry de Brass refers to him as a writer of great merit (*ibid.*, vol. XII, p. 93). I have found nothing to confirm Mr Michael Grant's observation that, according to Milton, Tacitus did not go far enough in support of the Republic (op. cit., p. 10).

[33] Rousseau, *Oeuvres*, t. III; d'Alembert, *Morceaux Choisis de Tacite*, t. I, p. 33.

[34] Butterfield, *Whig Interpretation of History*, p. 6.

[35] *P.H.E.*, vol. 32, p. 1040.

[36] Becker, *The Heavenly City of the Eighteenth Century Philosophers*, p. 98.

[37] Tacitus, *The Histories* (tr. Fyfe), vol. I, p. 6.

was the whig idea of the historian as a moralist.[38] For this, of course, almost any classical writer would do, for they had all inherited the lofty ethical attitude of the Stoics through Zeno and Plato. But even among them Tacitus, whom the whigs loved to quote more than any other author of antiquity, stood out as the foremost *maître de morale*. Gordon spoke for all whig historians in commending the *Annals* as a model work on 'private and publick Virtue.'[39]

There was nothing so very remarkable about the fact that Francis, like many other whigs of his time, derived his political education from the classics and from history. He seems, however, to have taken the classical insistence on 'publick Virtue' more seriously than most other contemporary politicians. His personal honesty was beyond question. Judged by the standards of his age – the standard by which Clive convinced himself and others of his moderation – the money Francis had made in India, about £3,000 a year and that, too, won mostly at cards, was a ridiculously small amount. His concern for petty savings during his retirement was the price he had to pay for his extraordinary self-denial in youth.[40]

Even more remarkable than this was the courage he often showed in refusing to give up what he considered a moral stand. His attachment to principles and causes which successful politicians had either abandoned or would not touch has often been interpreted as dogmatic and intransigent. But at a time when the Opposition indulged far too often in the habit of 'leading on the country to attack with an eye turned wistfully towards the Court',[41] it is wonderful to see Philip Francis shocking both the INS and the OUTS by suddenly declaring his conversion to an unpopular cause like the reform movement, or ruining his chances for a rich inheritance by opposing slave trade, or going out of his way to recant his views on the American War of

[38] Butterfield, op. cit., pp. 107–32.

[39] Gordon, *The Works of Tacitus*, vol. I: 'Political Discourses', p. 15.

[40] Brougham, *Historical Sketches of Statesmen who flourished in the Time of George III* (*Second Series*), pp. 96–7; P. & M., II, pp. 211, 398; Leslie Stephen's article on Philip Francis in *Dictionary of National Biography*.

[41] Brougham, op. cit., p. 96.

Independence long after the issue was settled. If this is eccentricity one feels almost grateful to this odd unbending character for providing a healthy diversion in a scene of universal political debauchery where no loyalties were sacred. In private life he was no respecter of persons: he did, in fact, snub the Prince of Wales for boring him with a tiresome story.[42] This was very much the spirit of his public conduct too. No personal allegiance, not even that of Edmund Burke, could ever induce him to deviate from a point of principle, and as a result, his political progress was marked by the wreckage of many friendships. He was indeed a very lonely man when he wrote in 1793: 'I am proceeding . . . in the same path, though not all in the same company, in which I set out in Parliament.'[43] There was something quite quixotic about the way in which he defied the climate of political opportunism around him to uphold the outmoded public virtue of consistency. His estimate of Charles James Fox clearly brings this out. With all his grudging admiration for Fox, he could never forgive him his 'apathy about consistency and character', his want of 'steady resolution'. He recalled how during a discussion about the *Crito* Fox had maintained that Socrates should have followed the advice of his friends to escape from prison instead of drinking hemlock. Francis himself admired the *Crito* because, as he put it, there 'Socrates is permitted to speak and act like a man of virtue, resolution, and sound judgment, undisturbed by the fear of death'. Would Cato have been immortal, he asked, if he had accepted the clemency of Caesar, or Brutus and Cassius if they had waited to be forgiven by Augustus? Nothing could be more alien to the contemporary standards of political behaviour than his definition of a hero:

> It is only at the summit of prosperity, on the pinnacle of fame, where you cannot move without falling, that the elevated persons called heroes, whether wise or unwise in preferring reputation to existence, are bound to take their own security against fortune.[44]

[42] *Ibid.*, p. 92.
[43] P. & M., II, p. 300.
[44] *Ibid.*, pp. 445, 447–8, 460.

Any politician who in the reign of George III proposed to judge himself and others in the light of such an ideal was not likely to succeed. Francis, too, broke his lance.

What takes away partly from the moral appeal of his idealism is the element of personal frustration which embittered it. Francis's career illustrates very well how failure often adds an edge to professed beliefs and turns them into dogma. In Bengal the death of Colonel Monson had the effect of hardening his opinion. Until then he had not been unwilling to compromise at least on minor points of policy. Even as late as the summer of 1776 he was pleading for moderation with some of his closest associates. When Rous, for instance, pressed to speak up for a complete and immediate Indianization of the Company's service, Francis soberly pointed out that 'it cannot be done at first, nor can it be done at once'.[45] He argued for a graduality of reform, for a recognition of the lag that must necessarily be there between perfection and practice in any exercise of power. 'We are limited', he wrote, 'by powerful Facts, which counteract Principles, and I fear will for a long Period prevent this Government from acting entirely up to those, which we profess.' This was when he was still hoping for the governorship of Bengal, for in the same letter he tried to tempt Rous with the prospect of promotion in the event of his plan being accepted as the official line. Monson died on 25 September 1776, and thereby placed Francis and his friends 'at the mercy of H. and B.'[46] Reduced to a minority, he began to fight on in the Council like a cornered beast. He no longer felt bound by that sense of responsibility which he had exercised so long in the hope of being eventually elected to the head of the government. In November he wrote to Lord North in a mood of rising anger: '. . . the death of Col. Monson has disarmed us of Power. But in the Case of Measures, which, in my Judgement, decide upon the Wellbeing of this Country,

[45] To Rous (Private, 22 June 1776). *Francis MSS* 77 (31) 8.

[46] To D'Oyly (26 September 1776). *Ibid.*, 47 (36) 118. The initials stand for Hastings and Barwell.

I can neither yield without Resistance here, nor answer the Trust which, I conceive, was reposed in me, if I did not give your Lordship Notice of them.'[47] The operative word here was 'resistance'. All his most choleric and uncompromising statements date from this time. The difference between the academic, impersonal exposition of his revenue plan of January 1776 and the virulence of his answer to his critics during the debate on his minute which began in November, is a measure of the galling effects of frustration. Monson's death, he was to write in retrospect, produced 'a total change of system.'[48] Judged by the influence which that event had on his own attitude and factional strategy, this observation was quite accurate.

In the field of English politics, too, the severity of his opinion increased in the same proportion as his sense of failure. By the end of 1786 he had already started complaining about his want of luck in India. 'I find myself farther from employment and profit than ever I was', he wrote to Sir Robert Chambers.[49] In April 1787 'the career of his public life received a check which was most sensibly felt.'[50] He was excluded from participation in the impeachment of Warren Hastings. He was still licking his wound when exactly a year later he had the great mortification of seeing another of his carefully laid plans falling through: in May 1788 the motion for the impeachment of his enemy, Sir Elijah Impey, was finally rejected by Parliament. After this Francis could no longer hope for any advancement in India,[51] and according to his biographers, all his subsequent speeches on the Company's affairs were marked by 'increased bitterness.' It was from 1789 onwards, too, that his views on politics not directly

[47] To Lord North (20 November 1776). *Ibid.*, 47 (36) 137.

[48] *Letter from Mr Francis to Lord North*, p. 21.

[49] To Chambers (20 December 1786). P. & M., II, p. 252.

[50] *Ibid.*, p. 243.

[51] He could not, of course, have foreseen at this date the situation which was to revive his hopes in this respect for a brief period in 1805–6 after Pitt's death and the consequent ascendancy of the Foxite whigs. *Ibid.*, pp. 350–1.

related to India began to show an inclination to extremes. The two major revisions of his earlier moderate stand, that is, those about the need for parliamentary reform and the justification of American independence, both date from this period. As he felt the brakes being applied on the progress of his career, he sought compensation in an accelerated shift to the left.

This interpretation of his politics does not, however, take away from the fact that frustration, far from weakening him, inspired a kind of nervous and desperate courage. Thwarted in his ambition in one respect, he might have tried for advancement in other spheres of English politics by using the perfectly respectable escape route of compromise; instead, he went on burning his boats. His radicalism, as it will appear from the following survey, was stretched to the farthest limits of the whig horizon.

On American Independence

His initial stand on the American question was far from sympathetic. The Boston incident had drawn from him 'an outburst of passionate declamation against the minority for its vacillating policy, urging the home government to act with prompt decision and to coerce the colonies into obedience'.[52] But already a few months before the declaration of American independence he started having second thoughts about it. England, he believed, had got herself involved in a completely useless war. What could she get out of it? 'Is it revenue? the present armament will cost the nation more than all the direct taxes that can be raised from America will amount to in a century. Is it commerce? You have a navy to guard the seas: the Americans have none, nor ever can have any. If neither of these objects be in question, it must only be the form of dominion, not the substance . . . The fate of nations must not be tried by forms.'[53] Up to this point his objection was based on grounds of expediency rather than of principle. Even as

[52] P. & M., I, p. 162.

[53] To D'Oyly (22 January 1776). *Francis MSS* 47 (36) 76.

late as July 1777 he felt that with all his sympathy for the American cause he was still unable to justify a solution by war with the mother-country. 'The Idea of the Destruction of America is more painful to me', he wrote, 'than any Thing can be but that of the direct Ruin of the English Constitution. Events have totally altered the original Question of Right. After the Sword has been once drawn, Speculation, Argument, and Justice too, perhaps, are at an End.'[54]

The pronouncement he was to make on the same subject two decades later was based on an entirely different notion of right. In one of his speeches in the House of Commons in 1796 he borrowed a celebrated motif from Chatham to declare: 'I rejoice that America resisted with success, because it was a triumph of unquestionable right over outrageous wrong, of courage and virtue over tyranny and force.'[55] The change in the whig doctrine of resistance from Burnet to Russell could find no better illustration than in this statement. It also shows the extent to which the moderate constitutionalism professed by Francis during the 1770s was vigorously revised under the impact of the French Revolution and personal disappointment.

On Slave Trade

These remarks on America were a part of Francis's answer to those who quoted the experience of 1776 'to deter us from acts which might alienate the West India islands'. The acts concerned the abolition of slave trade. It was for practical politicians like Dundas to urge caution on this subject in view of all the existing difficulties with France.[56] For Francis, however, it was entirely a moral issue. There was no personal or political consideration strong enough to prevent him from giving his support to Wilberforce's motion in 1791 and keeping it up throughout the subsequent period, when the cause of abolition

[54] To Godfrey (19 July 1777). *Ibid.*, 49 (38) 99.

[55] *P.H.E.*, vol. 32, p. 972.

[56] Lecky, *A History of England in the Eighteenth Century*, vol. VII, p. 378.

became dangerously identified with Jacobinism.[57] The self-conscious rectitude with which he spoke on this subject in 1791 indicates both courage and vanity. 'He believed he was not very likely to be suspected of receiving with special favour and partiality, any measure introduced and recommended from the other side of the House; that in his own situation in private life, every motive, by which the conduct of men is usually determined, was united on one side, and powerfully pressed upon him . . . against his opinion. Connexions of every sort; friends who were dear to him, and who thought that their fortunes were at stake; solicitations the most urgent, from persons, to whom he was bound by many ties; and possibly, the prospect of advantage to himself or to his family at a future day, to be forfeited or preserved; all these were in one scale, and nothing in the other, but the justice of the cause . . .'[58] In another debate on abolition five years later he mentioned how his views had, in fact, cost him a considerable legacy.[59] In April 1796, he proposed a motion for the regulation of slavery in the West Indies,[60] and again in 1804 we find him participating in the debate on the third reading of the bill for abolition. It was on this latter occasion that he defined the limit beyond which he was not ready to push his sympathy for the slaves: abolition, he said, must not necessarily lead to emancipation which, according to him, 'might be found neither safe, prudent, nor practicable'.[61] A fine example, that, of whig reserve! But even more characteristic of his social outlook was his idea of giving property to the slaves. 'Give him some tenure in the earth', he argued. This would turn the 'personal service' rendered by the negroes into 'a real service by attaching it to the soil'. In Sparta,

[57] Halévy, *England in 1815*, p. 455.

[58] *P. H.E.*, vol. 29, p. 286. Also see Francis's letter to C. D'Oyly (4 August 1791): 'I send you inclosed the Heads of what I said about the slave trade. I know the price I shall pay for having said so much and yet I am ashamed of having said so little.' *The Francis Letters*, vol. II, p. 391.

[59] *P. H.E.*, vol. 32, pp. 869–70.

[60] *Ibid.*, pp. 944–81.

[61] *P. D.*, vol. II, p. 864.

he maintained, 'the Helots were in fact proprietors of the lands', and the other historical precedent was, of course, his own effort, many years ago, 'to inculcate a similar principle on the English government of Bengal'.[62] In other words, it was not freedom but property which was to solve the difficult problem of slavery.

On the French Revolution

It was the French Revolution more than any other event, more even than the American crisis, which was a crucial test for English radical thinking. Ever since the days of Walpole the lower classes of England had been called upon from time to time to act against authority. But in general the politicians who counselled revolt 'were profoundly ignorant of the social consequences of a constitution overturned by violence with the aid of the lower classes'. However, the way in which the problem of power had been posed and settled in France in 1789 left no scope for ambiguities. 'It made all radicals define their attitude to it and, by implication, to revolutionary methods for achieving political ends.'[63] It is true that the lines of demarcation did not emerge sharply on this side of the Channel during the very first stages of the Revolution[64] and Burke was certainly exceptional in having no second thoughts about it. But as the enthusiasm of the street scenes of Versailles and Paris gave way to the grimness of Thermidor, opinions in England began to get sorted out and polarized. We know from the record of so many famous recantations that the change of sides was, on the whole, from the left to the right among intellectuals and politicians of Francis's own social class. But he himself survived the flux without taking back a single word he had ever said in support of the Revolution: he, too, like Burke, had no second thoughts about it. This is all the more remarkable in view of the pronounced anti-Gallican attitudes of his recent past. Only two years

[62] *P. H.E.*, vol. 32, pp. 958–63.
[63] Plumb, *England in the Eighteenth Century*, pp. 155–6.
[64] Brown, *The French Revolution in English History*, p. 37.

before the Revolution he had got up in the House of Commons to speak in the debate on the proposed commercial treaty with France, and shamed Pitt by pointing out how he was reversing the policy of his father whose 'glory is founded on the resistance he made to the united power of the House of Bourbon'. And France, he said, 'the object of every hostile principle in the policy of Lord Chatham, is the *gens amicissima* of his son'.[65] When the critic and his victim changed places after 1789, they were both, in their own ways, being true to themselves. For Francis had nothing against France except that he hated kings: the Revolution had removed that objection.

His enthusiasm for the Revolution followed, in the first place, from his opposition to monarchy.[66] 'Under a monarchical government', he wrote, 'the natural feelings and propensities of the mind are perverted by education or a total want of any instruction, and modelled by habit or by the fashion of society to act in a false direction, and to look *up* for the titular objects of their compassion; as if all our pity should be reserved for kings and queens, and other exalted persons, who never *pity us*, or even one another.'

The constitutional difficulties of George III's reign and the public celebrations of the centenary of the Glorious Revolution reminded him of the problems of 1640 and the solutions of 1688. The very last literary effort of his life was a long essay justifying opposition to monarchy by seventeenth-century precedents.[67] A survey of English history from James I to George III, it had the Revolution of 1640 as its central theme. Both Clarendon and Hume were accused here of having distorted history as a result of their royalist sympathies.

[65] *P.H.E.*, vol. 26, p. 422.

[66] The sources for this and the three subsequent paragraphs are the extracts from Francis's writings in P. & M., II, pp. 472–98, unless otherwise mentioned.

[67] The essay is incomplete. It was found among the Francis papers after the author's death and was, according to its editor, 'the composition of his very last years'. It has been reproduced under the title 'Characteristics of the Kings of England' in P. & M., II, pp. 464–529.

Francis pointed out how the latter ('the deep and treacherous Hume, I speak only of the historian . . .') had in the first edition of his *History* included some adverse remarks about Charles I, which were either left out or favourably amended in subsequent editions. Burnet, he thought, was a better historian, although somewhat uncritical of his own party. It was Milton whom he most admired. He was particularly unhappy about Dr Johnson's observation that Milton 'hated all whom he was required to obey' and that his republicanism was 'founded in an envious hatred of greatness'. In his manuscript notes on *Lives of the Poets* Francis angrily retorts: 'These severe remarks are all gratuitous and utterly unsupported. What authority have you for apprising that Milton hated all whom he was required to obey. Might it not be said with greater appearance of Truth, that Saml. Johnson professed slavish principles of submission to Monarchy Aristocracy and Hierarchy, because his Temper was tyrannical . . . Does any Man really love a Master, or a Superior, as such? Even Mr Burke said in the House of Commons, when he introduced the Impeachment, that undoubtedly if he were to be born again and could choose, he would be born in a Republic.'[68]

Not good enough as an argument against Dr Johnson, these comments still very truly reflect Francis's hostile attitude to monarchy as a form of government. In his essay he has not a kind word to spare for any of the Stuart kings: they are all equally abominable, and 'the manly character of England was saved by a civil war'. He justifies the execution of Charles I on both moral and political grounds. Charles was himself guilty of many brutalities towards his political opponents, but by far the ugliest example of his cynicism, according to Francis, was his sacrifice of Strafford who had defected in favour of the king.[69]

[68] Notes on Johnson's *Lives of the Poets* (p. 211, 8v., 1783). *Francis MSS* 63 (60).

[69] Francis had, of course, nothing but contempt for Strafford who started as a leader of the Opposition, but 'was bribed soon after by a peerage and an office, when prostitution in that way was uncommon'. As an obvious reflection on his own times Francis added: 'Many have followed his example,

Such being his record, the king could have no claim to sympathy. Above all, the balance of political forces existing at the time called for his complete liquidation. 'To reinstate and to limit the power of the crown in the same person, is a dangerous experiment, and has never yet been tried with success . . . Who can say that, if Charles had been reinvested with any portion, however limited, of the power he once possessed, he might not gradually have recovered the whole?' The public trial and execution of a king, says Francis, was indeed a great improvement on the traditional method of getting rid of a tyrant by assassination. 'The French, I am sure', he adds with a touch of grim humour, 'envied the English for being the first nation that brought a king to a formal trial for his life.' Both the nations, however, committed the same blunder and compromised their revolutions by the same kind of half-measures: the revolutionaries ought to have proceeded in each country to the complete abolition of the unlimited and hereditary form of monarchical government.

> When the English Parliament drew the sword against Charles, they should have abandoned all thoughts of reconciliation with him on any terms, and abolished the office of king in a single person . . . They failed by attempting to reconcile contradictions. They, in fact, proclaimed the king to be a tyrant by taking up arms against him, and then they negotiated with him; as if it had been possible to reduce a corrupt despotism to a limited monarchy in the same person, or even in the same family. The French made a similar mistake in 1791. Instead of resolving at once to extirpate the tyranny, they thought they could prune it, and that, when it was corrected and restrained, it might safely be reinstated. But they soon found that the pretensions of arbitrary power dispossessed are never relinquished.

These lines were written perhaps during the earliest days of the Restoration in France. They record the frustration of an old republican who had expected the French to avoid the shortcomings of the English

---

and nobody, that we know of, have been deterred by his fate.' P. & M., II, p. 486.

Revolution. Nevertheless, an irreducible core of optimism persists in him. His very last political remark, uttered on the morning before his death, was: 'The Bourbons will never hold out. Some great change is not far off.'[70]

In the French Revolution he saw not only the end of monarchical despotism but also of priestly power.[71] He owed his anti-clerical sentiments both to the circumstances of his early life and to his adult intellectual development which, in this particular respect, was distinctly influenced by the philosophical attitudes of Enlightenment. His father, though a clergyman, was not distinguished for virtuous living. He was 'a loose liver and a freethinker, one whose life under the cloth, and in the enjoyment of church preferment, was a mere recognised hypocrisy'.[72] He is, in fact, mentioned by the courtesan George Anne Bellamy as an associate of one of her 'protectors'.[73] No wonder that the young Francis grew up without acquiring any exaggerated respect for the sanctity of his father's vocation. The contest between the court of Portugal and the Jesuits backed by the Vatican during his service with the Kinnoul mission impressed him about 'the low politics of Italian priests'.[74] This attitude continued throughout his life and is very strongly expressed in several passages of the historical essay discussed above. But his distrust about priesthood was above all consideration of sect and denomination. In India he ascribed grave social evils like widow-burning to the power of the priests.[75] In his own country, he found the Church of England guilty of complicity with the first Stuart despot. 'In all Christian monarchies', he went on to generalize, 'the king and the bishop make common cause, that is, the dupe and the knave are united, at the expense of one of them

[70] P. & M., II, p. 403.
[71] *Ibid.*, p. 280.
[72] *Ibid.*, p. 412.
[73] P. & M., I, pp. 15–16.
[74] Letter to Dr Francis (22 August 1760). *Ibid.*, p. 42. Also see *ibid.*, pp. 47–8, 195.
[75] P. & M., II, p. 375.

for the benefit of the other, or in odium tertii, this they call Church and State.'[76] The French Revolution must have been particularly welcome to him for having disrupted this axis in the most Christian Kingdom of Europe.

Finally, he perhaps found in the events of 1789 a vindication of the whig doctrine of resistance to tyranny. A nation cannot revolt against oppression, he wrote, 'unless some public virtue be left in it, as there was generally in France in 1788, a little in the capital and none at all at Versailles'.[77] Under such circumstances 'despair is an active, vigorous principle. It leads the people to assert the birthright of a nation to oppose a tyrannical or ruinous Government by force of arms, and to discard a treacherous, ungrateful king, as it was exercised by the Whigs at the Revolution.'[78] It was this birthright which Wat Tyler and Jack Cade had exercised when forced to do so 'by grievances insupportable, by a vile government . . . by a rapacious clergy, and by an execrable nobility'. The jacqueries in France in the fourteenth century were to be justified on the same grounds. 'The crimes of the peasantry in the process, and their ruin in the result of their insurrection, prove nothing against the original right of their cause.'[79] This must have been the sentiment of many in England during the earlier phase of the French Revolution. For the sufferings of the peasantry under the Bourbons had received wide publicity on this side of the Channel. Even Arthur Young, whose views were moderate almost to the point of being conservative, spoke of peasant violence as an unfortunate necessity.[80] Francis, in his own doctrinaire way, rejoiced at the moral

[76] *Ibid.*, pp. 476–7. For other anti-clerical statements in this historical fragment, see *ibid.*, pp. 465, 467, 474, 494, 501, 513.

[77] *Ibid.*, p. 525.

[78] P. & M., II, p. 528. In his manuscript notes on *Lives of the Poets* Francis joins issue with Dr Johnson for his description of Hampden as 'the zealot of rebellion'. 'Vile . . . pensioned slave', he asks, 'was it rebellion to resist the levy of taxes not granted by Parliament?' *Francis MSS* 63 (60).

[79] *Ibid.*, pp. 464–5.

[80] See his essay 'On the Revolution in France' in *Travels in France*, pp. 322–4. As is well known, Young recanted in 1796.

punishment inflicted upon the *ancien régime* by the angry whig God of History. It is not that Francis condoned the cruelties of the Reign of Terror; only, he ascribed these 'to that infernal despotism under whose rod a mild and generous people have been perverted into a nation of savages'.[81]

However, it was not merely the demolition of the old order which Francis appreciated. He recorded his very positive admiration of the revolutionary regime in a letter written after his visit to France in the summer of 1791. 'I have seen, observed, and inquired', he wrote, 'into everything to the utmost of my power; and I think I may tell you with confidence, that France promises to be the most flourishing country in the world, excepting North America. Undoubtedly they still have great difficulties to encounter. But when was there anything great and eminent done in the world without labour, contest and hazard? Believe me, they know their own affairs best and they laugh at the flimsy criticisms, so much puffed and admired in England. I cannot answer for the event of external violence, tho' I see no appearance of its being attempted . . . The National Assembly, in my opinion, have done everything that brave and wise men could do to serve their country.'[82] No subsequent development made him ever doubt the fact of French progress under the new government. In 1794 in the course of a parliamentary debate he joined issue with Burke precisely on this point to say, 'I very much doubt whether the French in general are such sufferers as he conceives them to be'.[83]

On the question of 'external violence', however, Francis proved a poor prophet. In 1792 he spoke in the House of Commons in support of Fox's motion for sending an envoy to Paris to treat with the Provisional Government of France. His purpose in doing so,

[81] *P.H.E.*, vol. 30, p. 845.

[82] To D'Oyly (4 August 1791). *The Francis Letters*, vol. II, p. 390. Three days earlier he had written to another correspondent in the same vein and almost in the same words. Letter to L. Collings, 1 August 1791. P. & M., II, p. 296.

[83] *P.H.E.*, vol. 31, p. 382.

he said, was 'to assist in preventing a war if it be possible.'[84] But by February next year it seemed to him that there was no hope of avoiding a conflict: 'A war with France, I am inclined to think, is inevitable, because, on our part, provoked and intended.' But those who were clamouring for war, he thought, counted too much on the weakness of the revolutionaries and did not take into account 'the unconquerable powers of enthusiasm and the inexhaustible resources of despair'.[85] He himself continued to fight the losing battle for peace in the House of Commons. After having voted with the minority in support of the resolution of both Fox and Grey against war,[86] he wrote in a mood of dark foreboding: 'Two nights ago, I was one of forty-six against two or three hundred who I suppose thought it a very proper thing that the High Contracting Parties should settle a Plan of internal Government of France . . . If that be the object and if we adhere to it, it is possible that there may be a final pacification in the course of the next century.'[87] It really did take Europe more than twenty years to achieve this 'final pacification'.

Opposition to slave trade had cost Philip Francis a legacy; defence of the French Revolution cost him the invaluable friendship of Edmund Burke. He had met Burke in 1773, been in touch with him during his career in Bengal, assisted him in writing the ninth and eleventh reports of the Select Committee, advised him on the impeachment of Warren Hastings,[88] and since his return from India had in fact become one of Burke's most intimate associates and a friend of the family. There is a public record of Burke's appreciation of Francis in one of his speeches in Parliament.[89] The hyperbole of that tribute – Burke spoke of his friend's 'sunshine of the soul' – was

[84] *P.H.E.*, vol. 30, pp. 91–4.

[85] Letter to Mr Collings (February 1793). P. & M., II, pp. 300–l.

[86] *P.H.E.*, vol. 30, pp. 453–4.

[87] To J. Bristow, 21 February 1793. *The Francis Letters*, vol. II, p. 404.

[88] For Francis's own account of his relations with Burke, see P. & M., II, pp. 286–8.

[89] P. & M., II, pp. 221–2.

equalled by his true personal sentiments. 'I do not recollect, since I first had the pleasure of your acquaintance', he wrote in one of his last letters to Francis, 'that there has been a heat or a coolness of a single day's duration, on my side, during that whole time.' Francis, he admitted, was 'the only friend I have who will dare to give me advice'.[90]

Ironically, however, the particular piece of advice which had called forth this declaration of loyalty was the one that broke up the friendship. Burke who in his letters to Francis earlier in the winter of 1789 had already expressed a mild concern about 'the follies of France',[91] sent on 18th February of the following year a proof sheet of his *Reflections on the Revolution in France* for his friend's perusal. Francis wrote the following day to say that in his opinion it was a work unworthy of Burke in every respect: it was badly written; it would provoke a futile controversy; and as for its contents, 'all that you say of the queen is pure foppery'. The letter ends with a grave warning against publication. 'The mischief you are going to do yourself', says Francis, 'is, to my apprehension, palpable. It is visible. It will be audible. I snuff it in the wind. I taste it already. I feel it in every sense; and so will you hereafter.'[92] Burke, as is well known, did not retract. But how deep these reproaches had cut into his mind is indicated by the high-strung opening lines of his reply on 20th February, '½ after P.M.', 1790:

> My dear Sir. – I sat up rather late at Carlton House and on my return hither I found your letter on my table. I have not slept since.[93]

As the letter proceeds, agitation gives way to argument; he modestly speaks in justification of the style of the essay; refutes with a touch of indignation the charge of foppery; and announces his resolution

[90] *Correspondence*, vol. III, pp. 134–5.

[91] See the two letters of November and December 1789 quoted in P. & M., II, pp. 262–5.

[92] *Correspondence*, vol. III, pp. 128–32.

[93] *The Francis Letters*, vol. II, p. 380.

to expose the home-grown Jacobins 'to the hatred, ridicule and contempt of the whole world'. But it was no use arguing. The wires were already dead and not communicating. 'We differ only in every thing', he said, and concluded with still another protestation of friendship which, as he must have felt himself, could not continue much longer. 'Adieu! believe me always sensible of your friendship; though it is impossible that a greater difference can exist on earth, than, unfortunately for me, there is on those subjects, between your sentiments and mine.'[94] Correspondence was resumed ten months later.[95] Meanwhile, Burke's *Reflections* had already come out in print, and he and Francis had both taken up final and irrevocable positions. The latter had started reading the book, but found many things to complain about. The style was too heavy: 'The flavour is too high; the wine is too rich; I cannot take a draught of it.' The argument had many logical faults. Thus, according to Francis, there was not much sense in condemning the French for not having acted 'as we did in 1688'. For, 'they had no constitution as we had to recur to . . . Much less had they *the elements of a constitution very nearly as good as could be wished*'. In view of this, 'all that part of your "Reflections" which impeaches the French Assembly for taking new ground to act on, is a *petitio principii*'. Besides, it was unfair to hold the Assembly responsible for the violence of the mob. And was even that violence really unjustified?

> The loss of a single life in a popular tumult, excites individual tenderness and pity. No tears are shed for nations. When the provinces are scourged to the bone by a mercenary and military power, and every drop of its blood and substance extorted from it by the edicts of a royal council, the case seems very tolerable to those who are not involved in it. When thousands after thousands are dragooned out of their country for the sake of their religion, or sent to row in the galleys for selling salt against law, – when the liberty of every individual is at the mercy of every prostitute, pimp or parasite, that has access to the hand of power, or to any of its basest

[94] *Correspondence*, vol. III, pp. 134–41.
[95] *Ibid.*, pp. 162–77.

> substitutes, – my mind, I own, is not at once prepared to be satisfied with gentle palliatives for such disorders. Why? Because, as you say, it is not *natural* that it should.

Burke replied to this in a tone of remote and offended dignity. 'When and where, my dear sir, did you find me the advocate of any tyranny, either ancient or modern, either at home or abroad?' Only he was not interested in entering into a 'parallel of crimes' with anyone and refused to accept that the grievances of the people under an absolute monarchy gave them the right 'to ruin their country'. As for logic, well – to one scholastic brick thrown by his correspondent he could return at least four.[96] But there was not much use continuing the argument. For in Francis's letter he saw, perhaps wrongly, 'the method of controversy rather than of friendly admonition'. He would not polemize with his friend. In any case it would be futile to do so, for his mind was entirely made up. 'Therefore let us end here all discussion on the subject.'

The breach which thus began was never repaired. There is a good deal of evidence in Francis's private and public statements to show that on his part he regretted it as a great personal loss. For him it was still another painful instance of the price one had to pay for one's convictions. There is a sad reference to this subject in one of his parliamentary speeches on slave trade in 1796. 'Divided as we are', he said, 'by an irreconcilable difference of opinion on another important subject, and separated in private life as long as that unfortunate question continues, I still hope and believe that the bond of personal friendship and good-will between us will never be dissolved.'[97] His sincerity is proved by the fact that although he was against Burke almost on every single question in the House of Commons after 1790, he never mentioned the other's name except in terms of the

[96] In Francis's letter, wrote Burke, there 'are many arguments *ad hominem*; some, *ad verecundium*; some, *ad invidiamcreandam*; not a few, *ad captandum*'.

[97] *P.H.E.*, vol. 32, p. 968.

highest praise.[98] Burke continued to command his esteem even when towards the end of his life Francis had very little respect left for any other leader of the two major parties.[99] Till his last day he was not sure if Edmund Burke really believed all the nonsense he had written and said in defence of legitimacy. 'And yet such a man as Edmund Burke', he wrote incomprehendingly in that historical essay of his old age, 'could pretend to idolise the divine right of kings and queens, and lords and bishops, and all the royal families in the world, when in fact, and I know it, he thought of them just as I do.'[100] He was himself so well integrated in the eighteenth century that he could never understand his friend's defection. Consistency was for him such an important 'publick Virtue' that the politician he most admired could not be suspected of self-contradiction. The record of Burke's opportunism was, therefore, best regarded as political playfulness.

On Parliamentary Reform

> Let the occasion, the subject, the argument, be what it may, he has but one way of treating it. War and peace, the repair of a turnpike, the better government of nations, the direction of a canal, and the security of the constitution, are all alike in his contemplation. The French revolution is an answer to every thing; the French revolution is his everlasting theme, the universal remedy, the grand specific, the never-failing panacea, the perpetual burthen of his song; and with this he treats us from day to day; a cold, flat, insipid hash of the same dish, perpetually served up to us in different shapes . . . Has he no choice of topics? . . . Has he no way of opposing a reform of corruptions and abuses in our own system, but by telling us incessantly what mischiefs have been done by madmen in another country, acting in circumstances totally different from ours!

This was Philip Francis speaking in 1793 in the debate on Grey's motion for parliamentary reform.[101] The target of his ridicule was

[98] For an example, see *P.D.*, vol. 6, p. 758.

[99] Cf. references to Burke in 'Characteristics of the Kings of England'. P. & M., II, pp. 449, 451, 453 *et passim.*

[100] *Ibid.*, p. 520.

[101] *P.H.E.*, vol. 30, pp. 843–4.

of course an opponent of reform, but the description would have applied even to one of its advocates. For of all subjects between turnpikes and foreign policy the one which at this time was the most confounded with the French Revolution was the problem of parliamentary representation; and both friends and enemies of reform were fond of quoting the French experience to prove the validity of their respective positions. The former saw in it a warning against all systems based on a denial of popular rights. For the latter it proved how unsafe liberty was in the hands of the lower classes.

By his education Francis was ideally equipped to participate in a movement involving fundamental questions of law and constitution. For it had been 'his most singular pursuit' of youth to make a careful study of these problems. His early manuscripts dating from the period of his return from Lisbon contain much evidence of his familiarity with a wide range of views on these subjects all the way from Bacon to Samuel Johnson. The publication of Blackstone's *Commentaries* corresponded to the formative period of his intellectual development between his fifteenth and nineteenth years. Several entries in the catalogue of tracts and pamphlets collected in his library indicate his keen interest in the controversy over this work in 1769–70.[102] Its influence on his own ideas is clearly illustrated by the use he makes of Blackstone's authority in his Bengal minutes.

His initial attitude to parliamentary reform was by no means favourable. He had on two occasions voted in Parliament against Pitt's plan to disfranchise rotten boroughs.[103] But in March 1792 he happened to attend a meeting held in protest of a case of particularly gross electoral abuse. It was on this occasion that Francis 'openly declared that he now saw the necessity of a parliamentary reform'.[104] A few weeks later, during the debate on Grey's motion, he rose to say that he had 'something to retract and something to declare'. He referred to the negative view he had held on this subject in the

102 P. & M., II, pp. 427–8.

103 *P.H.E.*, vol. 29, p. 1339; P. & M., II, p. 302n.

104 Veitch, *The Genesis of Parliamentary Reform*, p. 196.

past, and proceeded to announce his conversion: 'It is the view and contemplation of doctrines and principles, introduced from day to day, and of transactions in the last and present parliament, which have removed my doubts of the necessity of a reform in the actual construction of the House of Commons.'[105] This is still another instance of Francis's refusal to drift with the tide in the characteristic manner of the more conservative sections of his social milieu. Here again he had to pay for his conviction in terms of broken friendships.[106]

The demand for reform originated in the belief that the three distinct principles of government as represented by the Crown and the two Houses of Parliament had ceased to act as a check on one another; that, in other words, 'the Constitution had been stultified'.[107] According to Francis, the danger lay particularly in the increasing influence of the Crown and the powerlessness of Parliament to prevent any possible abuse of the royal prerogative. He was against all the crowned heads of all countries at all times, and particularly against the ruling one in England. George III was, in his opinion, not merely stupid and mad, but also cunning as only an idiot turned insane could be. But what made his wickedness even worse was his German extraction.[108] Thus, both on account of his striving for personal rule and his foreign connections the king called for invocations of Stuart analogies. Francis played on the century-old theme not merely by direct appeals to the Bill of Rights (he once got a substantial part of it read out to the House of Commons during a debate), but by suggesting that the Crown was exploiting the weaknesses of an unrepresentative Parliament to recover the ground lost in memorable battles not so long ago. His appeal to Parliament jealously to reserve its control over

[105] *P.H.E.*, vol. 29, pp. 1339–40.

[106] *P.H.E.*, vol. 30, p. 848.

[107] Halévy, op. cit., p. 170.

[108] For Francis's views on George III and the Hanoverians, see his historical fragment, particularly P. & M., II, pp. 466, 468, 472–3, 476, 515, 516–17, 524, 525.

the army by amending the Mutiny Bill (1787); his warnings against admission of the Crown's right to introduce foreign troops in 1794 and 1804; his reminder during the debate on the Volunteer Corps Bill (1794) that the Crown had no right to levy money without the sanction of Parliament[109] were all a thinly veiled way of saying that George III was invading the rights of the people in the vicious manner of the Stuart despots. 'Under the House of Hanover', he wrote, 'the names and forms of the English Constitution have hitherto been preserved, and through the medium of a Parliament a power more absolute and ruinous than that which the Stuarts claim directly from God, has gradually centred in the Crown. Prerogative at first gave way to influence, and now the influence is ready to support whatever the king chooses to call his royal prerogative.'[110]

What was it that made the Crown so powerful? 'A passive House of Lords and an instrumental House of Commons', he said.[111] One was 'venal and contemptible', and the other 'rotten, odious'.[112] Thus constituted, Parliament's claim to represent the people was sheer mockery.[113] He illustrates the absurdity of the existing system by making fun of his own election for Appleby in 1802. This constituency had, for all practical purposes, only one Elector, that is, the Earl of Thanet, who was a patron of the borough and controlled the votes of all the one hundred burgage-holders. Francis was his nominee and described his electoral experience thus in one of his letters:

> . . . I was unanimously elected by one Elector to represent this ancient borough in Parliament . . . there was no other Candidate, no opposition, no Poll demanded, Scrutiny or petition. So I had nothing to do but to thank the said Elector for the Unanimous Voice with which I was

[109] *P.H.E.*, vol. 26, p. 642; vol. 31, pp. 5–6, 211–14. *P.D.*, vol. 2, p. 841.

[110] P. & M., II, p. 472.

[111] *Ibid.*, p. 518.

[112] *Ibid.*, p. 528.

[113] Letter to M/S Richardson and Riddell (19 April 1792). P. & M., II, p. 299.

> chosen . . . On Friday Morning I shall quit this triumphant Scene with flying Colours and a noble Determination not to see it again in less than seven years.[114]

Francis believed that it was the people themselves who had by their own vices reduced elections to such a farce: 'Electors are so corrupt and degenerate, that instead of choosing they sell.'[115] But it would be futile, he thought, to seek improvement in legislation against individual offenders 'who are no way distinguished from their neighbours but by the accident of being caught'. For, even if such partial correctives were useful in their own way, they would inevitably tend to divert attention from the general abuse. 'The effect of these pretended remedies, these occasional palliatives, I fear', he said in opposing a bill against electoral abuses at Stockbridge,[116] 'will be to lull and stupefy the people, already too dull and indifferent, on the subject of a parliamentary reform, and to deprive us of any chance of a real effective remedy.' He wanted Parliament to concentrate on the problem of 'a complete alteration in the construction of the House of Commons', and was one of the most ardent spokesmen for Grey's motion for a more comprehensive reform. This could not be achieved without rallying public support outside Parliament. He was, therefore, against all official measures aimed at muzzling criticism. In 1792 he severely criticized the King's Proclamation against seditious writings and in 1795 the continued suspension of Habeas Corpus.[117] In the very last publication of his life, *The Petition of the Freeholders of the County of Middlesex to the House of Commons* (1817), he pleaded for justice to all those who were victimized for their political opinion by the latter measure.

The platform he chose for the expression of his own views on reform was the Society of the Friends of the People. He was one of the

[114] *The Francis Letters,* vol. II, p. 493.
[115] P. & M., II, p. 498.
[116] *P.H.E.*, vol. 30, pp. 769–72, 774–5.
[117] *Ibid.*, vol. 29, pp. 1498–1501; vol. 30, pp. 1144–5, 1161–9.

signatories to the Society's manifesto adopted at its first meeting on 11 April 1792, and in his loyalty survived the defection of many of its other influential sponsors.[118] Whether he had a hand in formulating its principles or not,[119] they undoubtedly represent the exact measure of his reformism. The Society, as is well known, was a forum of advanced whig opinion. For Fox, who did not join, it was a shade too inclined to the left. So, it appears, it was for Grey who did join, but did not perhaps feel quite at home.[120] The Society was certainly a bit too right-wing for John Cartwright. It dissociated itself from his more radical views, and five of its leaders who belonged to his Society for Constitutional Information were promptly expelled from this latter organization.[121] The Friends of the People became easily the most exclusive of all associations favouring reform, and its high subscription rate – 2½ guineas for annual membership – as well as its political reservations were all characteristic of its links with the whig landed interests. From its very inception it took care to demarcate itself from those extreme opinions which might be suspected of Jacobinism, and this was as much an evidence of its fear of witch-hunting as of its social outlook. The limits of its demand for parliamentary reform were defined by Francis on many occasions. The point where he thought

[118] There is a brief, but poignant, reference to the early history of the Society in Francis's speech in the House of Commons on 28 May 1806. Here he mentioned by name some of the Society's first enthusiastic adherents who had since crossed over to the Treasury bench, and added sarcastically: 'A feeble memory is one of those human infirmities, which sometimes accompany the most exalted faculties.' Of himself he said, 'It was my lot too, sir, to be one of the Friends of the People; at all times the least considerable, and now, I believe, the last of them.' *P.D.*, vol. 7, p. 405.

[119] The authorship of this document, says Veitch (op. cit., p. 198), has been variously attributed to James Mackintosh, W.H. Lambton and Philip Francis. Francis's own claim is recorded in his speech in the House of Commons on 30 April 1792: 'I had some share in the construction of the Declaration and Address.' *P.H.E.*, vol. 29, p. 1340.

[120] Veitch, op. cit., p. 197.

[121] *Proceedings*, pp. 25–31, 47–52.

a line must be firmly drawn was the question of universal suffrage. This demand was a part of the London Corresponding Society's mass petition which he had once agreed to carry to Parliament after Fox had declined to do so on principle.[122] But his own opinion was most emphatically against it, as was that of the Friends of the People. When contrary imputations were made against both in Parliament in 1795, Francis refuted the charge in a vigorous speech.[123] His letter to the *Morning Chronicle* (20 February 1797) states fully and clearly:

> 1st, That, having been a Member of the Society of the Friends of the People, and having had a share in the conduct of their proceedings, I know of no Act, Order, Resolution, Proposition, Motion, or Proceeding of any kind, in that Society, in favour of individual or universal Representation.
>
> 2nd, That I am morally certain, that, if any motion to that effect had been proposed, it would have been rejected by a very great majority of the whole Society.
>
> 3rd, That, if it had been possible for such a motion to prevail, I would have quitted the Society and opposed their proceedings.
>
> 4th, That in fact a very different principle of Reform, and incompatible with that imputed to us, viz. by extending the right of voting to all householders paying parochial taxes, and stopping there, was unanimously adopted by the Society, on the 9th of April, 1794.
>
> 5th, That, on the 30th May, 1795, the Society unanimously approved of a Plan formed by me on this Principle, and recommended it to the consideration of the public . . .
>
> 6th, That I have, on all occasions, resisted and reprobated, to the utmost of my power, the idea of individual or universal Representation, particularly at a Meeting of the Society on the 8th of March 1794, at which I expressly treated it as *a dangerous chimera, set up on purpose to delude the lower classes of the People.*[124]

The emphasis in the last statement was his own. He was far too good a whig to admit the lower classes to a share of power 'by giving

[122] Veitch, op. cit., pp. 277–8.
[123] *P.H.E.*, vol. 31, pp. 1164–6.
[124] Quoted in *P.H.E.*, vol. 34, Editor's Note.

a vote to every hackney-coachman and chimney-sweeper in the kingdom'.[125] Universal representation was a folly. Even in the wisest of all republican constitutions, that of ancient Rome, 'the *proletarii* who were supposed to be good for nothing but propagation, and the *capite censi* who were counted by the head or by tale, belonged to no class, and had no vote or voice in any act of the people.' Just as in that republic a census or fortune was necessary to entitle a Roman to bear arms, so in England one must have property to be entitled to suffrage. He was, therefore, a 'moderate reformer', as he liked to describe himself, who wanted Parliament to represent only a relatively wider range of propertied interests. 'We hunted for property', he said, 'wherever it could be found, in order to support the vote.' This is how he defined his own platform of parliamentary reform. With just a slight change of words the definition would perfectly fit his Indian plan of 1776.

[125] For Francis's statements quoted in this paragraph, see his speech of 21 March 1806, in *P.D.*, vol. 6, pp. 511–13.

4

The Plan of 1776

THREE MEMBERS OF THE Bengal Council and four judges of the Supreme Court disembarked at Chandpal Ghat, Calcutta, on 19 October 1774. At the sight of the barefooted natives around them, one of the judges is said to have remarked: 'I trust we shall not have been six months in the country before these victims of oppression are comfortably provided with shoes and stockings.'[1] This has been quoted as an example of the reforming zeal of these nominees of the Regulating Act. But compared to what another member of the party, Philip Francis, had in his mind, these charitable sentiments read as tame as a resolution on the parish pump. For the mission that Francis had set to himself was, as he wrote to a friend soon after his arrival in Calcutta, 'to save this glorious empire'.[2] It was quite consistent with his character, his radicalism and his sense of self-importance, that he believed this and nothing short of this to be the real measure of his responsibility in India.

To save Bengal from what? From the ruinous policies of Warren Hastings's government. Before leaving England he had read all the East India literature about corruption and abuse under the Company's regime. He had gone through Clive's collection of papers on

[1] Marshman, *History of India*, vol. I, p. 346.

[2] To Bourke, 30 November 1774. *Francis MSS* 47 (36) 23.

India making notes and summaries from them,[3] and absorbing, as Weitzman says, Clive's plans and prejudices.[4] He had no doubt that he was being sent out to cleanse an Augean stable, and one can almost see him reaching out for the big broom when, less than fifty days after the first meeting of the Council, he promised to send home 'such an Account of the internal State as will make every Man in England tremble'.[5] Bengal was in a state of decay, and he was not going to concede that this was all due to the famine of 1770. 'The Measures since taken by Government have in this Respect been as fatal to the Country as the Famine itself.'[6]

The search for an alternative policy had therefore begun almost with the first verbal exchanges in the Council. It is true that Francis did not come out with his reply to the Hastings–Barwell plan of April 1775 until about nine months later. But we have all the evidence to show that he had for a long time been busy collecting materials for a general statement of policy. Vansittart, who was helping the Governor-General to prepare his plan, wrote to Graham in March that year that 'the new folks' too were busy working on a paper to represent their views.[7] Most of the propositions which were later embodied in Francis's minute of January 1776 are already stated, though not in quite the same order nor with equal refinement, in some of his letters to Lord North between January and March 1775.[8] A list of six questions which he sent to Wilbore Ellis as early as November 1774 also shows that he was already exercising his mind on all the relevant aspects of administration in order to equip himself for a comprehensive policy statement of his own. These, described by him as

[3] Some of these are to be found in the *Francis MSS* at the India Office Library. See, for instance, 46 (29) 3 and 65 (51) 8.

[4] Weitzman, op. cit., p. 20.

[5] To Strachey, 7 December 1774. *Francis MSS* 47 (36) 29.

[6] 'Draft of a Minute on the State of Decay in the Country'. *Ibid.*, 78 (6) 5.

[7] British Museum, *Add. MSS* 29136, p. 130.

[8] Letters dated 13 January, 24 February and 23 March 1775 in *Francis MSS* 47 (36) 47, 47 (36) 48 and 49 (38) 17 respectively.

'the Questions either now agitated or likely to be agitated between our Colleagues and Ourselves', related to (i) the general state of economic decay, (ii) failure of the farming system, (iii) decline in revenue, (iv) problems of internal trade, (v) the currency crisis, and (vi) the future procedure of revenue collection.[9] To all these questions, except perhaps the fifth, which Francis discussed in separate minutes, the answers he had to give were all fully stated in his famous 'Plan for a Settlement of the Revenues of Bengal, Bahar and Orissa' of 22 January 1776.

For many months after he had submitted the plan to the Council, Francis was still quite full of it. In his correspondence that year there are numerous references to it, and he speaks of it with the intensity and enthusiasm of an author who has just completed writing something highly creative and knows he has done it well. The plan, apparently, was a very great effort for him and he had put all his heart into it. It was, he said, 'the deliberate Result of all the Inquiry, Observation and Judgment that my Head is capable of'.[10] He had great confidence in it himself 'not so much from an Idea of its Perfection, as from its Capacity of its being made perfect'.[11] It had been, so far as he was concerned, an intellectual exercise of the highest order, resembling more a philosophical statement than a mere administrative minute, and he was not boasting when he presumed that it was worth 'the Judgment of Men whose Intellects are higher than the Standard of a Rupee'.[12] The lucidity and power of his political writings were recognized even by his critics, and in nothing that he wrote did these qualities come out more clearly than in the plan of 1776.

1. The Scope and Method of the Plan

The two most remarkable characteristics of the plan were that it was both comprehensive in its scope and consistent in its parts. Far too

[9] To W. Ellis, 30 November 1774. *Ibid.*, 49 (38) 5.
[10] To C. D'Oyly, 22 January 1776. *Ibid.*, 47 (36) 76 and 77.
[11] To H. Strachey, 20 March 1776. *Ibid.*, 47 (36) 86.
[12] To H. Strachey, 22 January 1776. *Ibid.*, 47 (36) 75.

often it has been studied as only a statement of land revenue policy. In the nineteenth century, when second thoughts about the Permanent Settlement grew into a major historical theme, writers and commentators found it convenient to treat Francis's fiscal theories apart from the rest of his ideas. Subsequently, as specialized research on Indian land problems developed, a point was reached when nothing was retained of the plan except a bare summary of the measures actually proposed by Francis for the restoration of zamindars. This surely is not how he expected his work to be interpreted. He was himself aware that the central ideas of his thesis exceeded purely practical considerations, that they 'will not unite with any practical Principles but those of Justice and Moderation'.[13] The practical recommendations were for him no more important than the moral premises, involving arguments of political economy and political philosophy from which they were deduced. The one-sided emphasis on the fiscal policy stated in his plan is, therefore, quite contrary to its spirit. Francis had written it not as a solution of the problem on hand, not as an answer only to the petty questions of policy raised by maladministration, but as a contribution to the task of 'forming or restoring the Constitution of an Empire'.[14] It was designed to lay down a line not only on revenue settlement, but also on many other aspects of finance, trade and taxation and again not on economic questions alone, but also on the general problem of British power in India – the problem of sovereignty, the relative positions of the Company and Parliament with respect to India, the social basis of English rule in the country and so on. The problem of 'Permanent Settlement of the revenues' gave Francis the occasion to formulate and pronounce his ideas on the 'Permanent Settlement of the Country', and the way in which he goes on using the two phrases interchangeably in his correspondence shows how he confounded the part with the whole.

[13] To R. Becher, 19 July 1777. *Ibid.*, 49 (38) 98.

[14] To C. D'Oyly, 22 January 1776. *Ibid.*, 47 (36) 76.

The plan thus transcended the limits of purely administrative consideration: looming large over the details of policy recommendations and altogether dwarfing them there stood out of its pages the ambitious edifice of a 'system' – a word Francis was fond of using – which could not be judged except as a whole. The operation of such a system did not depend on measures 'supported by occasional Acts of Power' men call laws. Its mechanics were based on human nature itself. Once set in motion the system, like the Newtonian universe, must move by its own volition without the assistance of artificial decrees. A nation could have too many laws. The physiocratic suspicion of positive law and its opposition to 'natural order' characterized his own definition of the plan as he wrote:

> If the Plan be what I intended to make it, when once instituted and fairly set in Motion it ought to execute itself. If not, it is defective in Principle, as every System of Government must be, which can only be supported by occasional Acts of Power. Men are governed by Manners, not by Laws. If the latter could supply the place of the former, the Rules and Regulations made within these few Years for the Use of Bengal, would be sufficient, in Number at least, to govern the World. The Truth is, We have too many already and there cannot be a surer Symptom of the Decline or Misrule of a Country.[15]

The author of these lines would have been outraged at the idea of his plan being regarded as simply a contribution to the land laws of Bengal. To add further to the already unmanageable volume of 'rules and regulations' was the last thing he had intended to do when he wrote his minute of 1776. His claim was that of a law-giver only in an elevated Solonian sense.

From the outset it had been his aim to look for 'some simple determinate Principles' upon which to base 'the Settlement of the Country'.[16] The plan, when written up and submitted, was described by him as 'plain and simple'.[17] This simplicity is syllogistic and derived from the fact that all the various parts of his argument, in spite of their

[15] To C.W.B. Rous, 22 June 1776 (Private). *Francis MSS* 7 (31) 8.
[16] To Lord North, 23 March 1775. *Ibid.*, 49 (38) 17.
[17] To C. D'Oyly, 22 January 1776. *Ibid.*, 47 (36) 76.

broad and comprehensive range, are bound together by one central idea of 'permanence of dominion'. He never tired of insisting that the ultimate strategic aim of his policy was to ensure 'permanence and duration' of the English power in India.[18] The point of all the criticism he had to make of the East India Company was that they had lost sight of their far-reaching and fundamental interests in the pursuit of immediate and temporary advantages. It was, again, in this, he thought, the essential difference between him and Hastings lay. For 'the Security of a permanent Possession' was the consideration from which all his own arguments proceeded. 'Opposing Views of moderate but permanent profit to those which offer immediate and Excessive Returns', he wrote, 'I am not likely to be a favourite with Men, who consider nothing but the utmost Emoluments of a temporary Possession. This is the true Line of Distinction between all Mr Hastings's Measures and mine. The Idea of it should accompany the Consideration of almost every Argument from hence.'[19]

It was precisely this approach that gave his plan its singular consistency, and his method of reasoning was fully matched to it. His disregard for facts, his deductive method, his use of generalizations and universals, have all been noted by his critics. But all these were characteristic of the writings of the eighteenth-century *philosophes*, and Francis's methodology no less than his ideas was an index of their influence on him. 'Mere facts are sufficient for a gazette, but teach nothing', said Francis in his essay on English history; 'What we want is moral example.'[20] One could quote scores of similar statements from the pages of Fontenelle, Grimm, Diderot or for that matter any other major writer of the French school of 'new history.'[21] Their method in its ideal form, as Professor Becker has analysed it, was to classify

[18] To Lord North, 23 March 1775. *Ibid.*, 49 (38) 17. To H. Strachey, 22 January 1776. *Ibid.*, 47 (36) 75. To R. Becher, 19 July 1777. *Ibid.*, 49 (38) 98. To W. Young, 5 July 1778. *Ibid.*, 51 (41) 41.

[19] To W. Ellis, 13 January 1777. *Ibid.*, 49 (38) 68.

[20] P. & M., II, p. 467.

[21] For some specimens of their views on this subject, see Becker, op. cit., pp. 91–2.

ideas and institutions into categories that cut across distinctions of time and space, leave out as irrelevant such elements as were local and temporary, process the remainder to form what Hume called the 'constant and universal principles of human nature', and present the result as a formula for social reconstruction.[22] This corresponds exactly to what Francis had to say about his own manner of argumentation. Introducing his plan to Lord North, he wrote:

> In proportion as I acquired local and particular Knowledge, it has been my constant Rule to compare facts with Principles; – judging that, if ruinous Consequences in Practice were proved to flow from false Principles in Theory, the Reverse might he fairly expected to follow from the Establishment of true ones. Hitherto I see no reason to question the Truth of those general propositions, which struck me at the first View of the deplorable State of this Country, and which, tho' drawn from the sources of European Policy, must hold good at all Times and in all Places, if as I believe, they are founded in Truth and right Reason.[23]

These 'general rules', he thought, embodied 'the common Judgement of Men' and were supported by the wisdom of responsible authorities. To regulate policy measures by them was therefore the only natural thing to do, and any deviation, he said, by turning the tables on his critics, must be supported by 'Extraordinary Proofs'.[24] The only claim he ever made about the plan was that it was 'right on principle'.[25] For the rest, he cared nothing. When it was known that Clavering had some objections to make on a number of points, he asked: 'The Question is, are they Objections of Principle or Detail? The first imply an incurable Defect – the second are open to Improvement or Correction.'[26] He would concede the latter so long as the 'leading general Principles' were not touched. 'If the Foundation be secure, and the grand Apartments judiciously disposed', he said, 'I shall not

[22] *Ibid.*, p. 100.
[23] 22 January 1776. *Francis MSS* 53 (49) 17.
[24] Note on 'Trade to Suez'. *Ibid.*, 64 (52) 9.
[25] To C. D'Oyly, 22 January 1776. *Ibid.*, 47 (36) 76.
[26] To Lord North, 18 March 1776. *Ibid.*, 47 (36) 88.

dispute with General Clavering, or any Body else, about Offices and Water Closets.'[27]

Methodological differences were, of course, more easily settled with Clavering than with the Governor-General. Here, as in almost every other respect, there was an irreducible opposition between Hastings and Francis. The latter liked to take a broad, comprehensive view of things, ignoring details, and spoke of his rival as being 'literally and exclusively a man of parts', who missed the wood for the trees.[28] Used to abstractions, he could never understand why Hastings and his partisans should resist his arguments deduced from first principles. 'To establish any Proposition whatsoever', he grumbled, 'we are constantly obliged to go back to the First Elements, and so deduce the Argument Step by Step to a regular Conclusion. When we do so, they first dispute the simplest Postulata, and at last they deny the Truth of the Demonstration.'[29] They could not have behaved otherwise, for nothing could be more alien to Hastings than such a mode of reasoning. The exchange of minutes that followed the plan of 1776 in course of that year was often enlivened by rival statements justifying the logic of either of the alternatives proposed as the best policy. Hastings summed up the difference quite correctly when he wrote in his minute of 12 November 1776: 'More used to the practice of business than to speculation, I beg to be excused from discussing these propositions as general and abstract questions; and instead of considering them as principles, which are equally applicable to any country, I wish to confine them merely to the revenue of Bengal.'[30] To this Francis replied by asserting again what he had learnt from the philosopher-historians of his age. 'With respect to general propositions', he said, 'I have yet seen no reason to admit that principles, unquestionably true in every other country, should not be applicable to Bengal. It is in the nature of justice and good government

[27] To H. Strachey, 20 March 1776. *Ibid.*, 47 (36) 86.

[28] P. & M., II, pp. 80–1.

[29] To W. Ellis, 22 February 1775. *Francis MSS* 47 (36) 51.

[30] *Sir Philip Francis's Minutes*, p. 128.

to deduce its arrangements from some undisputed points of original right. It is in the nature of arbitrary power to make exceptions.'[31] The sociology and the method indicated in this statement were both characteristic of the Age of Enlightenment. For further evidence of his intellectual affiliation in this respect one must, however, turn to the economic thesis of the plan itself.

2. The Political Economy of Permanent Settlement

(A) The Agrarian Programme

The impact of Blackstone's *Commentaries* on contemporary thought has been attributed by Asa Briggs to 'the dominance of law as the synthesizing element in the study of society', and he mentions the enthusiasm with which Adam Smith read the work as a young man and wrote about it.[32] In much the same sense Francis's passion for constitutional history was connected with his interest in political economy. An abstract of Locke's views on money and interest, extracts from the writings of Davenant, notes on the revenue and taxation systems of several European countries, and masses of commercial statistics were found among his papers dating from the period soon after his return from Portugal.[33] The year before he left for Calcutta he had translated Isaac de Pinto's *Traite de la Circulation et du Credit.*[34]

[31] *Ibid.*, p. 152.

[32] Briggs, *The Age of Improvement*, p. 90.

[33] P. & M., I, pp. 50–1.

[34] 'Autobiographical Fragment'. *Ibid.*, p. 366, and P. & M., II, p. 321. For Francis's letters to de Pinto about the translation, see *Francis MSS* 46 (29) 26 and 46 (29) 44. Isaac de Pinto is described in the English edition of his *Essai sur le Luxe* (1762) as a Dutch merchant 'distinguished for his taste and conversancy in polite useful literature'. His affinity with contemporary French thought is well illustrated by many of his ideas on economic and social problems discussed by him in the *Essai* and in the *Traite* written nine years later. For further details, see *Biographie Universelle*, vol. 33, and *The Universal Jewish Encyclopaedia*, vol. 8.

He was well acquainted with the works of contemporary French *économistes*, and quoted profusely from the writings of Quesnay, Turgot and the elder Mirabeau. Some of his earliest policy statements in India related to problems of money and banking. He knew his Locke well enough to come out with the suggestion that in Bengal the Company should introduce the use of gold coins as optional currency with silver as the standard of value.[35] In a rare fit of modesty he spoke of the works of Sir James Steuart as 'a solid Mass of Knowledge, not always to be penetrated without a severe Attention, or more Sagacity at least than I am Master of'.[36] But from his correspondence with Steuart about the latter's recommendations for currency reform he emerges as a highly knowledgeable and competent critic.[37]

It has been already noted by Firminger that Francis's economic thought was influenced by the physiocrats.[38] The contribution of this school has been recognized as the starting point of modern economics. Weulersse traced in it the doctrinal ancestry of both Adam Smith and Karl Marx.[39] The physiocrats were the first to attempt a proper study of the behaviour of capital in the labour process and the forms it assumes in circulation. On both points Adam Smith took over directly from them, and his admiration for François Quesnay, the leader of the school, was surely an acknowledgment of their merit,

[35] J.C. Sinha, 'Economic Theorists among the Servants of John Company (1766–1806)', in *Economic Journal* (March 1925).

[36] To Lord Barrington, 20 November 1776. *Francis MSS* 47 (36) 134.

[37] Francis got in touch with Sir James Steuart through Lord Barrington. *Francis MSS* 47 (36) 115 and 134. Francis's important minute on currency questions, his views on Steuart's recommendations, and their correspondence on the subject are recorded in *ibid.*, 49 (38) 48 and 80 (24), pp. 363–81; *Home Miscellaneous Series*, vol. 125; and Steuart's *Works*, vol. 5. There is an excellent summary of the debate in S.R. Sen's *The Economics of Sir James Steuart*, ch. X. 'Steuart's most distinguished and by far the most clear-headed critic was . . . Sir Philip Francis', says Sen. 'Even in matters economic Francis proved to be quite a match for the celebrated "political oeconomist". His analysis of the situation was precise and penetrating' (p. 174).

[38] Firminger, *Fifth Report*, vol. II, Introduction, p. xviii.

[39] 'Economics: The Physiocrats', in *Encyclopaedia of the Social Sciences*.

if not of his own debt to them.[40] Marx, on his part, spoke of them as 'the true fathers of modern economics'.[41] They represented one of the principal trends of the intellectual revolt against the *ancien régime.* The social criticism and philosophical assumptions in their theories were largely derived from the encyclopaedists with whom, in fact, they closely collaborated. Personally many of the physiocrats felt outraged at the actual turn of events in 1789, but that did not prevent the Assemblée Nationale from experimenting with many of their ideas in their programme of reform. It is easy to understand why Philip Francis, who had been so profoundly influenced by the intellectual ferment of contemporary France, should want to try out the physiocratic formula in Bengal.

Land, according to the physiocrats, is the source of all wealth. Their theory of value is based on an analysis of agricultural production in which, much more than in industry, the difference between the value of labour power and the value created by its use appears in its most tangible form. It is this difference, the *produit net,*[42] which is the surplus appropriated by the owner of land as rent. The physiocrats claimed to have invented the mechanism which in their ideal society would ensure the reproduction of this surplus and its correct distribution. The social philosophy upon which this doctrine implicitly rested 'consisted in placing above everything else private property, especially property in land'.[43]

The economic thesis of Francis's plan for Bengal, as stated in his minute of January 1776 and explained in parts in numerous letters,

[40] Roll, *A History of Economic Thought*, p. 146. It is known that Adam Smith would have dedicated his masterpiece to Quesnay but for the latter's death two years before its publication. Gide and Rist, *A History of Economic Doctrines*, pp. 22–3.

[41] *Theories of Surplus Value*, p. 44.

[42] The English equivalent of this phrase is actually used by Francis when in his minute of December 1776 he defines revenue as 'a fixed portion of the net produce'. *Sir Philip Francis's Minutes*, p. 147.

[43] Weulersse, 'Economics: The Physiocrats', in *Encyclopaedia of the Social Sciences.*

notes and memoranda, closely followed this model. The recognition of the right of the zamindars to landed property was, as he himself said, 'the main hinge on which the whole argument turns. My deductions will be found to flow regularly from this position.'[44] No government, he thought, could be assured of its revenue unless it was prepared to guarantee the rights of proprietorship, and in a letter to William Young he explained how the one was conditioned by the other.

> . . . without private Property [he wrote] there can be no public Revenue. I mean that regular and permanent Revenue, on which alone a wise Government ought to place its Dependance . . . Agency can never supply the place of Proprietorship, because many of the principal Duties of a Proprietor are such as an Agent has no personal interest in performing. But these Duties are essential to the permanent Prosperity of the Government itself, since they belong to the Care and Improvement of that Fund, from which the Government receives its Support. Now it is not the mere name of Proprietor that will engage any Man to perform these duties, if he has no real Security, that he shall not be robbed of the surplus Produce of his Industry and Labour; – that is, if he does not know, once and for all, how much he is to pay to Government, and be not assured that the remainder will be his own.[45]

Consequently, whenever he had an occasion to state the aims of his revenue policy, considerations about the amount and period of assessment would always yield pride of place to his insistence 'that the Zemindars should be restored to their hereditary Rights'.[46] It was not possible, however, to put forward such a view without challenging the basic assumption of the official line that the ruling power was 'proprietor of the soil'. It was considered by Francis as 'not less false

[44] *Sir Philip Francis's Minutes*, p. 147.

[45] To W. Young, 5 July 1778. *Francis MSS* 51 (41) 41.

[46] There are two letters in which the three articles of his land policy are enumerated in the same sequence, that is, (i) recognition of the zamindars as proprietors, (ii) moderation of the fiscal demand, and (iii) unalterability of the demand. To Clavering, 14 January 1776. *Ibid.*, 53 (49) 16. To W. Ellis, 13 September 1776. *Ibid.*, 47 (36) 114.

in fact than absurd in theory and dangerous in practice',[47] and the opposition between the concept of crown-ownership and zamindar-ownership dominates his argument. The plan of 1776 actually opens with an indictment of the other point of view:

> The Company, I believe, had conceived an early, but erroneous, opinion that by the constitution of the Mogul Empire the governing power was the proprietor of the soil; consequently that in the management of their territorial acquisitions, they ought not to content themselves with a fixed tribute as government, since they had a right to engross the entire produce as landlord.[48]

The theme recurs like a refrain throughout his writings, for this, he thought, constituted 'the great and . . . the voluntary Mistake of every Administration since our Acquisition of the Duannee'. He would grant that as Government 'we have a Right to Revenue', but would insist at the same time that 'we are not Proprietors of the Soil'.[49]

In arguing for zamindari rights Francis had to contend with a certain interpretation of Indian history underlying the other theory. In the seventeenth and early eighteenth centuries many European travellers had come to believe that in India all land belonged to the king. Bernier had indeed made a very definite statement to that effect, and his authority was often quoted in support of the view that under the Mughals there was no private property in land. Francis believed that this assumption was implicit in the official revenue policy of the East India Company. (The way James Grant was to work out the logic of this assumption in his defence of what was essentially the Hastings line confirms Francis.) The alternative he himself recommended could therefore be established only by demolishing the other view of Indian history.

Here again he drew largely upon the French *philosophes.* The security of private property was, according to them, an essential

[47] *Letter from Mr Francis to Lord North*, p. 7.

[48] *Sir Philip Francis's Minutes*, p. 19.

[49] To W. Ellis, 13 September 1776. *Francis MSS* 47 (36) 114.

characteristic of good society. They had also been writing about the superiority and excellence of the oriental governments, particularly of China and India. This latter notion could therefore be defended only by proving the travellers wrong in their opinion about the state of property in India. The writer who was most aware of this inconsistency was Voltaire, and it is interesting to see how over a period of seventeen years he proceeded to develop his attack against it in three successive statements. Already in 1756 in the first definitive edition of his *Essay sur l'Histoire Générale* the reader was warned against the notion 'que dans l'Inde le fruit de tous les travaux des hommes appartienne à un seul homme'. Some of the castes, he argued, retained their hereditary properties even after the Mughal conquest and estates acquired by the nobility as grants were enriched by them in the same manner as farmers did elsewhere. The Indian peasants, he said, were poor, but certainly not reduced to serfdom in the European sense of the word.[50] The thesis was developed still further in a subsequent edition of the work five years later. There he named the writers he thought were most responsible for popularizing this misconception: François Catrou, who believed that all the land belonged to the Mughal emperor, but contradicted himself by saying at the same time that the property of the Rajas was inherited by their sons; Tavernier, dismissed as a writer who addressed himself to the merchants rather than to the philosophers, and whose testimony about the opulence of the merchants was in any case quite incompatible – so Voltaire thought – with Bernier's description of the country consisting of only two classes, the aristocracy and the poor. The last-named writer, however, deserved more serious examination, for he was indeed a *philosophe*, although he made poor use of his philosophy on the question under discussion. Bernier, too, spoke of crown-ownership. Assuming that this was based on the king's right of conferring estates on his followers, Voltaire made a nice distinction between *donner* and *jouir* and went on to suggest that the custom of bestowing such grants

[50] *Essay sur l'Histoire Generale* (ed. 1756), t. IV, p. 304.

made the Mughal no more the owner of all the lands than the grants of *bénéfices* and fiefs could be said to make a European monarch the sole proprietor of all the estates in his domain.

> Il (Bernier) dit comme les autres que toutes les terres appartiennent à l'Empereur. C'est ce qui a besoin d'explication. Donner des terres et en jouir sont deux choses absolument différentes. Les Rois Européens qui donnent tous les Bénéfices Ecclésiastiques, ne les possèdent pas. L'Empereur dont le droit est de conférer tous les Fiefs d'Allemagne et d'Italie quand ils vaquent faute d'héritiers, ne recueille pas les fruits de ces Terres.[51]

In the *Essay*, Voltaire allowed his fellow-philosopher to get away rather easily, and even gave him the benefit of doubt by saying that Bernier had not really meant all that his interpreters read into his statement. His criticism in its final form, however, was quite severe when he returned to the attack twelve years later in *Fragments sur l'Inde.*The logic remained the same as before, that is, a distinction between ownership and the customary right of making land grants. But to the historical interpretation was now added a purely political comment – a sign perhaps of the gall that had already developed out of the intellectual ferment – that for a philosopher to write as Bernier did to Colbert was to furnish a despotic government with a most dangerous argument: 'Ç'eût été une imprudence bien dangereuse de parler ainsi à l'administrateur des finances d'un Roi absolu.' Voltaire also accused Thomas Roe of being as wrong on this point as Bernier: 'tous deux éblouis de la pompe du grand Mogol and de son despotisme.' He regretted that all French authors – the travellers, the missionaries, the hackwriters who produced fairy-tales for their publishers – were equally unreliable. He, therefore, turned to what was then the most recent literature on the subject in English, the histories and dissertations which had been coming out in a steady flow since the Company's acquisition of Diwani, influencing opinion not only in England but to some extent in France as well. Voltaire mentioned

[51] *Ibid.* (ed. 1761), t. IV, pp. 186–8.

Holwell and Dow, and actually quoted Scrafton in support of his own view that the custom of hereditary succession proved beyond doubt the existence of private property.[52]

Francis in his turn quoted Voltaire.[53] Like Voltaire, too, he considered inheritance as the best evidence of individual ownership, and enclosed with his plan a number of supporting statements from native officers and Hindu pundits.[54] 'The inheritable quality of the lands is alone sufficient to prove', he wrote, 'that they are the property of the Zemindars, Talookdars, and others, to whom they have descended by a long course of inheritance.'[55] He was, therefore, satisfied that in arguing for zamindari rights he was in fact pleading for a restoration of what had been subverted during the interregnum of British rule. This conformed fully to the eighteenth-century attitude of reverence for what all thinkers of the Age of Enlightenment believed to be the wisdom of oriental governments. There was also associated with this idea of reversion a certain myth-making quality characteristic of reformers – a certain manner of justifying the blueprint of a new order in terms of the past. The image of Rome dominated much of the ideology of reform in Europe at this time; out in the East, Francis used the image of Mughal India for a similar purpose. 'We shall revert to the ancient institutions of the country', he wrote to Lord North,[56] and was sure that this could be best achieved by his plan. For the security of private property, which it was his policy to re-establish in India had, indeed, been the underlying principle of that good old order under the Mahommedans.

'When the Moguls conquered Bengal', he wrote, 'there is no mention in any historical account, that they dispossessed the Zemindars of their lands.' Land was left in the hands of the original proprietors and was not taken away by the conqueror for distribution among

[52] *Fragments sur l'Inde*, pp. 34–7.

[53] *Sir Philip Francis's Minutes*, p. 72.

[54] *Ibid.*, pp. 66–71.

[55] *Ibid.*, p. 64.

[56] *Letter from Mr Francis to Lord North*, pp. 9–10.

his retainers either as an act of favour or in exchange of money. He referred to a historical note prepared for him by Muhammad Reza Khan in which the latter maintained that 'Princes have no immediate property in the lands'.[57] The grant of *jagir* and *wakf*, corresponding roughly to fief and *benefice* in the European sense, was explained away by him by the same kind of argument as Voltaire used: 'the land continues to be deemed a part of the Zemindary; the sovereign only grants the revenue of it.' How then could one account for so many royal *sanads* bestowing lands on the zamindars? Francis solved the difficulty by simply ruling out the fact that could not be fitted into his theory. 'It is true', he said, 'the forms of the royal Sunnuds, or grants, to the Zemindars, suppose them to hold of the sovereign *in capite*; but this I consider as a kind of feodal fiction, of which the sovereign in fact never pretended to avail himself, as constituting a right to assume or transfer the possession.'[58]

Otherwise unconvincing, this statement contains an important indication of Francis's idea of feudalism. In a feudal society, he thought, the monarch was the supreme proprietor, the overlord whose rights superseded those of the other landowners. Private property was never safe under such conditions. He was, therefore, keen on differentiating the zamindari tenure from the feudal land system. It is interesting to find him dwelling on this distinction at some length in a letter he wrote to C.W.B. Rous apparently in an effort to dispel his correspondent's confusion on the subject. Feudalism as a historical concept was still very young when Francis wrote about it. He followed the narrow legalistic notion popularized by Blackstone that crown-ownership was 'the great and fundamental maxim of all feudal tenure'.[59] But in spite of the inadequacy of his definition the

[57] 'Mahammed Reza Cawn's Description of the former and present State of the Country, the Causes of its decline and the way there is of recovering and bringing it again into a flourishing Condition', January 1775. *Francis MSS* 77 (31) 2.

[58] *Sir Philip Francis's Minutes*, pp. 64–5.

[59] Blackstone, *Commentaries*, vol. II, p. 53, and vol. IV, p. 106. There is a good deal of internal evidence to show that Francis was deeply influenced

insistence on some characteristic differences between the Indian and European patterns was certainly a most remarkable thing to do at that time, considering the urge for uniformity which was to dominate the sociology of medieval studies during the next century. To quote in part from this letter:

> If the Nature of the Zemindary Tenure be attentively examined by the Test of Facts, I think it will appear to have no real Relation to the Feudal, consequently that no Argument, in support of the Sovereign's supposed Property in the Soil, can be drawn from a Comparison of the two Systems. No Proprietorship of Lands in the Sovereign could be higher than that which the Principles of Feudal Government vested in him – It was a System of Conquest. The Chief of a victorious Army divided the Country in large Allotments among his superior Officers, by whom it was again distributed in smaller Portions to the inferior Officers and Soldiers. They all held their Lands originally of the Prince, on condition of performing military Service for the general Defence of the Conquest. The Descent was confined to Males and those of Blood only. In case of Failure of Heirs or Forfeiture, the Lands reverted to him who granted them. The Right of Females to inherit or of the immediate Possessor to introduce a Stranger by Adoption, was unknown to the Feudal Law and would have been utterly incompatible with the Principles on which it was founded. The tenure of landed Property in Bengal is quite upon a different Footing. The Mahometan Conqueror did not divide the Country among his Followers, nor did he make a new Grant of the Lands to the former Proprietors on condition of military Service. In general he left the Possession of the Lands where he found it, on the condition of a fixed pecuniary Tribute, with which he maintained a standing Army for the securing of the Acquisition.[60]

All this subtlety in sorting out the concepts did not, however, prevent some of his critics from imputing a certain feudal bias to

---

by Blackstone's ideas on feudalism. The way he dismisses the *sanads* as 'feodal fiction' is, for instance, literally an echo of the *Commentaries*, vol. II, p. 51. Blackstone's own ideas on the subject were not free from inconsistencies, and these, as Vinogradoff suggests, were in their turn the result of a projection of eighteenth-century concepts into the past. – *Villainage in England*, p. 9.

[60] To C.W.B. Rous, 22 June 1776. *Francis MSS* 53 (49) 26.

Francis.[61] In fact he sometimes spoke of the zamindars as if they were feudal landlords. He mentioned what he considered their 'manorial rights', described them as 'Lords of the Manor', defined their relationship with the ryots as that of 'reciprocal Obligations of protection and Dependence', and had no objection to their exercise of magisterial powers derived from 'the possession of landed property'.[62] Put together thus into one statement from bits and pieces scattered all over his writings, this might indeed read like a perfect contradiction of all that he had been trying to say about the zamindari tenure being non-feudal. But the important thing to consider is that even in this ambiguity Francis was being true to his physiocratic convictions.

There were some obvious contradictions in the physiocratic doctrine. It had taken shape as a part of the intellectual revolt against the *ancien régime* and was, in both its economic and social outlook, orientated towards capitalism. But the conditions of its origin were still predominantly feudal, and as a result the terms in which it expressed itself were often derived from experience characteristic of the old order. This gave rise to all kinds of contradictory and equivocal statements in physiocratic writings, and led in their turn to the many conflicting interpretations of the doctrine. Marx, with all his great admiration for this school, was also one of the first modern economists to seek an historical explanation of their inconsistencies which, according to him, reflected 'the contradictions of capitalist production when it is working its way out of feudal society and only interprets feudal society itself in a rather more bourgeois way, without having yet discovered its own peculiar form'. He pointed out how in physiocratic literature the correct analysis of surplus value as arising from social labour appeared side by side with the naive notion

[61] For Thomas Law's objections to Francis's policy on this account, see p. 176 below.

[62] *Letter from Mr Francis to Lord North*, pp. 8, 42, 46. To Lord North, 13 January 1775. *Francis MSS* 47 (36) 47. 'Minute on Farming of Lands by British Subjects', 12 May 1775. *Ibid.*, 72 (1) 24. To C.W.B. Rous, 22 June 1776. *Ibid.*, 53 (49) 26.

of value as a 'gift of nature', and how agricultural rent removed from its feudal context and studied as a surplus in excess of wages was still sometimes presented 'as if it were feudal, derived from nature and not from society, from man's relation to the land and not from his social relations'.[63]

This ambivalence is perhaps best illustrated in their concept of the landlord-entrepreneur. The physiocrats put it forward as their fundamental thesis that the greatest need for agricultural improvement was 'non pas tant des bras que des capitaux', and they could never insist enough on the desirability of inducing a general flow of capital into the land. An important condition of agricultural productivity would, therefore, be 'to encourage the development of a class of rich agricultural entrepreneurs or large-scale farmers who would lease large areas of land for long terms'.[64] The capitalist farmer was assigned such a key role in the physiocratic programme that Mirabeau went to the extent of recommending several kinds of official honours for the best entrepreneurs.[65] But the patina of feudalism was never quite taken off the image of the farmer even after his function as a capitalist had been so clearly conceived. Often the physiocrats wrote as if it was the feudal landlord whom they expected to invest capital into the land, carry out improvements, treat his peasant like a capitalist employing free labourers on his farm and earning his income in terms of *produit net* which, in the last analysis, looked more like a firm's profit than the rent from a typical French estate before 1789. 'In other words, this landlord is in essence a capitalist.'[66]

[63] *Theories of Surplus Value*, pp. 51–3. Many modern writers on the history of economic thought have closely followed Marx in their analysis of the physiocratic doctrine, and this equally applies to erudite interpretations like those by Schumpeter and Sweezy and to more elementary surveys like those by Roll and Gide and Rist. For a brilliant study of the contradictions in the doctrine, see Louis Salleron's essay 'Le Produit net des Physiocrates' in *François Quesnay et la Physiocratie*, t. I, pp. 131–52.

[64] Weulersse, op. cit., and *Les Physiocrates*, pp. 75 and 79–80.

[65] *Ibid.*, p. 90.

[66] Marx, op. cit., p. 52.

Some of the apparent inconsistencies in Francis's policy for Bengal were the outcome of a comparable process of confounding two distinct social images into a single vision. His idea of the Mughal agrarian system was in fact made up of concepts borrowed from contemporary England. 'Francis's scheme', says Firminger, 'while it pretends to be a return to the principles of the Mughal empire, is in reality parallel with the methods of those early English administrators in Ireland, who being so familiar with the land-holding by *contract* in their own land, simply could not recognise in Ireland the existence of land-holding by *status* . . . Claiming to be pleading on behalf of . . . native laws and customs . . . Francis in fact popularized in England, if not in Bengal, a view of land-holding in India which was hopelessly at contradiction with the facts of history.'[67] He apparently believed that the structure of rural society in Bengal before the English conquest was similar to that of England in the eighteenth century. 'A violent and arbitrary reduction of some thousands of noblemen, gentlemen and freeholders (for such ranks there were in Bengal as well as in England) to a competent subsistence, that is, to the level of the peasantry', he wrote, 'might perhaps excite some degree of remorse and compassion in England.'[68] Such statements were perhaps meant to appeal to the whig sense of property,[69] but this does not take away from the fact that Francis was speaking out of conviction. The spectacular progress of English agriculture was at this time greatly admired by the French *économistes*, and their followers on the other side of the Channel shared this attitude. Pattullo, who wrote on the agrarian question of France as well as of Bengal, had recommended the English model for both countries. It is understandable that in his Indian plan Francis too had allowed himself to be influenced by his native experience.

The central figure in the English agrarian scene at this time was the gentleman-farmer; he was the agent of all improvement – it was his capital that was invested in the land, his enterprise that made it

[67] Firminger, *Fifth Report*, vol. I, p. cccviii.

[68] *Sir Philip Francis's Minutes*, pp. 172–3.

[69] Firminger, op. cit., p. ccciii.

productive, and often his inventiveness that provided it with new techniques. Francis's zamindar was conceived after this image. With him as with other writers of the school to which he belonged, the feudal landlord, 'the Lord of the Manor', provided the point of departure; but after attributes and functions had been defined, the end product of the analysis was the zamindar appearing in the role of an entrepreneur. For it was the great aim of Francis's plan to help in the agricultural recovery of Bengal from the state of its decline since Diwani. He anticipated Cornwallis by his emphasis on the idea of improvement, and Thomas Law by suggesting that a concrete measure of achieving it would be for the Europeans to cultivate sugarcane instead of paddy in waste lands leased out to them.[70] But this, of course, could not

[70] 'Improvement by Europeans', *Francis MSS* 64 (52) 8. This note is not dated, but a copy was apparently sent to W. Ellis on 20 November 1776. Francis anticipated Thomas Law by recommending the cultivation of sugarcane. As Law was to do later, he too produced a rough estimate showing how a bigha of land growing paddy 'to the Value of five Rupees' would yield crops worth six times as much if 'cultivated in Sugar by a European'. He was also years ahead of Law in relating the problem of agricultural improvement directly to that of exports. 'If the Sugar be exported', he said, 'there is a clear Gain of 20 Rupees to the Country, allowing 5 to the original Produce and 5 to the Improver's Profit'. The note then goes on to describe some other economic advantages of growing commercial crops: 'Thus far the Gain to the Country is capable of Computation. That, which cannot be computed, is perhaps still more considerable. The Employment of the poor and Idle, and even of Women and Children; – the Habits of industry which such Employment creates; – the Encouragement to useful Population by furnishing it with Nourishment thro' the Medium of Employment; – and the general Increase of Circulation, which, as long at least as the Work continues, must go on: (and the Work must continue, or the first Improver cannot realise his Fortune).' Francis concludes the note with a warning that the European farmers of waste lands mentioned by him must not be 'confounded with those to whom Power and Station have given the Means of exhausting the Country directly of its Wealth without making it a Return of any Kind'; that, in other words, farming of lands by the Company's officials must not be permitted. 'The Expediency of granting Parcels of Waste Land to Europeans for the purpose of raising Articles not now produced, nor brought to perfection

be recommended as a general policy, however beneficial its practical results were. For 'the Soil of right belongs to the Natives', and if lands other than waste, that is, those already under cultivation were allowed to be farmed by Europeans, 'the Land-holders will consider us with Jealousy and Hatred as the Invaders of his Rights and Property'.[71] It was the zamindar, therefore, who was to promote improvements. For that he would require capital, and there were two ways in which Francis thought this might be available.

First, he expected the Permanent Settlement to revive the collaboration between 'the landed and monied property'. Each of these two classes had 'a natural and permanent interest in the prosperity of the other' before the zamindars began to decline under the impact of British rule. In those days 'while the credit of the Zemindars was supported, merchants and others, acting as bankers for them, lent them large sums, which formed a maintenance to the merchant and assisted the Zemindars in improving their lands'. Once that credit was restored as a result of Permanent Settlement, the lands would 'absorb the idle money thrown into the hands of private persons by the discharge of the bonded debt', if of course the government were willing to assist the process by fixing a definite rate of interest and a proper system of security, whether by mortgage or otherwise.[72]

Secondly, the sale of lands, he was sure, would further facilitate the flow of capital, and 'when the quit-rent is fixed, there can be no doubt of purchasers'. Some of the zamindars would lose their estates either for reasons of poverty and incapacity or from sheer distrust of the government and reluctance to come to a settlement. In all such cases, 'a transfer of landed property to monied people, who are

---

in Bengal' also occurs in Francis's note 'Trade to Suez', *Francis MSS* 64 (52) 9.

[71] 'Minute on Farming of Lands by British Subjects', 12 May 1775. *Francis MSS* 72 (1) 24.

[72] *Sir Philip Francis's Minutes*, pp. 57–8. The prospect of a revival of indigenous banking as a result of Permanent Settlement was emphasized at a later date by Thomas Law. See *A Sketch of Some Late Arrangements*, pp. 71, 75–7.

able to make improvements, will be in some degree advantageous to Government and to the country'. The development of a land-market was thus an important condition for the progress of his plan and the success of the improvements visualized by it. In effect, it was Francis's idea that all zamindars with whom the settlement was to be made according to his plan would be bound by a common interest in agricultural enterprise, but that there would be among them both those who represented 'monied property' and others who represented 'landed property'. On the balance it would perhaps appear that Francis's sympathy lay with the latter. Consequently, even when he was forced by the logic of his doctrine to admit of the necessity of a land-market, he wanted it to operate in a manner that would have the least dislocating effect on the established zamindari families. In the case of sales, he said, a preference should be given to the next heir. If more than the amount of the debt or revenue arrears was obtained by a sale, the excess should be credited to the original proprietor. In any case he hoped that the prospect of sale would have a chastening effect on the zamindars, and 'they will be roused from their present supine and hopeless state to exert every endeavour for the preservation and improvement of their estates, now rendered of real value to them'.[73] It is this attitude that accounts for much of the ambiguity of Francis's concept of the zamindar. He conceded, on the one hand, that investments in land must turn it into a commodity; but on the other, he was not quite prepared to face the consequences and accept that the laws of demand and supply must inevitably tend to eliminate an effete aristocracy and replace it by 'monied interests' having no hereditary connection with the land and often described by Francis as 'strangers' and 'adventurers'. In this respect he was not half as ruthlessly bourgeois as Thomas Law, who during the next decade was to work out fully the implications of the Permanent Settlement in terms of the land-market.[74] For himself, Francis, with the image of the English gentleman-farmer fixed at the back of his mind, remained

[73] *Sir Philip Francis's Minutes*, pp. 51–2.

[74] See Chapter 5 below.

hopefully committed to the idea of the traditional Bengali zamindar emerging in the role of Tull and Townshend.

The anti-feudal orientation of Francis's zamindari plan is equally obvious, in his insistence on the 'Distribution of landed property into a greater Number of Hands'.[75] He agreed with the recommendation of Hastings and Barwell that 'the large Zemindaries should be divided, and the small ones should be preserved entire',[76] but from a somewhat different motive. His rivals had conceived this primarily as a political measure, for 'the proprietors of the very extensive Zemindaries . . . possess influence which they employ in opposition to Government, and in case of war they might even become formidable, as was the case in former times'. Francis, on the other hand, was eager to emphasize the economic importance of small properties. By the eighteenth century this had come to be recognized as a principal condition of the development of capitalism in agriculture. In France it was regarded as one of the basic tenets of the physiocratic doctrine; in England it was justified by Blackstone in terms of legal theory, and by Hume in political economy. The latter provided a perfect quotation for any thesis on the permanence of landed property and Francis did not miss it: 'Such moderate estates', he wrote, 'as require economy and confine the proprietors to live at home, are better calculated for duration.'[77] It is significant, too, that Francis's emphasis on this principle was a shade different from that of the Hastings–Barwell plan. His recommendation had the edge more deliberately turned against the economic power of feudalism, and as a result the dismemberment of the larger estates was for him a matter of still greater urgency than the integrity of smaller properties. 'The Preserving the little Zemindaries intire would certainly be attended with many Conveniences', he wrote; 'but this is not an Object of near so much Importance as dividing the great Ones.'[78] He shared the view

[75] To C.W.B. Rous, 22 June 1776. *Francis MSS* 53 (49) 26.

[76] *Sir Philip Francis's Minutes*, p. 15.

[77] *Ibid.*, p. 53n.

[78] To C.W.B. Rous, 22 June 1776. *Francis MSS* 77 (49) 26.

of the other party that a new law of inheritance would be required to achieve this, and the rule of primogeniture, customarily held valid for the larger estates and not the smaller ones, must be applied in reverse so that 'the great Zemindaries should be divided equally among all the sons and the small ones descend to the eldest on condition of supporting the younger children'.[79] However, he improved upon the Governor-General's proposal by suggesting that the surest deterrent to the concentration of landed property would be to take away from the big zamindari families the power of adoption in case of a lapse in direct succession.[80] Here again was still another concept relating to the Permanent Settlement which its later protagonists directly inherited from Francis. The idea came up again and again in the writings of its leading advocates during the next decade. Shore spoke about the superiority of the small proprietor to the big landlords in a famous minute.[81] Cornwallis considered the rule of primogeniture a real nuisance.[82] Law, the best theoretician of the three, championed the right of the talukdari estates to secede from zamindaries and justified himself by quoting Blackstone.[83]

Francis stood on this question at a middle point roughly equidistant between the two extremities of the physiocratic doctrine. The elder Mirabeau, who had never quite succeeded in shaking off his aristocratic bias, represented the orthodox view that primogeniture was an important condition of social stability. But it was precisely on this ground that the more advanced opinion within the school, best expressed perhaps in a pamphlet by Ange Goudard, wanted abolition. It could do no harm if, as a result, the aristocrats ruined

[79] *Sir Philip Francis's Minutes*, pp. 14–15, 52–3.

[80] 'Remarks on General Clavering's Observations on the Plan proposed for a new Settlement'. Not dated, but copies sent to Lord North and H. Strachey on 13 May 1776. *Francis MSS* 77 (31) 5. Also letter to C.W.B. Rous quoted above.

[81] Firminger, op. cit., vol. II, p. 530.

[82] G.G.C. to C.O.D., 6 March 1793, para. 8. *General Letters to the Court of Directors: Revenue Department*, vol. 7.

[83] T. Law's Minutes in Proceedings, B.O.R., 7 and 9 June 1790.

themselves by transferring their lands: 'ce désordre particulier serait la cause d'un bien général: vendues par les portions, les terres seraient mieux cultivées.'[84] Francis's position was by no means so radical. As his reaction to the sales following the Permanent Settlement was to indicate many years later,[85] he did not visualize the revolutionary effect that the abolition of primogeniture could have on the land-market. He did not gloat like Barwell and Shore on the degeneration of the native aristocracy,[86] nor was he happy, as Law was, at the prospect of the old class of landlords being swept away in the process of the transfers. He only wanted to reorganize landed property on somewhat more rational lines without shaking its foundations. One way of achieving this, he thought, was a middle-of-the-road policy on primogeniture that could help in removing its abuses without doing away with the system altogether; abolished in the case of the larger zamindaries but allowed for the lesser ones, the custom could assist in a redistribution of property without subverting the basis of property itself.

The assumption underlying this attitude was that the landed aristocracy of Bengal had still great potentialities of social leadership left in them. For Francis, like all physiocrats, was a great believer in inequality. A well-known slogan of the school was – *la Liberté, la Sûreté, l'Inégalité*, the last being as important as the other two. Weulersse mentions how Quesnay himself, preoccupied as he was with the problem of circulation of wealth, bypassed the problem of its distribution with utter indifference. The idea of equality had a place in the doctrine only by being emphatically denied. Inequality was a part of the natural order, and it was not for man to try to correct it. On the contrary, as an important writer of the school,

[84] Weulersse, *La Physiocratie à la fin du règne de Louis XV*, p. 42.

[85] See p. 234 below.

[86] In his minute of December 1776 Francis did, in fact, roundly accuse Barwell of exaggerating the worthlessness of the zamindars. This, he thought, was done to prove that they were 'dangerous members of society' and could therefore be easily excluded from any title to proprietorship – *Sir Philip Francis's Minutes*, pp. 172–3. For a discussion of Shore's views on this subject, see Chapter 6 below.

Morellet, put it, 'la société n'est instituée que pour protéger et defendre ces disproportions élémentaires.' For no society could exist without agriculture and no agriculture prosper without inequality. The resources of the rich and the cheap labour provided by the poor were both essential for the success of enterprise in land. Inequality, therefore, was an economic necessity. The physiocrats in their love of abstraction formulated this in terms of what they called the 'law of property': 'Elle [la loi de propriété] décide tous les cas, borne toutes les jurisdictions, établit et consacre tous les devoirs: ceux du père, ceux du fils, ceux du maître, ceux du salarié . . . surtout ceux de la subordination, attachés a l'obéissance, aux états serviles, aux travaux grossiers et de sujétion. Tout cela est pris dans la nature, tout cela est borné . . . par la constitution de l'ordre social le plus parfait.'[87] The constitution of the 'perfect social order', as Francis defined it, was also based on a very similar principle of inequality. It provided for a general division of society between an enlightened minority in whom all authority was vested and a mass of people labouring for the few who acted as their guardians. 'The scheme of every regular Government', he wrote, 'requires that the mass of the people should labour, and that the few should be supported by the labours of the many, who receive their retribution in the peace, protection and security, which accompanies just authority and regular subordination.'[88] In terms of the actual conditions of Bengal this meant a society of zamindars and ryots, where 'the authority is natural on one side – the obedience voluntary on the other'.[89] He held it in the strongest terms against the government of Warren Hastings that its policies had the effect of levelling down the classes of Indian society to one uniform state of decline: 'by confounding and degrading all Orders of Men, [it] has forced the highest to act upon the Principles of the lowest.'[90]

The dialectic of authority and obedience operating in a good

[87] Weulersse, *Les Physiocrates*, pp. 183–5; *La Physiocratie à la fin du règne de Louis XV*, pp. 83–4.

[88] *Sir Philip Francis's Minutes*, p. 116.

[89] To Lord North, 13 January 1775. *Francis MSS* 47 (36) 47.

[90] To W. Young, 5 July 1778. *Ibid.*, 51 (41) 41.

society gave it a certain regularity of structure like that of a pyramid consisting of various ranks graded in descending order from summit to base and having assigned to them corresponding shares of rights and obligations. It was not merely the physiocrats with their never-ending song about the 'societe reguliere' from whom Francis might have derived the idea, but also from Blackstone. He actually quotes a passage from the *Commentaries* in which the ideas of obedience and regularity are juxtaposed in precisely the same manner as he himself does in his minute (with the difference that Blackstone makes a nice distinction between obedience 'limited only by absolute will and pleasure' as under a despotic government and the other kind of obedience which 'is grounded on the principles of society and is extended no further than reason and necessity will warrant'). Blackstone writes of 'a due subordination of rank and a gradual scale of authority' being 'the most stable foundation of legal and rational Government'.[91] The idea frequently occurs in Francis's minutes. In his plan of 1776 it appears in a reference to 'those intermediate gradations of rank, authority and responsibility, by which all great civil societies are held together'.[92] It is taken up again in his minute of November that year and he speaks of 'those successive ranks of subordination in society, through which the operations of Government descend, by regular and easy gradations, from the summit to the base'.[93] Much of the ambivalence in his attitude to the aristocracy was due to the vital middle position he assigned to them in this social order. 'To stand between the Crown and the people' was a function conforming to 'the true principles of an aristocracy'. In England this was indeed the importance of 'a real nobility in the ancient and rational sense of the English constitution', before they were crowded out by the 'new peerages lavished by the executive power'.[94] In Bengal it was the

[91] Blackstone, *Commentaries*, vol. IV, pp. 104–5. Quoted by Francis in his minute of 5 November 1776. *Sir Philip Francis's Minutes*, p. 112.

[92] *Sir Philip Francis's Minutes*, pp. 54–5.

[93] *Ibid.*

[94] P. & M., II, p. 528. John Shore, who shared many of Francis's views on the nature and importance of landed property in Bengal, also spoke

zamindars who best fitted into this role. They were the transmission belt helping economic power and political authority to circulate in society. It was to them that all 'intermediate profits between the Ryot and the Government' belonged.[95] They also 'are or ought to be the instruments of government in almost every branch of the civil administration'.[96] Unfortunately, however, the official policy based on the 'ill-founded idea' of crown-ownership of lands made it impossible for the zamindars to assume these important functions, and 'converted them into Collectors'.[97] It was by damaging this spinal column, these 'simple and natural channels of authority', that the government of Warren Hastings had threatened the very basis of political power in India. For 'a system which professes at once to destroy that medium, might as well profess at once the dissolution of the state; unless by the word *state* we are only to understand the oeconomical relation of master and slave, not the political union of a Government with its subjects.'[98]

All the criticism Francis had to make of the farming system followed from his conviction that it 'annihilated every idea of private property'. It was based, he thought, on the assumption 'not less false in fact than absurd in theory and dangerous in practice' that all land belonged to the State. The policy 'adopted as the act of a proprietor' by the East India Company had dispossessed the hereditary and lawful owners, and farmed the country to men having no real interest in the land – that is, to Calcutta *banyans* acting either for themselves

---

appreciatively of this pattern as constituting one of the chief virtues of the English social system. England was superior to France, he said in a letter to Charles Grant (7 March 1795), in 'that there is a due gradation in the ranks of society which connects the extremes, without exhibiting them in perpetual contrast, that the middle order of society in England is respectable, and that property is more equally diffused than it was in France.' Teignmouth, vol. I, p. 314.

[95] *Sir Philip Francis's Minutes*, p. 111.

[96] *Ibid.*, p. 54.

[97] *Letter from Mr Francis to Lord North*, p. 45.

[98] *Sir Philip Francis's Minutes*, p. 55.

or for their European masters. These men 'hoped to make money by disposing of their Leases to others; for, if they kept the farms in their own hands, by grinding the Ryot, with as little regard to prudence as to mercy'.[99]

The insecurity of property under such circumstances deterred all incentive to improvement: 'Improvements in such a state of things are not to be expected; for who will employ his money or his labour in the cultivation of a soil that does not belong to him, or when he has no security that the whole produce may not be extorted from him by a new assessment?'[100] The method of sale by auction exposed all the fruit of a proprietor's investment in his estate to the greed of the highest bidder. Besides every increase in output was likely to be followed by a proportionate increase in the revenue demanded by the government.[101] Landed property was thus subjected to a triple strain. It was to provide at the same time for the zamindar, the farmer and the under-farmer.

> In this state of the Leases [he wrote] almost every Farm has now three Persons to support, instead of one, viz. the Zemindar or Talookdar, who must have a Pension in lieu of his manorial Rights – The new Farmer must squeeze the Ryott in order to reimburse himself for the Fine he probably paid at his Admission, and to secure his expected Profit – The Agent at last, or under-farmer, who is an Alien on the Farm and who has only a temporary Interest in the Improvement of it, strains the last drop of Blood from the wretched Peasant, and does it hastily for fear that Time or Accident should produce some change to his disadvantage.[102]

Was it surprising then that the zamindars should in such conditions be interested more in running down the resources of their lands than in adding to them? The farming system had indeed succeeded in turning the old class of native landlords into 'the enemies of government'

[99] To Lord North, 13 January 1775. *Francis MSS* 47 (36) 47. *Letter from Mr Francis to Lord North*, pp. 33–4.

[100] *Letter from Mr Francis to Lord North*, pp. 35–6.

[101] *Sir Philip Francis's Minutes*, p. 44.

[102] To Lord North, 13 January 1775. *Francis MSS* 47 (36) 47.

without reducing their influence over the tenants. 'This influence they employ to embarass Government, by making private collections for themselves; raising complaints against the farmers, and putting their Ryots to flight during the season of the collection.'[103] Depopulation of villages and desertion of the peasantry were not the only evils of this system. It resulted also in an enormous increase in litigation, and the number of undecided suits went on accumulating in the civil courts so fast that they could no longer be tackled by the normal machinery of justice. 'The introduction of a mysterious science under the title of the Farming System', he wrote, 'with its endless train of principal farmers, securities, counter-securities, agents and cutkinadars, has not only perplexed the business of collections, but increased the number of suits in the Dewanny Courts and the difficulty of deciding them. The difficulty is so great . . . that, in reality, it amounts to a denial of justice.'[104]

The worst of all difficulties, however, was that the farming system was unprofitable for the government itself. The policy led inevitably to the lands being overassessed for revenues, and this 'over-ratement' was followed by an accumulation of arrears and their eventual remission – the three component evils feeding on each other in a vicious circle. In a letter to Lord North he quoted from Swift to impress the Irish parallel that it was customary for a farmer to offer more for an estate than he knew he could ever be able to pay and then, in his desperation, end up by paying nothing at all.[105] That was what happened far too often in Bengal also. In the last analysis, therefore, the farming system, by denying the right of private ownership, did no less harm to the government itself than to the zamindars. 'I am most deliberately of opinion', he wrote, 'that if private property be not once for all secured on a permanent footing, the public revenue will sink rapidly with the general produce of the country.'[106]

[103] *Sir Philip Francis's Minutes*, p. 44.
[104] *Letter from Mr Francis to Lord North*, p. 39.
[105] To Lord North, 12 July 1777. *Francis MSS* 49 (38) 93–4.
[106] *Letter from Mr Francis to Lord North*, p. 36.

Philip Francis's own plan of a permanent settlement for Bengal was built up, plank by plank, in total opposition to the farming system which he so thoroughly denounced. No two policies, both put forward to solve the same set of problems, could be more contradictory and mutually exclusive. To the concept of crown-ownership of land was opposed the right of private property; to the view of zamindars as mere officials, their status as hereditary landlords; to short-term leases, permanent and inheritable tenures; to high revenue demands subject to frequent revision, moderate amounts unalterably fixed.

The alternative Francis had to propose related to three principal questions concerning the settlement of land revenues, that is, assessment, lease and lessees. On each of these he set out from an initial position not nearly so decisive as the manner in which it was later to be stated in his plan. He still allowed practical considerations to appear in the company of his vision of the ideal. This gave some of his letters written early in 1775, especially those to Lord North, the appearance of thinking aloud. Doubt would be too strong a word for it, because his mind still continued to be under the pressure of dogma. Nevertheless, it is remarkable how on each of these problems he climbed down from the high pedestal of abstract principles and stooped, however briefly, to consider the earthy side of the matter. This excursion into common sense was not, as we know, to last long. In the plan submitted to the Council in January next year there was nothing that was not mercilessly argued out, nothing that could be suspected of a weakness for the other point of view. Even if the two hostile worlds of opinion sometimes met at a tangent and appeared to suggest an incidental point of agreement, Francis at least on his part would rush to point out the very different premise from which he had proceeded. What was it that happened during these nine or ten months to bring about the change, harden his attitude and induce intransigence? The war in the Council had already been going on for quite a few months, the Majority had been formed and clashed on many issues, while Francis was still posing and debating the alternatives in his letters to Lord North. It was, therefore, not a question of any truce being over that started him off again on his uncompromising course. Was it then the assurance of victory, the hope of being able to carry through his plan, lock, stock and barrel, that stiffened his back and made him withdraw all previous concession to expediency?

Francis seems to have been always convinced that the best revenue system was one which was subject to no revision of assessment. In one of his earliest references to the problem in a letter to Lord North he spoke of the excellence of the system by which all conquering powers 'except the last' had limited their demands on the natives to 'a fixed Tribute'. The 'Mahommedans, Tartars and Marathas who pretend to none of our political Refinements', had all adopted such a policy, which was both simple and effective. 'A simple Tribute, easily paid and easily collected', he said, quoting Montesquieu, was superior in every sense to 'that continued Series of Vexations which the subtle avarice of their present Masters has invented'. The ideal was thus already defined in these words in 1775. Only he was not yet quite sure whether this could be applied to Bengal as it was at the time. 'The only difficulty that occurs to me', he wrote as if arguing it out with himself, 'will be to fix the quantum of the Tribute.' The country was too poor at the moment to be able to stand up to any great demand on its resources, but 'in a few Years it would unquestionably recover and of course admit of a higher Assessment'. This was a dilemma that arose from a discrepancy between the actual and the potential, and for once, as a rare concession to common sense, he suggested a solution in terms of expediency: 'In these Circumstances, some Expedient must be adopted that will for the present satisfy the Landholders that they are not exposed to an arbitrary Increase of the Assessment, yet not entirely preclude the Governing Power from advancing, *in one single Instance more*, the present Tribute to a reasonable proportion with the future Improvement of the Country.'[107]

Not a trace of this careful weighing of alternatives remained in the plan when fully worked out. A week before it was submitted to the Council, he wrote to Clavering 'that the Assessment, once settled

[107] To Lord North, 23 March 1775. *Francis MSS* 49 (38) 17.

should be fixed *in ceterum*, and as immovable as the Land, from which it was raised'.[108] The idea of permanence had decisively won. It is emphasized in the plan itself that the jumma once decided upon 'must be permanent and unalterable'.[109] The great point about his policy, he was to claim later, was 'to fix the Demand upon the Country'.[110] This was 'the Foundation of my Plan, *sine qua non*'.[111]

Both the proprietors and the government were to benefit from such a measure. For, in the first place, the assessment 'once fixed, must be a matter of public record', and if possible, put beyond revision by an Act of Parliament. As a result, everyone would know what he had to pay and regard the surplus as his own. 'And, if he grows rich, the better for the State. He will then have a natural Encouragement to excite his Industry without any Motive to conceal the Produce of it.' Thus in direct contrast to the farming system which killed all incentive, the plan would have the effect of encouraging investment in land and improving agriculture, 'because the proprietor will be satisfied he is labouring for himself'.[112] Secondly, this would also help in stabilizing the administration of revenues. The demand being subject to no change would ensure a regularity of fiscal receipts, and thus break that vicious circle – 'I mean, that of making annual Settlements to the amount of two millions and a half – of granting remissions and relinquishing Ballances.'[113]

But it was not enough to make the jumma permanent; it had to be moderate too. The idea was not new. 'I think we ought not to exact one farthing more from this Province', wrote Clive to Verelst as early as 19 April 1766.[114] The Resident at Durbar and the Controlling

[108] To Clavering, 14 January 1776. *Ibid.*, 53 (49) 16.

[109] *Sir Philip Francis' Minutes*, p. 47.

[110] To H. Strachey, 20 March 1776. *Francis MSS* 47 (36) 86.

[111] To C.W.B. Rous, 22 June 1776. *Ibid.*, 53 (49) 26.

[112] *Ibid.* To Clavering, 14 January 1776. *Ibid.*, 53 (49) 16; *Sir Philip Francis' Minutes*, p. 47.

[113] To W. Ellis, 13 September 1776. *Francis MSS* 47 (36) 114.

[114] *Clive–Verelst Correspondence*, no. 19.

Council of Revenue at Murshidabad received from the Supervisors numerous reports about overassessment in the various districts of Bengal. The very heavy demands on the country in 1770, the severity with which collections were made during the famine, and the consequent loss of both resources and revenues, had all added up to make the volume of assessment a matter of great concern when Warren Hastings took over. But the principle of his Quinquennial Settlement tended, inevitably, to increase the amount of the jumma rather than reduce it, for lands were auctioned and only the highest bidders allowed to farm. 'The last settlement, made by the Committee of Circuit', Francis wrote, 'promised an immoderate increase of revenue at a time, when the famine had swept away one third of the inhabitants, and when the country was represented to be in a general state of decay.' The result was that a large part of the revenue remained uncollected. For 'the plain truth is that overratement and remission play into each other's hands'.[115]

Francis was convinced that 'the desire of increase invariably and inflexibly pursued'[116] was an essential feature of the revenue policy of Warren Hastings's government. This applied not merely to the first Five-Year Settlement made in 1772. When towards the end of that period it became known that the Governor-General was preparing a plan for another term, Francis rushed to condemn it in anticipation, alleging that its purpose was 'to appropriate . . . out of the Revenues, the enormous Sum of one hundred and sixteen Lacks to the Investment and Commercial charges, exclusive of Salt and Opium'. This, he darkly predicted, would be 'the finishing Stroke to the Country'.[117]

Apart from other considerations, he was opposed to maximization of the revenue demand as a matter of principle. For this, he believed, constituted a threat to all private property: 'A system of taxation, which avowedly aims, or is supposed to aim at raising the

[115] *Letter from Mr Francis to Lord North*, pp. 34–5.

[116] *Sir Philip Francis's Minutes*, p. 43.

[117] To W. Ellis, 20 November 1776. *Francis MSS* 47 (36) 140, 141.

greatest possible revenue, is in its nature hostile to every species of private property'.[118] He quoted Montesquieu to the effect that the moderation of the tribute had made conquest by the Mahommedans popular with their subject peoples and accounted for the stability of their empires everywhere. In India, too, 'the assessment fixed by the Mogul Government on these provinces, was light and moderate in comparison with ours'.[119]

He was therefore against every measure which, he thought, might add further to the fiscal demand. This brought him directly in conflict with the operative rule of the farming system, which was to equalize the amount of revenue and the actual value of the land. To the extent that the government sought to achieve this by economic methods – by auctioning the farms and settling the lease with the highest bidder in each case – Francis opposed them by his proposal for a permanent jumma. To the extent that purely administrative measures were employed for this end, he fought over every inch of the ground to defeat them. He abhorred the very idea of a cadastral survey and scrutiny of titles. One of his first successful assaults on the official policy had been to prevent an enquiry into the charity lands of Dacca. 'We have put a Stop', he wrote reporting the victory, 'to a Measurement of Lands at Dacca and to an Inquisition into Titles, which, in the particular Instance would have depopulated Dacca, and have spread a general Alarm productive of the same Effect thro' all the Provinces.'[120] On a later occasion he protested against the appointment of an Amini Commission on similar grounds. 'Whatever Colours may be given to the Measure', he wrote then, 'the true Object of it is, and can only be, to grasp the intire Rents of the Country, and annihilate every Right, Interest and Property between the Ryot and Government.'[121]

[118] *Sir Philip Francis's Minutes*, p. 109.

[119] *Ibid.*, pp. 25–6, 141.

[120] To Lord North, 24 February 1775. *Francis MSS* 47 (36) 48. To W. Ellis, 22 February 1775. *Ibid.*, 47 (36) 51. Minute, 7 February 1775. *Ibid.*, 72 (1) 20.

[121] To Lord North, 20 November 1776. *Ibid.*, 47 (36) 137.

He was opposed to such investigation into the value of lands both on practical and theoretical grounds. Administrative measures could hardly succeed where economic methods failed. What possibly could the Amini Commission hope to achieve when the experiment of auctioneering leases had made such a mess of the Quinquennial Settlement? Was it not also somewhat too optimistic to expect that the natives, who had learnt to distrust the government so much, would willingly hand over the information desired? The farmers, most of whom had been applying for remission all the time, would not. Nor would the zamindars whom the government had dispossessed of their lands. The ryots, who had their own grievances against the regime, were far too numerous to be individually consulted for such an enquiry.[122] When it was pointed out that the idea was by no means an invention of the Company's government in Bengal, but as old as the Mughal administration, he was quick to deny it 'as a matter of fact'. It was his understanding of Indian history that 'such a measure never was practised . . . under the original Mogul government', except in one case – 'the single case of Cossim Ally' who, he said (with the faintest suggestion of a parallel with Hastings's regime), 'knew that his tenure of the government was precarious and . . . was determined to make the most of an uncertain, temporary possession'.[123] Such an interpretation was of course perfectly consistent with his doctrine. For having credited the Mughals with the defence of private property he could not admit, on logical grounds, that they had ever undertaken a measure so alien to the spirit of private property as an 'inquisition' into the value of lands. The objection was thus related to his fundamental premise from which all arguments followed. 'An accurate valuation of private property is the act of a proprietor, not of a Government', he observed. 'As Government, we have no right to inquire into the value of any man's estate, or to oblige him to tell us what profits he draws from it. The information cannot be obtained without a vexatious inquisition; nor is it necessary, unless we mean to

[122] *Sir Philip Francis's Minutes*, pp. 108–10.
[123] *Ibid.*, pp. 149–50.

rack the country.'[124] These views were, of course, duly buttressed 'by those of men already in possession of the public respect and esteem', namely, Montesquieu, Mirabeau, Steuart and Smith.[125]

How then, if not by an actual valuation of resources, should a government formulate its fiscal demand? Francis's own answer was derived from his favourite author. A week before the plan was submitted to the Council, he wrote:

> My first and simple Principle of Taxation is that laid down by Montesquieu, 'qu'il ne faut pas mesurer le Tribut par ce que le Peuple peut donner, mais par ce qu'il doit donner – ou en le mesurant par ce qu'il peut donner, que ce soit au moins par ce qu'il peut toujours donner'. I quote the Words from Memory, but this is the Sense of them.[126]

The idea was repeated on numerous occasions in his plan, in all his subsequent statements of policy and much of his correspondence, often as almost a literal translation from Montesquieu's French as, for instance, in his minute of 5 November 1776 when he said, 'Let us proportion our demand to *our* necessities, not to *their* utmost abilities.'[127]

He knew that an assessment based on such a rule would be open to two objections; first, that it would be unequal; and secondly, that it would be unrealistic. He quickly dealt with the first by denying its validity. He did not doubt 'that there will be considerable inequalities in an assessment formed on this principle', but was not prepared to accept this as 'an inconvenience to be regarded'. It was neither necessary nor possible to remove such inequalities, and he had a vague

[124] *Ibid.*, p. 170.

[125] *Ibid.*, pp. 113–15.

[126] To Clavering, 14 January 1776. *Francis MSS* 53 (49) 16.

[127] *Sir Philip Francis's Minutes*, p. 117. See also *ibid.*, p. 170. The formula occurs fairly early in his correspondence, even at a time when he was still groping for an alternative line, but had not come to define it yet. Thus he wrote to Lord North on 23 March 1775: 'In fixing the whole amount of Tribute I would consider nothing but the Necessities of this State within itself, and the Necessities of its Subjects.' *Francis MSS* 49 (38) 17.

feeling that these would eventually level out 'provided all parties know with certainty the utmost they are to pay, and are assured that they shall not be exposed to an arbitrary increase of demands on future improvements'. Again he quoted Montesquieu and Steuart in self-justification, and as a last word in the argument mentioned that 'the assessment of the land tax was grossly unequal' in England though nobody objected to it.[128]

The answer to the other line of attack on his method required an actual estimate of 'our necessities'. He started with the assumption that 'we know the amount of our expences'[129] which, taken together with a fund to cover all future contingencies, was to represent the total amount of assessment. As it was stated in the plan: 'The whole demand upon the country, to commence from April 1777, should be founded on an estimate of the permanent services, which Government must indispensably provide for, under the great heads of civil and military establishment, and investment; with an allowance of a reasonable reserve for contingencies, I know not for what just or useful purpose any government can demand more from its subjects.' The estimate he made on this basis amounted to Rs 31,064,232 including Rs 3,711,547 as an 'unappropriated surplus' to pay for any further expansion of the services if required.[130] It is not quite fair to criticize him, as Firminger does, on the ground that 'until the new system [of administration recommended by Francis] had been some time in working order, it was impossible to ascertain whether or no the unappropriated surplus of Rupees 37,11,547 allowed for by his plan would be realised'.[131] No economic planning would be possible if such doubts were allowed to stand in its way. Francis had at least as good a reason to name a moderate fiscal target and hope to realize it as Hastings or any of his predecessors who, in most cases, had never succeeded in bringing the collection up to the amount of the jumma.

[128] *Sir Philip Francis's Minutes*, pp. 49, 112–15, 152–3, 158.
[129] *Ibid.*, p. 112.
[130] *Ibid.*, pp. 47–8, 98–9.
[131] Firminger, vol. I, p. ccc.

Considering the state of the accounts at the time it is quite remarkable that with all his very inadequate knowledge of the resources of the country he had succeeded in working out a figure within ten million rupees of Shore's more informed calculation thirteen years later. Again, compared with the amount of land revenue actually collected from Bengal, Bihar and Orissa in 1790-1, the year when his plan had already been substantially adopted in practice, his estimate was a masterpiece of prescience. The total amount received from these provinces for that year was, according to the *Fifth Report*, Rs 26,800,989. The 'Ways and Means' mentioned by Francis in his plan (Appendix IX) included income from Benares as well as from sources other than land, that is, from duties on opium, Calcutta customs, etc. (item nos. 3–8). Leaving out the latter, the total amount of his estimate arising from land revenue alone would be Rs 27,645,732. The difference between this and the collections for 1790–1 is less than eight hundred and fifty thousand rupees.

All this, however, does not take away from Firminger's more valid criticism that to have been guided by Francis's estimate would have been for the government 'a disastrous miscalculation'. For within a few years the cost of administration was to exceed by far the paltry reserve allocated in the plan and described by its author as 'liberal'. When this occurred Francis himself was quick to acknowledge the fact without, of course, drawing the obvious conclusion. In a speech at the House of Commons on 16 June 1784 he observed 'that either the Ways and Means of 1784 had fallen short, or the services had exceeded those of 1776, to nearly the amount of £2,200,000'.[132] He did not perhaps realize that this amounted to an unwitting censure of his own estimate. Whatever might be said of the 'Ways and Means' of 1784, there could be no doubt that those of 1776, calculated by himself, had blundered by a large margin.

The problem of assessment was closely related to the problem of lease. How long should a lease be? The physiocratic answer was based

[132] *Ibid.*

on one of the essential tenets of their doctrine – security of property.[133] Under the *ancien régime* leases were usually limited to short periods of three to nine years. This, as the physiocrats pointed out in language reminiscent of the critics of the farming system in Bengal, discouraged improvements and, still worse, led the farmers to rack-rent the peasants and plunder the resources of the land in their drive for the greatest possible profit in the quickest way. The longer the lease and the more secure a farmer felt in his ownership of the land, the better it was for agriculture, and in this, as on many other points of their programme, they wanted France to emulate the English example. In one respect, however, they were particularly cautious. Under the existing conditions, when the revenues had reached rock bottom, they were not in favour of protracting the leases so far as to make it impossible for the government to help in the progress of agriculture. To advocate permanent leases was, they felt, going a bit too far.[134] It is a curious though little-known fact on this question Francis, on his part, had not quite made up his mind even as late as less than a year before completing his plan for Bengal. Writing on 24 February 1775 to Lord North, he still spoke of granting leases 'either in perpetuity or for Life'.[135] It would be futile to speculate what made him ponder over these alternatives at the time. It might have been the influence of the doctrine; it might have been just common sense. Whatever it was, there was no trace of indecision in his policy as it was finally set out in the plan. The idea of permanence had won. To some extent, no doubt, this was the result of his driving logic, the insistence on reducing everything to a 'simple' scheme of things – and the notion of permanence has, indeed, such a false appearance of simplicity about

[133] Quesnay's dictum on this point was: 'La sûreté de la propriété est le fondement essentiel de l'ordre économique de la société.' *François Quesnay et la Physiocratie*, t. II, p. 950.

[134] Weulersse, *Les Physiocrates*, pp. 103–4, 183; *La Physiocratie à la fin du règne de Louis XV*, pp. 33–4, 83; *La Physiocratie sous les ministères de Turgot et de Necker*, p. 56.

[135] *Francis MSS* 47 (36) 48.

it. But the factor that must have turned the scales eventually in favour of emphytheotic leases was the assurance of support from a large body of expert opinion within the administration. The question about the term of lease to which Francis was venturing an answer had been posed in Bengal long before him. Already in 1765 Verelst had indicated an alternative when he assured the farmers of Burdwan 'that if they exerted themselves in the improvement [of their lands], they should never be dispossessed'.[136] Clive himself had vaguely sensed that the stability of the Company's power was to some extent conditioned by the stability of landed interests in the conquered provinces. 'For my own part I think', he wrote to Verelst in 1766, 'that if Bengal was let out for 3, 5 or 7 years it would be for the Advantage of the Company, of Individuals and add Stability to our Possession by inspiring the Inhabitants with just Ideas of our Justice and Moderation.'[137] At a lower level of the administration the Supervisors, too, had from time to time begged for power to offer farms within their districts for longer terms. In a way Warren Hastings's idea of introducing a five-year settlement was itself a recognition of this need. Francis knew which way the wind was blowing when in 1775 he noted that three of the most experienced officers, Middleton, Dacres and Vansittart, had advised the government to 'grant Leases for Life'.[138] The fact that in the summer of 1776 four members of the Patna Council jointly signed a letter saying that they would be only too happy to be allowed to try out a mukarari settlement in Bihar,[139] and that his plan received support from officers like Becher and Goodlad who were by no means allied to his faction,[140] must surely indicate that in

[136] Firminger, vol. I, p. cxlv.

[137] *Clive-Verelst Correspondence*, no. 19.

[138] 'Account given by Messrs. Middleton, Dacres and Vansittart of the State of the Country etc. in reply to the Queries of the Council. 1775.' *Francis MSS* 74 (3) 5.

[139] Letter from I. Sage, E. Law, E. Golding and W. Young, 21 May 1776. *Ibid.*, 77 (31) 3.

[140] Letters from R. Goodlad (10 February 1776), and to R. Becher (19 July 1777) and W. Young (5 July 1778). *Ibid.*, 77 (31) 7, 51 (41) 41 and 49 (38) 58 respectively.

recommending permanent leases Francis sought to formulate in terms of policy something that was not for once unrelated to experience. Ironically, too, in this one instance experience drove him beyond the limits of moderation approved by the physiocratic doctrine.

Francis had preconceived notions about zamindar-ownership. This has led all writers on the subject to assume that he had always been exclusively in favour of a zamindari settlement. A close look at his correspondence during the germinal year 1775 gives quite a different impression. 'The Land should be granted to the Zemindars, Talookdars, or even to the Ryotts', he wrote to Lord North in February.[141] He had then already started working on his plan, and at rare moments of perception come to recognize how facts, stubborn things that they were, refused to fit into his model. The disparity between the ideal and the actual was nowhere more pronounced than in the condition of the Bengal zamindars. By the 1770s this ancient class had already lost its wealth, power and competence. He had recorded in his journal how during a visit to Krishnanagar he had been to see the Raja of Nadia, a broken destitute figure huddled in a corner of the palace.[142] That was the image of a common degradation, and even as late as November 1775, that is about two months before the Council was to receive his statement in its final form, he was still not sure whether these miserable remnants of the native aristocracy could really be chosen to lead the coming agrarian resurgence in the country. To his confidants he thus expressed his doubts:

> The Zemindars, from the Moment they were converted into Pensioners, have gradually sunk into a state of Sloth, Stupidity, Beggary and Contempt. Being almost universally overwhelmed with Debts, and few of them having any Knowledge of their Affairs, they of course have lost all Dignity and Consequence in the Eyes of the People. I am assured, and inclined to believe that the greatest Part of the younger Generation

[141] 24 February 1775. *Ibid.*, 47 (36) 48.

[142] Journal, 15 May 1777: 'Visit from the Old Raja, which I returned, and saw an immense Palace in ruins, and the Prince of the Country, a venerable old Man, lodged in one Corner of it, in a State of Beggary and Misery, not to be believed.' *Francis MSS* 66 (64) pp. 1–2.

> are likely to be Idiots . . . Here lies the great Objection to trusting the Zemindars with the Management of their Lands. Yet the Choice lies only between this and the farming System.[143]
>
> . . . I know not in whose Hands the Lands can be safely trusted. My Principles and inclinations lead me to revert to the Zemindars; but by this Time the greatest Part of them are Beggars and in Debt . . . We come the Day after the Feast, and must cook a Dinner out of the Scraps.[144]

John Shore was faced with exactly the same dilemma years later, and having more regard for facts than for theories, proposed a solution that would make it possible for the government to revise the settlement if, after a term of years, the zamindars proved really incapable. In the case of Francis, however, 'Principles and Inclinations' eventually decided the issue in favour of an unconditional settlement with the zamindars. Once this position was reached, there could be no question of considering any other claims. So far as Francis was concerned, the recognition of the zamindars as the party most eligible for a permanent lease excluded necessarily all other alternatives whether advanced in favour of the inferior landlords or of the direct producers. He knew that his opponents had set out to make a very strong case for the latter. He therefore went out of his way to argue at great length against a settlement with the ryots.

It is not that he ignored the importance of the ryot. As a physiocrat he could not have professed indifference towards the man behind the plough. 'Without his assistance', he admitted, 'the land is useless to the Zemindar.'[145] The physiocrats never imitated those of their contemporaries who were fond of explaining all agricultural backwardness in terms of the weaknesses of the peasant character – indolence, extravagance, parasitism and want of the right sort of moral values. The decline of agriculture and degeneration of the peasant were, according to them, equally the result of poverty.[146]

[143] To Lord North, 21 November 1775. *Ibid.*, 47 (36) 82.

[144] To H. Strachey, 23 November 1775. *Ibid.*, 53 (49) 15.

[145] *Sir Philip Francis's Minutes*, p. 117.

[146] Weulersse, *Les Physiocrates*, p. 75.

Something of the same attitude is there in all those numerous passages where Francis deplores the misery and impoverishment of the ryot, the ruin and depopulation of villages, and desertion under the pressure of rack-renting and brutality of the farmers – all due to the short-sighted policies of the Company's government. The agrarian decline was, in his opinion, caused by the fact that the peasant was forced to work on the land without hope, without incentive: 'The Ryot having nothing and never expecting to gain anything cultivates the soil from mere necessity, and no more of it than will supply a bare subsistence for himself and his family.'[147]

But the solution was not, as Hastings and Barwell had proposed, 'to secure the Ryots the perpetual and undisturbed possession of their lands' and on that basis, conclude a settlement directly with them. This, he suspected, was merely a tendentious argument introduced 'to countenance and give a colour to acts of violence and injustice against the Zemindars and other superior ranks of the natives'.[148] He did not believe that Hastings was at all serious about those 'many fine Things . . . said of his care of the Ryots'; but if he was, this would mean making a gift of 'the Property of other People' to those who had no claim to it.[149] For, the problem of lease, like all other problems, could be settled only in terms of ownership: 'Before we give *perpetual possession*, we ought to determine the *property*.' Once this was done, there could be no room for ambiguity. The ryot was not the proprietor; 'it is not even necessary that he should be so, either for his own benefit or that of Government'.[150] It was, therefore, not necessary for the government to conclude the Permanent Settlement with him. Francis's view on this point was fully in accord with that of the physiocrats except that the latter were against a direct deal with the cultivator on economic rather than legalistic grounds. They thought that there could never be a sufficiently large number of

[147] *Sir Philip Francis's Minutes*, p. 45.
[148] *Ibid.*, p. 116.
[149] To W. Ellis, 20 November 1776. *Francis MSS* 47 (36) 141.
[150] *Sir Philip Francis's Minutes*, p. 116.

peasant-proprietors rich enough to make such an arrangement practicable; a settlement with them would be useless if they did not have capital enough to employ in agriculture.[151] Another way of saying the same thing was that the ryot was not entitled to a permanent lease because he had no property.

Settlement with the ryot was, therefore, strictly the business of the zamindar and not of the government. The government must 'not limit the Zemindar in his Agreement with his Tenants'.[152] For that would amount to 'an invasion of the rights of property in the first instance'.[153] Secondly, to 'descend to the Ryots' was 'a business of detail which no way belongs to Government, which we are in no sense equal to, and which carries a vexatious scrutiny, and an arbitrary exertion of power upon the face of it'.[154] Thus on grounds of principle as well as of administrative convenience Francis recommended the adoption of what Firminger calls a *laissez-faire laissez-aller* attitude towards the zamindar's relation with his ryot.[155] The policy was thus defined in his plan:

> The land is the hereditary property of the Zemindar. He holds it by the law of the country, on the tenure of paying a certain contribution to Government. When this condition is complied with, he is master of the land to re-let it to whom he thinks proper.[156]

Cleared thus of official interference the relation between landlord and peasant would assume the form of a voluntary agreement. 'If they are left to themselves', he wrote, 'they will soon come to an agreement, in which every party will find his advantage.'[157] The land-to-manpower ratio at this time was still considerably in favour of the cultivator, and

[151] Weulersse, op. cit., p. 104.
[152] To C.W.B. Rous, 22 June 1776. *Francis MSS* 53 (49) 26.
[153] *Sir Philip Francis's Minutes*, p. 117.
[154] *Ibid.*
[155] Firminger, vol. I, p. ccciv.
[156] *Sir Philip Francis's Minutes*, p. 55.
[157] *Ibid.*, p. 117.

the ryots were in excellent position to bargain for terms. The great decline in population as a result of the famine of 1770[158] as well as of 'the Measures since taken by Government'[159] was a weighty argument in favour of his thesis: 'In the present state of the country the Ryot has in fact the advantage over the Zemindar. Where so much land lies waste, and so few hands are left for cultivation, the peasant must be courted to undertake it.'[160] So the peasant was – for the time being. Francis did not realize how short-sighted he was in his perspective; how all the improvements he expected to follow from his plan, if they really did take place, must in course of a few decades set the demographic curves shooting upwards until the growing pressure on land would inevitably reverse the balance in favour of the zamindars. In this one instance he did not extend the logic of his argument far enough, and as we know, within fifty years of the enactment of Permanent Settlement the inevitable happened.

Underlying the concept of a 'voluntary agreement' there was the idea of a labour market operating on the basis of demand and supply. The zamindar and the ryot were the two free contracting parties, the one coming forward with his capital to buy the labour-power required for his estate and the other bargaining for wages that he thought would be remunerative enough if he were to accept a job on the farm. In other words, here was the capitalist farmer confronting the rural proletariat, and there is no trace of feudalism in it so far as it goes. The *laissez-faire* attitude was admirably suited to this concept. For such contracts were best worked out when the parties concerned were left to

[158] In his 'Minute on Farming of Lands by British Subjects' (12 May 1775) Francis wrote: 'I understand it to be the general Opinion that at least two thirds of the whole Surface of Bengal and Bahar are in a State of total Depopulation.' This is exactly twice the area mentioned by Cornwallis in 1789 as being still in a state of wilderness (Firminger, vol. II, p. 512). Shore was apparently not wrong in claiming, against Cornwallis, 'that since the year 1770 cultivation is progressively increased' (*ibid.*, p. 516).

[159] 'Draft of a Minute on the State of Decay in the Country'. Incomplete and not dated. *Francis MSS* 78 (6) 5.

[160] *Sir Philip Francis's Minutes*, p. 117.

themselves to thrash out the terms of agreement without any external interference. Regarded thus, rent would appear as a firm's profit. It was not for the government to restrain a businessman from making as much as he could on a particular deal. Similarly, it was not for the Company's administration to try and put a ceiling on the amount of rent a zamindar was to receive from his ryots. 'It is not meant', said Francis, 'to prevent the Zemindar from drawing a larger rent from the constituent parts of the Zemindary than its proportion of the assessment, and rendering it of more value to himself, if he improves the land it contains. This would be absurd and defeat the intention of the present plan.'[161] And just as many of the earlier advocates of capitalism believed that the wise employer must out of self-interest treat his workers well, Francis too counted on the zamindar being kind and fair to the ryot. 'In general I judge that, if the Zemindar be not rigorously treated by government, he will for his own sake be just, if not indulgent, to his Ryots; because, his estate being then of value to him, it is essentially his interest to prevent complaints.'[162] It is well known how during the next century Francis's analysis was disproved on every point by the facts of economic development under the Permanent Settlement. The zamindars' income from land increased beyond all proportion to what the government earned from the same source, and consequently the problem of assessment had to be reconsidered in order to correct the enormous disparity between revenue and rental. On the other hand, population increased at a rate much faster than that of agricultural expansion; the zamindar could freely and on his own terms draw upon a large army of agricultural workers standing by; therefore, he did not have to be just to the ryots 'for his own sake', as Francis had complacently predicted.

However, the plan of 1776 did not rule out official intervention altogether. It was not for the administration to come between zamindar and ryot in such a manner as to influence the terms of their

[161] *Ibid.*, p. 51.
[162] *Ibid.*, p. 175.

contract, but once this was decided to their mutual satisfaction, the government had to undertake to enforce it. This was to be done by the issue of a uniform *patta* containing the terms of the agreement which must be respected by both the parties. It is not clear how serious Francis was about this, for he took away much of the force of this recommendation in his plan by suggesting at the same time that in the good old days before the British conquest the security of the ryots was derived not so much from the *pattas* as from 'the natural interest and relation by which they and the Zemindars were mutually bound to each other'.[163] The assumption about the existence of a 'natural Relation between the Proprietor and the Ryot' occurs throughout his writings. This was 'dissolved' under the farming system.[164] To restore it, as his plan proposed to do, would be for the ryot the best guarantee of security – 'this security, so much superior to any formal engagements, the present system promises to restore'.[165] Some even among his close adherents felt unhappy about this indifference to 'formal engagements' and the want of adequate safeguards for lesser landlords and ryots in his plan. Anderson, one of the most knowledgeable revenue officers, expressed this common misgiving in an otherwise appreciative and friendly letter about Francis' proposals:

> Great Care has been taken to satisfy the Zemindars and Talookdars with respect to the future Security of their Tenures. But the Desires of Government will be but in an imperfect Degree accomplished unless equal Security can be given to their inferior Landholders . . . And in this I think consists one of the greatest Difficulties which remains to be surmounted. The Zemindar's own Quit Rent is by the present plan fixed in perpetuity: but his Demands on his inferior Landholders and Renters must in many Cases annually fluctuate and consequently must often produce Disputes that will require the Interposition of Government.

[163] *Ibid.*, p. 55.

[164] 'Draft of a Minute on the State of Decay in the Country'. Incomplete and not dated. *Francis MSS* 78 (6) 5.

[165] *Sir Philip Francis's Minutes*, p. 55.

> . . . Whilst the Ryott possesses his land on a precarious Tenure or whilst he is Continually subject to new and arbitrary Demands, Industry must languish and Emulation cannot exist . . . these Evils must in some Measure be obviated before the Country can regain its former affluence and prosperity.[166]

If such was the feeling of his friends, his enemies naturally were quick to concentrate their attack on what was really the weakest spot of his plan. Hastings and Barwell both picked it out as their most obvious target in their minutes of November 1776. It was only at this later stage of the debate that Francis came out with a somewhat clearer statement about the whole question. 'It does not follow', he said, 'that because the Ryot has no direct permanent property in the lands, he should therefore have no rights, or that no care should be taken to protect him.'[167] However, except for a shade of added emphasis, this reiteration contributed very little to his former stand. He remained firm as ever in his opinion that official intervention must go no further than 'to inforce the execution of their respective engagements'. Even after all that great debate he was left unconvinced that the ryots could not really do without *pattas.* 'I do not find that, in general, Pottahs have been applied for by the Ryots, or that a refusal to grant them has been the subject of any general complaints,' he defiantly observed.[168] On the whole, Francis appears never to have fully grasped the relevance of this entire problem. It was for him a matter of detail which must spontaneously fall into its place once the 'system' had been put into operation. 'A great part of this business, which seems difficult and perplexed in detail', he wrote with exquisite naivéte, 'will gradually execute itself, when once it is perceived, that a wise and solid system is adopted at the Fountain-Head and steadily adhered to.'[169]

166 'Extract of letter from Mr Anderson', October 1776. *Francis MSS* 77 (31) 9.

167 *Sir Philip Francis's Minutes*, p. 117.

168 *Ibid.*, pp. 175–6.

169 *Letter from Mr Francis to Lord North*, p. 40.

The Permanent Settlement of Bengal has often been criticized for its failure to safeguard the interests of ryots; this was, in fact, the aspect on which the revisionist attack in the nineteenth century and later was largely concentrated. But the failure is easily explained if one remembers how Francis's ideas on the subject were faithfully, if without acknowledgment, echoed by Lord Cornwallis. He too had understood 'the word permanency to extend to the jumma only and not to the details of the settlement'.[170] The security of the ryot, he thought, was a problem requiring no immediate solution, and any measures that might be necessary could ge introduced 'occasionally, as abuses occur'. In his opinion too the government had no business to insist that the zamindar 'shall not raise the rents of his estates'.[171] No wonder that his Regulations of 1793 inherited so many of the weaknesses of the parent plan of 1776.

3. The Political Economy of Permanent Settlement

(B) The Commercial Programme

The scope of Francis's policy for Permanent Settlement was much wider than the title of his plan suggests. Its central theme was naturally the agrarian question, because land, according to him, was the source of all wealth and the Company's administration in Bengal was itself based on the mangement of revenues. But an answer to this fundamental problem had implications for what was the most important auxiliary sector of the economy, that is, trade. These were briefly dealt with in the plan itself, and then worked out in great detail in his other minutes and correspondence. However, his ideas on this subject are by no means as clearly physiocratic as those on property and land revenue. Remnants of mercantilism are here intermingled with more advanced concepts and the result is a lack of consistency characteristic of much of English economic thought in the period

[170] Minute, 18 September 1789. Firminger, vol. II, p. 513.
[171] Minute, 3 February 1790. *Ibid.*, p. 533.

which separates Thomas Mun from Adam Smith. Towards the end of this period, when a good deal of solid argument against mercantilism had already been formulated but the material conditions were still not mature for its final overthrow, Francis was not alone in professing a political economy alloyed by diverse and even contradictory elements. He was after all a lesser mind than Sir James Steuart, from whom he had borrowed so much, including his eclecticism.

Commerce, according to the physiocrats, is sterile; it merely involves an exchange of equal values and therefore produces nothing. The concept of utility was entirely foreign to them. Quesnay in developing this thesis with great power and wit in his famous dialogue 'Du Commerce' – described by his most recent editor as 'the last blow dealt to mercantilism'[172] – went even further. Commercial transaction, he pointed out, could be 'non seulement *stérile*, mais *nuisible*'[173] because it tended to inhibit competition. He had no sympathy for merchants and traffickers: 'On doit même observer que plus ses gains sont grands et que plus les fortunes se multiplient dans le commerce, plus il soustrait de richesses de la masse des richesses productives.'[174] It was his opinion, however, that these men, the *marchand* and the *trafiquant* who were engaged in the pursuit of useless exchange, must not be confused with the honest *négociant*.[175] The latter had it as his function to help in the direct transport of agricultural goods to foreign markets and sell them at a 'good price'. This was a process which really contributed to increase of production and added to the 'richesses productives' of the exporting nation.

[172] *Francois Quesnay et la Physiocratie*, t. II, p. 815.

[173] *Ibid.*, p. 858.

[174] *Ibid.*, p. 586.

[175] Quesnay was very fond of word-play. In the dialogue mentioned above he makes his interrogator naively ask 'N'est-ce pas gagnerque de ne pas perdre? N'est-ce pas perdre que de ne pas gagner?' Then with evident relish he proceeds to explain how, according to grammarians, 'l'énonciation exacte des idées n'admet presque point de synonymes' (*ibid.*, pp. 817–18). There are other examples of this sort throughout his writings.

There are passages in Francis's writings which might give the impression that he, too, understood the importance of Bengal's export trade as consisting only in the transfer of agricultural commodities. 'It will not be denied in the abstract', he said, 'that Consumption creates Produce; – that, without a Market, there will be no Supply; – that the Wealth of a State depends on the Industry of its Subjects, and that a free unlimited Export Trade is the surest Way to improve and give Value to the Soil.' It was on this basis, he thought, that the foreign trade of the country had developed before the British conquest and made it 'a Commercial Nation of the first Order'. Other countries which traded with her were, in this sense, only 'the Agents of her fundamental Industry and the Retailers of her Original Produce'.[176]

Any interpretation of Francis's ideas built entirely on such statements would, however, be misleading. For the physiocratic notion they represented was outweighed by numerous pronouncements in an opposite direction. The decline of Bengal's foreign trade figured as a most prominent article on his charge-sheet against the regime.[177] What he regretted was not any loss of export in raw materials. A disciple of Quesnay, adhering strictly to the doctrine of the master, would have done that. Francis, on the contrary, was concerned that the demand for Indian manufactures in England was being increasingly replaced by a demand for raw silk. His sympathy was ranged on quite the 'wrong side', that is, the branch of economy regarded by the physiocrats as utterly unproductive, and he wrote thus of the danger of its being subverted by what 'at the first view implies Cultivation and Improvement – I mean the extraordinary Increase of Bengal raw Silk within these few years':

> This Country once the Staple of the richest and most delicate Manufactures, is gradually departing from that Line of Art and Industry, which naturally belongs to it, which led to wealth and Population, and imposed

[176] Note: 'Trade to Suez' (n.d.). *Francis MSS* 64 (52) 9.

[177] *Ibid.* To Lord North, 24 February 1775. *Ibid.*, 47 (36) 48. To W. Young, 5 July 1778. *Ibid.*, 51 (41) 41.

a voluntary Tribute on the rest of the World. In the present Course we shall see the Land Diverted from the production of Cotton, the Loom deserted, and the Country covered with Mulberry Trees. Instead of supplying the rest of the World with the Manufactures of Bengal you will find e'er [sic] long that raw Materials make the Chief Article of Exportation . . . The Consequence will be that the Manufacture will be lost, and the Raw silk will not sell.

In the Investment of last Year this Article amounted to 3/8 of the whole. In the present year it amount(s) to two-fifths.[178]

It is quite dear that in spite of the faith he professed in the primacy of agriculture, Francis had not succeeded in integrating this concept into his trade theory, and as a result, ended up by being in direct opposition to physiocracy. This is further confirmed by what he had to say about the importance of commerce. Far from being a sterile occupation it had, in his opinion, many advantages to offer. A merchant did not live off the fat of the nation; on the contrary, the profit he made in his transactions added to the existing stock of capital. This was an emphatic rejection of the physiocratic thesis that all commercial 'gain' involved a corresponding loss for the community. The idea was in fact derived from the repertoire of late mercantilist thought as represented by Sir James Steuart. Francis's view of profit as a surplus was the nearest thing to what Steuart called 'positive profit' arising 'when somebody gains and nobody loses' as distinct from 'relative profit' when one man's profit was necessarily another's loss.[179] Francis enunciated it thus in his note on 'Trade to Suez':

. . . it is not in the Nature of Things, that a Fortune can be acquired by any fair Enterprize in Commerce, or exertion of Industry whatsoever, without benefitting all the Parties employed in the support of it. A Merchant, who carries on Trade from a Country where he resides to another, does it with part of the stock of the former, which he borrows. From his Returns he pays the Loan made him with Interest: the Profit, if any, rests with him, and out of it he pays for his Maintenance by the Country. It is not to

[178] To W. Ellis, 13 January 1777. *Ibid.*, 49 (38) 68.
[179] Sen, *The Economics of Sir James Steuart*, p. 73.

> be disputed that, if the amount of the ultimate Profit were not remitted to Europe, Bengal would be so much the more enriched: – But it does not follow, that such Profit is made at the Expence of Bengal. On the contrary, the operations, by which it is acquired, must have improved, and enriched the Country. The Merchant creates a Thing, which would not have existed without him: – he increases the Capital of the Country, his Profit is a Portion of that Increase, and he leaves a new Channel of Industry and Improvement open to his Successors.[180]

But together with the refinement of 'positive profit' there also appears in this passage the more primitive notion of identity between capital and money. Francis, unlike the physiocrats, was not anti-money, and on this, no less than on the problem of the origin of profits, his attitude reflected all possible trends of mercantilist thought. At times he spoke almost in the language of Hume in defining money 'as the common and universal equivalent of all things alienable'. As such, its value was determined by the relation between its quantity and the quantity of goods for which it was to exchange. In other words, the value of money was fictitious: 'it may at different times be the price of a greater or smaller quantity of the same commodity without any increase in the demand.' In an argument with Hastings he went on to demonstrate this by pointing out how an influx of precious metals would produce a corresponding increase in the 'nominal price' of corn without altering the 'real price' at all.[181] In spite of such sophistication, however, he held fast at the same time to the crude concept of money as an active force 'lubricating the wheels of business by means of the importation of coin and bullion'.[182] The imagery of money as a life-giving flow – 'Fortunes circulating in a multitude of little Channels'[183] – came easily to his pen. To secure an increase of wealth in this form was the great advantage of foreign trade. 'The

[180] *Francis MSS* 64 (52) 9.

[181] *Sir Philip Francis's Minutes*, p. 178.

[182] Schumpeter, *History of Economic Analysis*, p. 350.

[183] Note: 'Opium'. *Francis MSS* 64 (52) 10. See *Letter from Mr Francis to Lord North*, p. 82.

essential Property of Commerce', as he defined it, was 'selling', that is, to obtain an excess of exports over imports. It was precisely this surplus, the 'natural Tribute' imposed by Bengal on the rest of the world and received in specie, that had been the cause of her former prosperity. With all his reading of the French *économistes,* Francis was on this point as firmly attached as Alexander Dow to the classic mercantilist concept of balance of trade. He wrote:

> The Consumption of foreign Commodities by the Natives of Bengal, is very inconsiderable. Cotton, the chief article of Import, is the Material of Manufacture of Exportation. But the Productions of Bengal have been in request in almost every Part of the World. The Returns were received in Specie. The parsimonious Industry of a simple unenlightened People imposed a natural Tribute on the Indolence or Luxury of the most powerful and polished Nations. In these Circumstances, the growing Balance of Trade accumulated, and the country flourished under a despotic Government.[184]

The overthrow of the former despotic government by British power had reversed the balance of trade and turned it into a 'drain of wealth'. This was 'an evil attached to the political situation of Bengal'.[185] Francis was breaking no new ground in thus relating economic decline to loss of sovereignty; other critics of the East India Company had said the same thing before him. Where he excelled them all was by producing what must be regarded as the clearest contemporary analysis of the factors constituting the 'drain'. His note 'Trade to Suez'[186] dealt with this problem at great length and gathered into one

184 'Trade to Suez, *ibid.*, 64 (52) 9. The balance of trade notion, expressed sometimes simply as 'tribute', constantly occurs in Francis's notes and correspondence. See, for instance, letters to Lord North, 24 February 1775, *ibid.*, 47 (36) 48; to same, 23 March 1775, *ibid.*, 49 (38) 17; to W. Ellis, 13 June 1777, *ibid.*, 49 (38) 68.

185 *Letter from Mr Francis to Lord North*, p. 52.

186 *Francis MSS* 64 (52) 9. The discussion on pp. 169–74 below should be read as primarily based on this source unless otherwise mentioned. It is surprising that no writer of this period of Indian history has taken any notice of this document so far. Even the most knowledgeable among them, Miss

single statement the numerous observations on the subject scattered all over his writings of the Indian period. In view of the importance of the document and the little use made of it so far, it would be worth while considering his argument *in extenso.* There were four 'articles of Tribute' which, he said, constituted the drain of wealth from Bengal. The first two of them, as enumerated below, were 'direct', that is, appropriated by the government itself. The others were 'indirect' and pumped out of the country through non-official channels.

(1) *The East India Company's Investment*

'The Company's Investment is a clear acknowledged Tribute from Bengal to England; and if a direct Tribute must be remitted to the Governing Power, this mode of paying it is the easiest in its operation, and least prejudicial in its Effects to the Tributary State; supposing always that the Part of the Revenues appropriated to the Purchase of the Investment be fairly laid out, – that the several Articles are provided without Violence or Monopoly, and that the Manufacturer, after paying, in Quality of Subject, a direct contribution to the support of Government, be not exposed to particular Hardships or Restraints in the Exercise of his Profession. With all these Conditions the payment of such a Tribute from Bengal to England must gradually impoverish the Province that pays it. No Country can stand it any longer.' In his own copy of the minute Francis subsequently added a marginal note saying that 'from 1775 to 1780 a great Surplus of territorial Revenue was applied to the purchase of an Investment for India'. He gave no figures.

Weitzman, does not mention it. Francis himself regarded it as an important record of his ideas on the subject. In a letter to W. Ellis (18 November 1777) he wrote: 'The Minute I drew up in consequence of a Proposal made by Mr Hastings to give some Encouragement to a Plan of exportation to Suez, contains every Thing that my Experience and Observation here, united with the Principles on which I set out, have suggested to me on the Subject of the export Trade of Bengal'. *Francis MSS* 50 (39) 28, pp. 242–3.

(2) *Remittances to Other Presidencies*

'The annual Supplies remitted to Bombay and the other Presidencies' were another direct Tribute. He did not develop the point any further, and in view of the undoubted need of the administration in other parts of India had apparently been resigned to the idea as a necessary evil. In his estimate of the 'services to be provided for' in his plan of 1776 he included a sum of two million rupees on this head, but added that taken together with the large sums of money sent to Europe, this would amount to 'a drain on these provinces which they are by no means able to bear'. He, therefore, asked for a reduction of this 'allowance', though he did not mention by how much.[187]

(3) *The Transfer of Private Income to England*

'The Third to England is indirect and unavowed, but very considerable in its amount, and more ruinous in its operation and consequences than the first. I mean the private Fortunes carried home by Men in Power and Station. The Quantum of this Tribute must necessarily decrease Every Day; but it will be equally felt, as long as it is paid in a Degree proportionate to the Existing Wealth of the Country.' What made this particular form of drain so harmful was that the private wealth transferred to England was acquired mostly, perhaps exclusively, 'out of the mass of the Revenues' by those serving in the revenue branch of the Company's administration in Bengal. The result was 'that less and less of the public Revenue returns every year into Circulation'.[188]

(4) *The Transfer of Income from Private Trade*

'The Returns for the Private Trade of the Company's Ships constitute a fourth article of Tribute to England. This is now a considerable object, and from the actual State of the Manufactures here, not unlikely to increase.' Bengal goods were no longer as well produced nor as cheap

[187] *Sir Philip Francis's Minutes*, pp. 98, 101.
[188] To W. Young, 5 July 1778. *Francis MSS* 51 (41) 41.

as before. This 'precludes the possibility of a Profit on Exporting them'. For private traders, therefore, 'the alternative left is to carry home Specie'. According to what he described as a reliable though 'very moderate' estimate, the quantity of specie extracted on this account amounted to no less than 1.2 million rupees every year.

Francis never tired of warning the government about the catastrophe that must inevitably follow if the drain of wealth was allowed to continue. Bengal 'will sink at last' under the burden of all these enormous 'tributes', he darkly predicted. 'It is impossible that the internal resources of any country should answer a constant demand on one side without a proportionate supply from other quarters. The fact is against Bengal in both instances . . . A country that gives, must receive, or its power of giving must soon be at an end. But our principal Indian markets are lost in the ruin of Persia and Indostan, and Europe returns nothing.'[189] The remedy had therefore to be sought in both preventive and compensatory measures. It was necessary, on the one hand, to reduce, if not altogether stop, the outflow of specie from the country, and on the other, to add to its depleted stock of wealth by acquiring an export surplus and thereby to stimulate internal trade and promote agriculture. Francis had both these objectives in view in formulating his recommendations.

Taking up the problem of 'indirect tributes' he said, 'The first Thing to be done is to prevent the private Fortunes, actually acquired and not remitted home, or which may be accumulated hereafter, from being carried in Specie out of the Country.' This he did not think could be achieved 'by any possible Act of Power'. In Spain and Portugal the authorities had not succeeded in stopping the export of bullion even on the pain of capital punishment. In any case the imposition of such grievous penalties would be alien 'to the wisdom of the British

[189] *Letter from Mr Francis to Lord North*, p. 52.

Constitution'. An appeal to good sense, he thought, would be much more effective than legal measures. Europeans who had money to send home could be easily persuaded that they had nothing to lose, but in fact a good deal to gain, if instead of remitting their wealth they invested it in agriculture and industry in Bengal and then reaped the harvest by exporting rich commercial crops and manufactured goods. This would have the double advantage of building up the resources of the country and allowing the merchant at the same time what was due to him, that is, 'a positive profit'. Alternatively, those who had money to spare could lend it to traders of other European nations in Bengal and 'thereby enable them to provide their Investments without Importing Bullion from Europe'. This also would partially help in encouraging manufacture, although it could never have quite the same effect as the English themselves putting their money into local production. The success of this latter policy, of course, largely depended on official encouragement: it was necessary that the government should permit Europeans to participate freely in private commercial activities (he certainly did not visualize the stimulus in the form of direct industrial investment) and to farm waste lands 'for the purpose of raising Articles not now produced, or not brought to perfection in Bengal'. Between these two possible ways of making use of the wealth owned by his compatriots in Bengal Francis's emphasis was clearly in favour of commercial enterprise, for it was his view that Europeans had neither any proprietary rights in land nor the required understanding of native agronomy, and would therefore have to limit themselves to the cultivation of waste lands. On the other hand, the very bright prospect of fertilizing Indian 'Industry and Circulation' with money provided by European merchant-financiers was thus described by him in a series of rhetorical questions:

> . . . shall we encourage those Europeans, who still have Fortunes to remit, to take away the value of them in Manufactures, rather than to compell them to do it in Specie? . . . In other words, shall the Amount of such Property be left to circulate in the Country, encouraging Industry, employing and paying the Manufacturers, and creating the Commodity, with which that Portion of the foreign Tribute is to be paid; or shall we

> cut off the source of so much Industry and Circulation, – shall we, so far forth, deprive the Manufacturer of Employment and the Country of the Benefit of all these united operations, and all their Consequences? In plainer Terms, shall we part with the seed, or the Fruit?

It would not be possible, however, to induce the Europeans, that is, those who were 'not employed in the collections or in offices of authority', to take part in commercial transactions without lifting the ban that still kept the inland trade out of bounds for them. This was introduced at a time when the Company's servants had nearly cornered the entire trade of Bengal by abusing the privilege of the *dustuk* and had consequently involved the English in disputes with the native government. Conditions had changed since then: the Company no longer permitted its employees to trade within the country and 'dual rule' was gone. The prohibitory regulations, therefore, no longer served any purpose. In his plan Francis forcefully argued the case for their abolition.[190]

His solution for the other problem of 'indirect tribute' lay partly in an attack on the circumstance which promoted it and partly in an attempt to prove, on theoretical grounds, that this was really not so harmful after all. He started with the assumption that the revival of Bengal's foreign trade depended entirely on European effort. The native had no aptitude for such enterprise. 'It is no more compatible with his Interest than with his Genius, Constitution and Habits of Life, to be a Mariner or an Adventurer in the Retail of Commerce.' He added the weight of a historical figment to this extraordinary view by saying 'that there is no period of Time, at which the Foreign Trade has been conducted by any but Foreigners'. If then it was the high price and debased quality of Bengal manufactures which made European traders return home with specie rather than merchandise, the remedy obviously was to produce more and better goods. This should be possible to some extent at least, if Europeans came forward to assist indigenous production with their resources as proposed above. Even then there would be serious bureaucratic difficulties

[190] *Sir Philip Francis's Minutes*, p. 63.

to overcome. What these were, is best illustrated by a merchant's letter which Francis carefully filed with his papers.[191] Fergusson, the merchant, writes that in December 1773 he arranged with his agents, Messrs Russell and Hunter, to provide an investment of over one hundred thousand rupees for the Basrah market, 'but then I found from the Change of Men in Power and Measures that the Quantity I first ordered could not be depended upon.' His agents, too, 'plainly saw that the Restraint of Government only prevented the Contracts from being fulfill'd'. At the same time he was warned by his friends from Dacca 'that not a Piece of Goods fit for exportation were to be got but thro' the means of the creatures of the Chief who put any price they pleased on them'. At first he asked his agents to submit to these terms, but eventually 'found the Goods so dear that I could not possibly take them'. The letter ends with a statement of the loss sustained in this transaction: 'The bad Consequences of this have been that ten Months interest on about one Lack and Thirty Thousand Rupees intended for the Investment has been lost, I have been obliged to send an improper Assessment of Goods to Bassorah on Freight, and for want of a sufficient Cargo for the Ships destined there, was necessitated to sell her, and instead of effecting at least a saving if not a Profitable Remittance by Goods to Bombay of a Lack and a half via Bassorah for the Provision of Cotton etcetera I have been forced to do it by Bills and in Sicca Rupees to an evident Loss of 18 pr Ct. Others have I know laid under the same Inconveniences, and our Friends at Dacca of long established good Character have been nearly ruined.' The tale of poor Fergusson's woes confirmed much that Francis said about the difficulty of obtaining articles of good quality at a reasonable price for export and the little choice the merchants had between sending out low grade commodities and remitting specie. Once such difficulties were removed, Europeans would be greatly encouraged to engage in the export trade to

[191] From J. Fergusson to G. Smith, 5 April 1775. *Francis MSS* 74 (3) 30.

other parts of India and abroad. In the process, he said falling back on his theory that commerce was not unproductive, they would enrich the country and be able at the same time to make a profit for themselves. Surely under those conditions they could export the surplus constituting their wealth without in any way weakening the economy of Bengal: 'if ultimately they carry away their Fortunes, they will leave the Country in a better Condition than that in which they found it.' In other words, given the condition of a revival of foreign trade and European participation in it, there should be no reason to object to the second form of 'indirect tribute'.

Francis had little to say about 'direct tribute' in the form of remittance to other Presidencies, except that he wanted it to be reduced and hoped that the revival of export trade would allow Bengal to 'lay the rest of India under Contribution'[192] and thereby make up for what it paid out in subsidies.

It was the drain by investment which was his principal concern, and engaged his attention almost as much as did the land question. The harm it did was in his opinion no less serious and far-reaching than the irrational system of revenue administration, and the measures he suggested for its remedy were as fundamental to his 'system' as his agrarian formula. The evils arising from these two sets of problems complemented each other. They were expressions of the same policy in two different sectors of the economy: the farming system was based on the assumption that all land belonged to the State; the method of investment on the assumption of absolute commercial monopoly by the government. In practice, too, they were closely related: 'The Company, in the first place, let the lands upon Farm to the best Bidder. The next Thing their Servants do, is to farm the Produce.' In each instance his judgment was equally categorical: 'Farm and Monopoly, both in Word and Deed, let the immediate Consequences be what they may, must be banished for ever.'[193]

[192] 'Trade to Suez'. *Ibid.*, 64 (52) 9.

[193] To Lord North, 24 February 1775. *Ibid.*, 47 (36) 48.

The monopoly, on which the organization of investment was based, was total, and covered both production and marketing. It was established by revolutionizing the traditional *dadney* system which allowed the peasant and the manufacturer to produce without being dictated by anything except the demands of an open market, and permitted no other influence on prices except that of free and unrestrained competition between buyers. It was on this basis that the English, like all other foreigners, traded in Bengal until 1765, when the assumption of political power by the East India Company resulted directly in its subversion in favour of their monopolistic control. In effect, this amounted to a quiet, though not painless, transition from the loose, relaxed procedure of English mercantilism in India to a more thorough and grasping mode of operation, and should surely disprove much that has been written about the 'factory system' without any distinction being made between its two phases – before and after the grant of Diwani. The change is well described in a document apparently written for Francis by one of his advisers. It is entitled 'Of the mode of providing the Company's Investment', and says:

> Before the English had acquired Influence, the Company's Investment was provided by Contract with Native Merchants who received Advances (in the Country language Dadney) and from thence, were called Dadney Merchants. They or their Agents went to the different Markets, purchased the Goods of the Manufacturers, and delivered them at the Company's Warehouses.
>
> After the Company became possessed of Territory, their demand for Investment increased, and their mode of providing it changed. They put themselves in the place of the Dadney Merchants, making the advances immediately to the Manufacturer . . . The Company went to market as Sovereigns and Tyrants. Instead of seeking a preference by paying better, they forced the manufacturers to Work for them and to work at an under price, at the same time that they prohibited all private Merchants from dealing in the Assortments required for their Investment, and from attempting to employ any Man retained by them. Thus a general Monopoly was at once rigorously established.[194]

[194] 'Of the mode, etc.' *Ibid.*, 74 (3) 41.

The Company's monopoly extended to production both in agriculture and in manufacture. 'There is hardly an Article either of the Produce of the Earth (including even the first Necessaries of Life) or of the Industry of the Manufacturer, which is not, in some Shape or other, made subject to a Monopoly.'[195] Francis was guilty of no exaggeration when he wrote thus to Lord North. His own list of the articles 'engrossed' shows how numerous these were and how they affected the economic life of the people in most of the major districts of Bengal. The monopoly was absolute and universal in salt, opium, salpetre, silk and cloths. In addition to these there were regional monopolies which in the northern districts included tobacco, hemp, mustard seed, gunny, timber, rice, wheat, gram and oil; in the eastern districts – betelnut, dry fish, tobacco and cotton. Some of these 'are forced on the Ryots at such prices as is thought proper to fix them at, without any Regard being paid to the Market Price'. Some others were 'bought there and sold again on the Spot'; the articles in this case were rice, wheat, gram and oil, and should serve to demonstrate how effectively the peasant was prevented from marketing the staples he grew.[196]

The monopoly which Francis singled out for particularly severe criticism in a number of minutes was that of salt and opium, and the demand for its abolition was highlighted in his plan.[197] He accused the government of maintaining the salt monopoly in defiance of all the orders of the home authorities on this subject since 1766. The result was not merely a fall in the output of salt, but depopulation of the salt districts. 'The cultivation of the lands in those districts is performed by the same hands, which work the salt; and when the Molungee is driven to desertion, the state proportionably feels the loss, not only in its manufacture, but in its agriculture.' Similarly, the opium monopoly was the cause of the 'present state of universal poverty and depopulation' in Bihar, while it had adverse effects both

[195] To Lord North, 24 January 1775. *Ibid.*, 47 (36) 48.
[196] 'Monopolies'. *Ibid.*, 72 (1) 40.
[197] *Sir Philip Francis's Minutes*, pp. 61–2.

on the foreign trade of the country and its revenues. He was convinced that 'the single act of throwing open the trade in salt and opium will . . . in a few years give a totally new face to the country'.

This was, of course, easier said than done. So many powerful interests were involved in the system of monopolies that it resisted all attempts at reform. It was these that made it difficult for the government to implement even its own decisions for reform. Thus, it was officially declared in April 1773 that all weavers and manufacturers should have the 'liberty to work for whom they pleased'. But, as the anonymous officer who prepared the note on investment policy for Francis observed, the declarations made little difference to practice. For instance even at Dacca, which was 'half populated with Weavers', a private merchant could not during a whole season get anyone to work for him. There the weavers 'continued in a state of Bondage', in spite of the official order guaranteeing them freedom of employment. 'Everywhere the Delols, Gomastahs, and Banians employed in the Company's Business with many of whom it has become hereditary, have so extended their connections and influence over the Workmen: the influence of Station in the service is likewise conceived to be so much a matter of Right, that a Chain of Interest is formed which may be shaken, but not easily broken.'[198]

It was, however, idle to expect that conditions being what they were, the Bengal administration would take the initiative for any radical change in the system. 'Their servants', wrote Francis, 'derive too many advantages from the Company's monopoly to wish for an avowed and general freedom of trade, in which others might participate.'[199] So momentous an act of reform could be introduced only by the Court of Directors. But unfortunately there was no indication that they were themselves prepared to give up their narrow monopolistic attitude. Even as late as in their letter of 3 March 1775 they had instructed the government to 'prohibit all persons . . . from

[198] 'Of the mode, etc.' *Francis MSS* 74 (3) 41.

[199] *Letter from Mr Francis to Lord North,* p. 75.

trading in any of those articles which compose their [the Company's] investment, directly or indirectly, until it was completed'. The order provoked Francis to write one of his most savage indictments of the investment policy. Commenting on the terms of the Directors' letter he said: 'Here therefore is as compleat a monopoly of the whole Produce and Industry of the three Provinces, as can be imagined. – No Class of People to trade, – no Articles free for Purchase, – no Period of Time, at which Purchases can be made: The Company must then be the sole Trader.'[200] This only proved what he had always maintained, that 'the Powers at home neither understand the Question, nor give themselves any Concern about it'. They saw a large investment sent to Europe every year from Bengal, and on this basis 'by some new Rule of Proportion infer that much must remain, because a great deal has been taken away'.[201]

Underlying it all was the very short-sighted view which, he thought, the Company took of their own commercial interests. It was the aim of an exclusive trading corporation like that to try 'to make the greatest possible Profit on the smallest possible Outset or Expence'. But if they increased their imports beyond a certain point, it was possible that the proportionate rise in profit would be less than the additional amount of outlay. If the market failed, as he believed it had actually done to a large extent for Indian goods in England, the imports would lie dead in the warehouse and the money spent on freight etcetera altogether lost. On the other hand, to try to sell off the goods at any cost must result in a glut and lower the prices. This too had happened, and in 1775 the prime cost of Indian imports was, according to his information, forty to fifty per cent higher than it had been a few years ago, while the quality of the goods deteriorated to a corresponding degree. 'Where can such a System end?' Francis had nothing but the gloomiest prediction to offer for an answer: 'It appears to me that the Company, considered as a Commercial Body,

200 Minute on investment, 8 January 1776. *Francis MSS* 75 (4) 45.

201 To W. Young, 5 July 1778. *Ibid.*, 51 (41) 41.

must infallibly be ruined by the Magnitude of their Investment united with the Mode of providing it.'[202]

A matter for still greater concern was that this policy amounted to killing the goose that laid the golden eggs. No sector of the economy of Bengal, between the plough and the loom, escaped from its disastrous impact. The monopoly on which it was based produced a chain reaction.[203] In the first instance it was, as Francis philosophically put it, 'an Invasion of the natural Right of every Individual to dispose freely of the Produce of his Labour'. It armed the monopolist with an arbitrary power 'to fix the Price of the Labour and Industry of Men who have already paid for the Protection of Government by the Tax on their Lands'. Consequently, producers were obliged to work without any incentive. The result, in manufacture, was a serious debasement of quality which badly affected exports as well as the inland trade; in agriculture – want of improvement and large-scale desertion of the ryots, leading in their turn to fiscal deficits.

In the second place, monopoly constituted not merely 'a Violation of private Right', but also 'of every Principle of Justice.' Being exercised by the government itself, 'it unites an Interest and a Power, which ought never to meet in the same Hands, and in the Case of Oppression of the Ryots, whether real or pretended, constitutes the Plaintiffs Parties against Government, and leaves no indifferent Tribunal to administer Justice to them.' In this particular form, therefore, monopoly was 'more liable to Abuse and less capable of Check and Controul than any exclusive Privilege granted to an Individual'. Francis described these abuses in a language reminiscent of Bolts:

[202] To Lord North, 24 February 1775. *Ibid.*, 47 (36) 48.

[203] To W. Young, 5 July 1778. *Ibid.*, 51 (41) 41. 'Opium' (not dated but, as indicated by a note in the India Office Library copy, probably written in 1775 or 1776). *Ibid.*, 64 (52) 10. 'Remarks on General Clavering's Observations on the Plan proposed for a new Settlement' (not dated but, as indicated in the India Office volume, copies of the note were sent to Lord North and H. Strachey on 13 May 1776). *Ibid.*, 77 (31) 5.

> . . . chiefs, superintendents and banians, detached from the Presidency, armed with despotic power to support the pretended commercial interests of the Company, have taken possession of the markets, excluded all competition, enslaved the manufacturers, and in some instances obliged private merchants to purchase from themselves, at an immoderate advance of price, the same goods which they had seized and set the Company's seal upon the loom, under pretence that they were wanted for the public investment.[204]

The force of this condemnation of monopolies was only equalled by his emphasis on 'a perfect Freedom of Trade'. This emphasis appears in his writings almost simultaneously with his very first pronouncements on the right of private property in land. Since the farming system and the monopoly in investment were intertwined, the solution to the difficulty they together produced had to be sought at the same time in permanent rights in land and free trade. He wanted the government to have nothing to do with the commercial process except 'to secure an Equivalent for the present Revenue by a moderate Duty to be paid by the first Purchaser', that is, in the form of the usual export duty. If this was ensured, the act of 'throwing open the Trade' would be followed by consequences exactly the reverse of what resulted from the regime of monopoly: 'the Ryot and Manufacturer, who are now obliged to sell to a Monopolist, will be restored to their natural Right of selling to whom they think proper; . . . they will of course receive a better price for their Labour; . . . the Country will be enriched, and . . . as the Merchant will purchase on easier Terms at an open Market, the Trade of Bengal, in the most beneficial Article of all its Exports, will be so far forth improved'. There was no doubt that the drain of specie would altogether cease under these conditions, and even if by the use of non-economic pressures the government still persisted in continuing 'the drain of Manufactures only', the country would be better equipped to bear the strain for a relatively longer period.[205]

[204] *Letter from Mr Francis to Lord North*, p. 63.
[205] To Lord North, 13 January 1775, *Francis MSS* 47 (36) 47; 24 February

It should be noted here that Francis' plea for free trade was much more radical than the demand for a partial relaxation of the Company's monopoly already voiced before him by many Europeans in Bengal, some of them private traders having no other interest than to clear for themselves a little corner in which to continue their own business. Some of these advocates of limited free trade had urged the government to stop direct procurement and revert to the former mode of providing goods for investment by contract with the native merchants. In fact, the administration of Warren Hastings was not altogether opposed to this, and if its efforts in this direction had made so little progress, it was, as Francis' own adviser informed him, mainly because the native contractors were discouraged by the high prices and were shy to come forward.[206] This favourable attitude to *dadney* did not represent on the part of the government any departure from the system of monopolies, but was on the contrary designed to make it more effective. Francis, however, considered the return to *dadney* as a necessary transitional step towards free trade. The replacement of direct procurement by open contract would, he thought, create conditions which must eventually make it possible for the Company to enter the market on equal terms with other purchasers and provide for their investment by relying on no other influence than 'that, which the superior Weight of their Purse would naturally give them.'[207] As he put it in his open letter to Lord North: 'The investment must be provided by contract, as it was heretofore, until the general increase and improvement of the manufactures will admit of its being provided by ready-money purchases.' What he was driving at was the need to stimulate by this method 'the competition of sellers at Calcutta' and 'the competition of purchasers at the Aurungs', in other words, full

---

1775, *ibid.*, 47 (36) 48; 21 November 1775, *ibid.*, 47 (36) 82; 18 March 1776, *ibid.*, 47 (36) 88. To W. Young, 5 July 1778, *ibid.*, 51 (41) 41. 'Opium', *ibid.*, 64 (52) 10.

[206] 'Of the mode, etc.' *Ibid.*, 74 (3) 41.

[207] To Lord North, 21 November 1775. *Ibid.*, 47 (36) 82.

competition – the characteristic aim of all post-mercantilist doctrines of free trade.[208]

In fact, the concept of free trade in Bengal had taken a big leap forward between Dow and Francis. The latter had set out to analyse the economic drain in terms of the old-fashioned theory of balance of trade, but ended up by producing what, on the whole, was a physiocratic programme of free trade. According to the school of Quesnay, the function of commerce was merely to exchange the values created by agriculture for equal values, at home and abroad, either in money or in goods. It was necessary therefore that this mechanism of exchange should be allowed to operate in the cheapest way and without any hindrance in the form of state interference or otherwise. This implied, first, perfect freedom of competition, and secondly, the removal of all forms of local prohibitions and inland duties. For Francis, too, these were indispensable conditions for free trade in Bengal.

It was Quesnay's opinion that in commerce freedom of competition was the best policy: 'la police du commerce intérieur et extérieur la plus sûre, la plus exacte, la plus profitable à la nation et à l'état, consiste dans la pleine liberté de la concurrence.'[209] How was this to be organized and for what purpose? Through open competition with foreign merchants and in order to secure the best, that is, the highest possible price, he said. Francis, too, hoped that 'the competition of sellers' and 'the competition of buyers' throughout the country following the abolition of monopolies would make it possible for the producers to 'receive a better price for their Labour'. It is true that he often expressed his anxiety about the rising prices in Bengal. But this must not be interpreted as a mercantilist affection for lower prices. In his arguments with Warren Hastings he maintained that the upward trend was imposed on the market, so to say, from outside: it

[208] *Letter from Mr Francis to Lord North*, pp. 64–6.

[209] 'Maximes Generales'. *François Quesnay et la Physiocratie*, t. II, p. 955.

had been caused by the 'heavy, insupportable taxation, which racks the landholder, and obliges him to raise the price of every article of his production upon the consumer'.[210] It was, in other words, an uneconomic increase which he naturally regretted. But he never doubted that under the ideal condition of free competition *le bon prix* necessarily meant higher prices. It was primarily on this ground that he wanted foreign traders to be given free access to the Indian market. 'Foreign commerce, if the door be thrown wide open to her', he said, 'will give the highest venal value to the productions of the soil.'[211] And here again he sought historical justification for a contemporary economic idea in an imaginary Mughal precedent. He believed that 'the ancient government' of the country, too, had adopted an open door policy, 'or why did they encourage every European nation to frequent their ports, by exempting their export and import trade from duties?'

Equally emphatic was his demand for the withdrawal of inland duties. The customs houses were for him the worst symbol of state interference and their abolition was, therefore, a most necessary condition for the freedom of trade. 'They check the operations of foreign trade in a country which properly *sells* to all the world and *buys* nothing, except some raw materials of manufacture and necessities from England for the consumption of Europeans. The inland customs fetter the industry of the natives in all its minutest branches.'[212] The revenue collected on this account could hardly compensate for what was taken away from the value of foreign exports and indigenous production. But supposing the government still wanted to make up for it, 'the amount might be levied, with less convenience, directly from the land'. For, 'the fund of this country is land. Nothing else ought to be taxed. There ought to be no custom-house.'[213] Underlying

[210] *Sir Philip Francis's Minutes*, p. 179. For other statements to the same effect, see *ibid.*, pp. 43–4, 180, and letter to W. Young, 5 July 1778, *Francis MSS* 51(41) 41.

[211] *Sir Philip Francis's Minutes*, p. 177.

[212] *Letter from Mr Francis to Lord North*, pp. 66–7.

[213] *Sir Philip Francis's Minutes*, p. 176.

this was the assumption that agricultural rent was the only form of economic surplus, and consequently, taxes levied on other forms of income must ultimately fall on landed property, but indirectly and in a manner harmful for production as a whole; and that taxes should therefore, be entirely passed on to the land, so that at one stroke both industry and trade were freed from state interference. In other words, what Francis was pleading for was the replacement of indirect taxes by the physiocratic *impôt unique*. Quesnay and his disciples had based their policy of taxation on this central concept, and believed that once it was introduced, 'landowners and farmers will adjust their burdens by raising the price of raw materials, every consumer of which will thus pay a share of taxation with the minimum expence for cost of collection, and the whole cumbrous apparatus of existing fiscal machinery will be swept away'.[214] Francis spoke in very much the same language in describing the possible advantages of the single tax system for Bengal. 'The land-holder then will in effect tax every other order of the state', he said, 'and bring into the treasury a net contribution, greater in amount, yet lighter to the contributer, and easier in the mode of collection, than it is possible through any other medium.'[215]

It should be evident from this summary that Francis's political economy was not carved out of one single piece. It was eclectic and several widely different strands were woven into it. His theory of international trade was mercantilist, but even as such it included an assortment of very divergent notions ranging from the crudities of bullionism to the subtleties of Sir James Steuart. In striking contrast to this was his physiocratic programme of reform of the land system. To the extent that the agrarian problem dominated his interest and its solution was for him the key to all improvement, he was a physiocrat. His ideas on free trade and taxation were a further proof of his doctrinal affinity with the French *économistes*. In the political

[214] Higgs, *The Physiocrats*, p. 44. Also see Weulersse, *Les Physiocrates*, p. 164; *La Physiocratie à la fin du règne de Louis XV*, p. 72.

[215] *Sir Philip Francis's Minutes*, p. 177.

philosophy of the Permanent Settlement, too, there was a good deal to indicate the same influence.

4. 'Who is King of Bengal?'

Francis had never intended his plan to be a mere statement of economic policy. That would have been taking a very narrow and partial view of things. It was not in his nature to consider the 'streams' without relating them to the 'fountain'. As a fundamentalist, he ridiculed Warren Hastings's proposal for judicial reform as 'a pleasant Idea to give a Nation a Court of Judicature before you gave them a Constitution'. For, there could be no laws without a sovereign. His own aim was no less than that of 'forming or restoring the Constitution of an Empire', and this involved him in an attempt to solve what was the most basic problem of all, that is, the problem of power. 'Does any Man in England know, or think it worth his While to enquire, *Who is King of Bengal?* he asked.[216] It was implied that he alone was the Oedipus who could answer the riddle.

In his opinion the difficulties in the government of Bengal were all due to the fact that the question of sovereignty had been left undecided. 'In the present State of Things', he wrote to Lord Clive on 21 May 1775, 'there is properly no Sovereign, nor of course can there be any regular Government in the Country.'[217] The result was a confusion of 'right, fact and form . . . in almost every operation of Government'. The elements of this strange disorder were clearly analysed by him in the plan. Under the existing conditions the country was being governed by an 'arbitrary succession of acts of power without right, flowing from different sources and excluding every idea of unity, regularity, or system'. These sources were:

> (the) native prince, claiming the rights of Subadar; whose government the Company tells us, 'they are engaged by solemn stipulation to

[216] To C. D'Oyly, 22 January 1776. *Francis MSS* 47 (36) 76.
[217] *Ibid.*, 47 (36) 59.

> support'; – the Emperor, whose rights, as Lord Paramount, inherent in the constitution of the empire, have been for a number of years acknowledged by the Company; – the Presidency of Fort William, who hold the sword by agreement with the Nabob, as they do the purse by grant from the Emperor; – and lastly, a Court of Judicature, exercising an unlimited jurisdiction through the provinces, in the name of the King of Great Britain.[218]

There were two points in this 'Labyrinth of Contradictions' on which Francis concentrated his attack. First, he maintained, that 'it has been the policy of Mr Hastings to abolish the Sovereignty of the Mogul in fact, and to deny it in Argument'.[219] Considering that the Company coined money in the name of Shah Alam and collected revenues by virtue of his grant, it was only fair that the country should be administered either in his name or that of his representative, the Nawab of Bengal. But Hastings had no sense of justice. He had adopted 'the dangerous measure' of trying to bring about 'the total Annihilation of the Soubah's Rights' before the government of His Majesty the King of England was prepared to assume power in Bengal.[220] The result had been to create a political vacuum hidden behind a facade of dual sovereignty, and 'the People at present have either two Sovereigns or None'.

Secondly, the confusion was worse confounded by the establishment of the Supreme Court of Judicature. 'The Introduction of the Supreme Court of Judicature, without any precise Limits being fixed to their Jurisdiction, or any express Declaration of the Sovereignty under which they pretend to administer Justice, has only added to the general Confusion.'[221] And true to his habit of spreading an argument all the way between a point of principle and private grievance, he suggested that at the root of both the contradictions lay the Governor-General's greed for power: that Hastings had deliberately created a political void

[218] *Sir Philip Francis's Minutes*, pp. 23–4.

[219] To Lord North, 24 February 1775. *Francis MSS* 47 (36) 48.

[220] To Lord North, 21 November 1775. *Ibid.*, 47 (36) 82.

[221] To Clive, 21 May 1775. *Ibid.*, 47 (36) 59.

in order to promote the Supreme Court, and the latter was, of course, a mere instrument of his personal despotism. His interpretation of the judicial plan proposed by his opponent in January 1776 bore this characteristic factional slant. It was stated there that '*the whole and sole Sovereignty* of these Kingdoms is *completely vested* in his Majesty', but this, according to Francis, meant nothing in view of the reservation made in favour of the 'just Rights, Claims, and Titles' of the Nawab of Bengal and other Indian princes. These rights and titles were all derived from the constitution of the Mughal Empire, and therefore, 'his Majesty's Sovereignty cannot exist, either in Fact or Form, consistently with the savings stated in the Bill'. In other words, Hastings's plan could in no way help to remove the 'inconvenience attending a divided Sovereignty'. Why then was it proposed at all? The answer which Francis volunteered was tipped with the usual dose of malice: what the plan sought to achieve, he insinuated, was 'singly to extend the Jurisdiction of the Supreme Court and to give to that Court a compleat and effectual Control over the Country'.[222]

Francis was convinced that there was only one way of solving all these problems arising from a division of power. This was for the British government to come out with 'an immediate Declaration of his Majesty's Sovereignty over the Kingdoms of Bengal, Bahar and Orissa'.[223] He had no doubt that 'this single Operation will clear the Way and relieve us from a multitude of Difficulties'. The best procedure should be, of course, 'to obtain from Shah Allum a formal Surrender of these Provinces to his Majesty, to be held hereafter in full Sovereignty, and pleno Jure'. Would this involve still another revolution in 'the Form of the Country Government'? On the contrary, Francis went to the extent of suggesting that its authority should be further strengthened, and he maintained that the transfer of sovereignty from the Mughal to the British in Bengal need not

[222] From majority of the Council to Lord North, 16 May 1776. Public Records Office, T. 49/10, no. 49.

[223] To Lord North, 24 February 1775. *Francis MSS* 47 (36) 48.

necessarily be made at the expense of the Nawab. 'The Nabob', he said, 'may then hold by grant from the King, as he is now supposed to do from the Mogul.'[224]

Francis thus put forward what was in fact a new formula for the solution of the problem of sovereignty in Bengal. His was a middle path between the two extremities represented by Verelst and Hastings on this question. The former pleaded for an uneasy self-denial, the latter forthrightness. Firminger, in his eagerness to distinguish between 'the bolder and more congenial line' adopted by Hastings in 1775 and the restrained attitude of his opponents in the Council, makes the mistake of identifying Francis's position with that of Verelst. 'Francis and his party in reality carried on the traditional views of Verelst', says Firminger; 'while, on the other hand, Hastings' whole administration is an open denial of Verelst's assertion that 'we cannot be more without being greater than sound policy allows.'[225] There is nothing in Francis's recorded views to justify this observation. He was no doubt very firmly against all attempts made by Warren Hastings to undermine the authority of the Mughal Emperor, and his protest against the Governor-General's refusal to continue payment of the annual tribute to Delhi was quite consistent with his general position. But Bengal was a problem of an altogether different order. Here he was absolutely clear in his demand 'that the undivided sovereignty shall be assumed and declared by his Majesty . . . and that, at all events, Bengal is to be held as a Province of Great Britain'.[226] The neat device of obtaining 'a formal surrender' of the province from Shah Alam was invented precisely with the idea of making the direct assumption of power there consistent with respect for the Emperor's authority. Verelst had spoken about 'that supreme line, which, to pass, would be an open avowal of sovereignty'. For Francis, Bengal was situated well below this 'supreme line', though not Delhi.

[224] To Clive, 21 May 1775. *Ibid.*, 47 (36) 48.
[225] Firminger, vol. I, p. xxi.
[226] *Sir Philip Francis's Minutes*, p. 24.

The need for such differentiation arose simply from the fact that in one case the English could claim the sanction of the sword behind their power; in the other, they could not. Firminger, following the logic of his initial misunderstanding, interprets Francis's views 'to show how little conscious the English were of any conquest of the country by English military power'. He suggests that the idea of a right of conquest in Bengal which 'exercised an influence over the popular imagination' at a later date, had not really occurred to those pioneer politicians for whom the battle of Plassey was still a living memory.[227] This certainly does not apply either to Francis or to Hastings. The former spoke on numerous occasions about the need to introduce 'a System of Government under which the Natives shall be considered as a conquered People, and which shall have for its first Object the Security of a Conquest'.[228] In doing so, he thought, the English would only be imitating the wisdom of all former regimes and continuing a tradition to which the country was fully adapted. For 'the Natives of Bengal have for Ages past considered themselves as a conquered People, and . . . they have been treated in every successive Conquest, except the last, as a conquered People ought to be'.[229] He was convinced that the English could claim the right to make institutional changes 'if Conquest conveys a Right of any Kind'.[230] To leave nothing to doubt, it would be enough to add to these a statement he made in the House of Commons in 1806. 'There was no power in India', he said, 'but the power of the sword, and that was the British sword, and no other.'[231] On this point, he was in complete agreement with his great rival who also had referred to the sword as the most valid title the British had to sovereignty in India. There was thus no quarrel between them about the quantum

[227] Firminger, op. cit., pp. iii, xxi.

[228] To Lord North, 24 February 1775. *Francis MSS* 47 (36) 48.

[229] To Lord North, 23 March 1775. *Ibid.*, 49 (38) 17.

[230] 'Remarks on General Clavering's Observations, etc.' *Ibid.*, 77 (31) 5.

[231] *P.D.*, vol. VII, p. 392.

of power which the conquerors could legitimately assume in Bengal, but only about the uses to be made of it.

If the government of Bengal was to be placed directly under the control of the British State, it followed that the existing status of the East India Company would require a drastic alteration. With a clarity and candour reminiscent of Adam Smith, Francis wrote about the fundamental inconsistency of the Company's position as merchants and rulers. Smith's great work was not published until 1776, too late to have influenced Francis on the subject.[232] Already as early as January 1775 he had lightly touched upon this problem in a letter to Lord North, and then within a few months followed it up by an explicit statement about the need for a separation between the mercantile and political functions of the Company:

> If ever there is to be a division of Rights between Government and the Company, I would wish it to be seriously considered, whether it would not be a beneficial Measure, both for the Country and the Company, to give the latter a fixed Sum out of the Revenues; and then let them go to Market for their Investment, without any Authority as a governing Power, or any other Influence over the Market, but that, which the superior Weight of their Purse would naturally give them.[233]

Thus months ahead of the publication of *Wealth of Nations* Francis had very nearly anticipated its central thesis relating to the East India Company. If anything, this was an indication of what he owed to that formidable body of anti-mercantilist opinion which had been gathering strength over the decades in England and was most articulate in the late 1760s.' In this sense he may be classed with those who set the pace for Adam Smith rather than with his disciples.

This acknowledgment of Francis's originality must not, however, be stretched so far as to suggest that he did not respond to the great

[232] Firminger, vol. II, p. xviii.

[233] To Lord North, 21 November 1775. *Francis MSS* 47 (36) 82.

debacle of mercantilism: the loss of half of its empire in America and the *pronunciamento* issued on behalf of its rival school in England. On the contrary, these developments directly encouraged his criticism. Adam Smith was at once entered into the list of his authorities and quoted for the first time in a minute in November 1776. His denunciation of the Company's dual role as merchant-sovereigns was more emphatic than ever when he took up this question again with Lord North early next year. There could be no reform, he said, 'as long as the Interests of the Company and those of Bengal are committed to the same Hands . . . they are in fact incompatible. If the territorial Acquisitions are to be preserved, it must be under a System of Government which does not refer all its Measures to the supposed Rights or Interests of a Body of Merchants . . .'[234] After this it was for him only a question of choosing the correct tactical hour to launch a full-scale offensive. He did not have to wait long for a turn of political opinion at home in his favour, or what in fact amounted to the same thing, against his rival. The Rockingham party in Parliament was clearly hardening in its attitude to Warren Hastings, who came under fire from many speakers of the Opposition in 1777; and in June that year Burke sent his first letter to Francis, which though quite unrelated to any of the great issues of common interest to them, was still a most welcome sign of the thaw the latter had been eagerly looking forward to.[235] He no longer had to be as circumspect as he was two years earlier when he still spoke of the Company's monopoly as a subject 'too delicate and dangerous in my Situation'.[236] His letter to Lord North written in September 1777 was very bold indeed. Here he accused the Company's administration of being guilty of 'injustice in its fundamental principle', which was 'that of uniting the character of Sovereign and merchant, and exercising the power of the first for the benefit of the second'. Since profit was the only object of a

[234] To Lord North, 14 February 1777. *Ibid.*, 53 (49) 40.

[235] Sutherland, *The East India Company in Eighteenth-Century Politics*, pp. 324–5.

[236] To Lord North, 13 January 1775. *Francis MSS* 47 (36) 47.

trading company, it also became the sole object of government, 'when the two characters were united'. All abuses followed from this single cause, for it allowed the same power to 'take the rents of the lands as proprietor, – engross all the merchantable produce as monopolist, and all the industry of the manufacturer for the pretended supply of their investment'. The most essential condition for the success of his own measures for reform was 'that the government is not to be continued in the hands of a mercantile body'.[237]

Twice during the next two decades the problem of the East India Company's status emerged as a grave political issue in England. On both occasions Francis spoke up against its pretension to power. During the agitation following the defeat of Fox's bill and the dissolution of Parliament, he took the field with his favourite weapon of anonymous pamphlets, and wrote in one of them:[238]

> The chief disorders of the Company's affairs have arisen from the junction of the incompatible characters of Sovereign and Merchant in the same persons, which led them into a ridiculous mixture of the great and the little in the conduct of their business. For example, the great views of the Sovereign made it necessary for them to have an army in the Carnatic; but the little views of Mercants, to save expence, tempted them to employ it only in collecting the revenues and taxes. Until General Stewart arrived at Madras, the army was, for the purposes of collection, cantoned all over the dominion, in threes or fours in a place, like so many Excise-officers, instead of being kept together in a body, and to do duty as soldiers. To put an end to this incompatible junction, the bill separated the two departments of government and trade.

The rejection of Fox's bill was, according to him, the result of a deliberate confusion created by 'the secret advisers of his Majesty' about the meaning of chartered rights. It had 'only proved the facility, in some cases, of substituting words for meaning, and of totally overturning

[237] *Letter from Mr Francis to Lord North*, pp. 6–7, 13, 53–4, 56.

[238] *We have been All in the Wrong*, pp. 46–7. I have relied on Weitzman's authority (op. cit., pp. 158–9) in ascribing to Francis this and the other anonymous pamphlet *Popular Topics*, written on the same theme.

the sense of the sound. The charter of a monopoly was confounded with the greater charter of our freedom, and that single word *Charter* decided the question.'[239] Charter or no charter, Parliament had every right to make 'such regulations as they thought fit'. He came forward to defend this right both on grounds of precedent and of principle.[240] 'In the years 1772 and 1773', he said, 'Parliament with the entire consent of the Buckingham House . . . entirely changed the Company's Constitution and disfranchised the far greater part of the Proprietors.' But even granting, for argument's sake, 'that Mr Fox's bill was the very first Parliamentary interference', there was no good reason for objecting to it. 'Is any man weak enough', he asked, 'to conceive that Parliament ever gave a Charter conferring power which they never were to control, and establishing a monopoly which they never were to correct? If the power is abused by corruption or oppression, are they not bound to resume it?'

Again, in 1793, speaking in the House of Commons in reply to Dundas, he asserted that the renewal of the Company's charter 'not only does not involve, but ought to exclude' all claim to political power. For, 'by the nature and principles of their institution they were fitted for trade and unfitted for Government'. Returning to a line of argument he had already used in 1777, he said that it was not in the Company's own interest that they should exercise sovereign rights in India. All their 'difficulties, debts and distresses', and the ruinous wars in which they had been involved from time to time, were 'owing to their being burdened with the possession of a territory which it was impossible for them to manage or govern either for the benefit of the people or for their own advantage'.[241]

This constituted one of the essential points of difference between him and Warren Hastings. Francis often spoke of the Governor-

[239] *Philip Francis's Speech in the House of Commons on Tuesday, 7 March 1786*, p. 42.

[240] *Popular Topics*, pp. 21–4.

[241] *Heads of Mr Francis's Speech in reply to Mr Dundas on the 23d of April 1793, etc.*, pp. 3–5.

General as the representative of the commercial interests of the Company and as such, committed to the narrow view taken by Leadenhall Street of power being a condition of profit. Their differences on the question of the Company's status, as recorded in their respective minutes, were described by him as 'the Argument on both Sides'. As the opposition began to grow between the Court of Directors and those groups in Parliament from whom he expected support, he went on adding stroke after stroke to his characterization of his rival as a creature of 'the other side'. There is much play on this theme in many of his letters written in 1777. Since 'Mr Hastings's Resolution is to raise the greatest possible Revenue here, and to send the greatest possible Investment to England during the Continuance of his own Administration', he insinuated to Lord North, 'your Lordship will judge what Favour he courts and what Protection he appeals to.'[242] To General Fraser he was more explicit: Hastings, he said, had been advised by his agents in England 'to rest all his Hopes of Protection and Safety on the Support of the Company in their commercial Character'.[243] By contrast, he considered himself as representing the interests of the 'nation'. The opposition between him and the Governor-General was, therefore, beyond conciliation. The Regulating Act had failed precisely because 'it obliged Men to act together who, besides a considerable Difference of personal Character, represented different Interests, therefore, never could unite, unless it were in Collision'.[244]

Once the question of power was thus decided by the transfer of sovereignty from the East India Company to His Majesty the King of England, it only remained to find an appropriate form of government for Bengal. Called upon to lay down a policy, he began, in his characteristic manner, with an abstraction as his point of departure.

[242] To Lord North, 14 February 1777. *Francis MSS* 49 (38) 76.

[243] Weitzman, op. cit., p. 315.

[244] To Lord North, 14 February 1777. *Francis MSS* 53 (49) 40.

The key word in his agrarian programme was 'permanence'; in his political settlement, it was 'simplicity'. All that he had learnt from the French philosophers warned him about the evils of 'governing too much'.[245] His cultivated aversion to state interference and positive laws inclined him to take this view. To govern well was to govern little, and to govern little was to govern simply.

As a form of government nothing could be simpler than despotism which, as Quesnay pointed out in the very first of his celebrated maxims, could entirely dispense with the clumsy apparatus of counterbalances. The sovereign, he said, must be paramount; his authority must be held higher than any other in society, 'car l'objet de la domination et de l'obéissance est la sureté de tous et l'intérêt licite de tous'.[246] China had been for Quesnay the exemplary seat of this *autorité unique*.[247] For Francis it was Bengal, before, of course, that 'wise, simple and benevolent System of Government' had been 'completely overturned by the Company's Servants'.[248] In his plan he spoke admiringly about the 'summary and simple principles of Asiatic policy', and quite early during his stay in Bengal when he was still groping for a definition of government, he observed that 'Eastern Empires are not to be governed by intricate or refined Systems of Law or Policy'.[249] What he had in his mind was the model of a benevolent despotism, living in splendid isolation from the subject people, but sternly exacting from them obedience and tribute. This was how he recommended it to Lord North:

[245] The phrase is Diderot's: 'Il ne faut se mêler de rien; tout s'ordonne de soi-même . . . pas trop gouverner'. The same idea was expressed by d'Argenson in a famous aphorism: 'Pour gouverner mieux il faudrait gouvener moins'. See Weulersse, *La Physiocratie à la fin du règne de Louis XV*, p. 85 note, and *Les Physiocrates*, p. 182.

[246] *François Quesnay et la Physiocratie*, t. II, p. 949.

[247] See his 'Despotisme de la Chine', particularly chapter VIII, section 3. *Ibid.*, pp. 918–20. For the sources of Quesnay's information about China and other interesting observations on this work, see Maverick, *China a Model for Europe*, pp. 111–38.

[248] To Lord North, 23 March 1775. *Francis MSS* 49 (38) 17.

[249] To Clive, 21 May 1775. *Ibid.*, 47 (36) 59.

> The English Power should stand Paramount, and hold the Sword over the rest; – watching the Administration of Men in Office; – contented with a gross Tribute, and guarding the Country from being ruined in Detail by Europeans. This simple System, so natural to the Genius of the People, seems best calculated to resist an external Force and has no radical Defect within itself. The Difficulties of establishing such a System, considering all Circumstances, are undoubtedly very great; – perhaps not to be intirely surmounted; – but it may be useful to keep the Model in View and approach to it as near as we are able.[250]

This 'simple System' could be effective only on one condition: that there was no interference on the part of the ruling power in the life of its subjects. The two spheres in which Francis thought the Company's government had interfered with disastrous consequences were administration of justice and the management of the revenues. To begin with, it was the attempt to replace native laws by a foreign code and native courts by the Supreme Court of Judicature which constituted the undesirable act of intervention. The initiative in the first case came from the Governor-General himself; in the other he was a willing accomplice. It has been said of Warren Hastings that he 'believed in English interference, but along the lines of native practice'.[251] Whatever that was, he never allowed himself to be outdone by Francis in professing respect for 'the Ancient Constitution' of the country. Tactfully – almost apologetically, one might say – he referred to his own judicial reforms as a minimal adjustment. His critics were assured that it was not his intention to go beyond 'such modifications and such only as were absolutely necessary to accommodate it ['the ancient constitution of Bengal'] to the genius and principles of our own'.[252] This, Francis retorted, was an absurd undertaking. 'Accommodating the forms of a simple despotic Government to the genius and principles of a most refined and perfect system

250 To Lord North, 21 November 1775. *Ibid.*, 47 (36) 82.

251 Weitzman, op. cit., p. 67.

252 Forrest, *Selections from the Letters, Despatches, and other State Papers preserved in the Foreign Department of the Government of India, 1772–1785*, vol. II, p. 456.

of civil liberty, or . . . blending the jurisprudence of the ignorant, unimproved native of Bengal, with that of, perhaps, the most enlightened and polished nation upon earth', could produce nothing but inconsistencies.[253] In trying to achieve the impossible, Hastings was rashly forcing the accumulated wisdom and experience of ages to yield to 'the crude ideas of a few foreigners (for such the English are in Bengal).'[254] The establishment of the Supreme Court of Judicature only carried the process of subversion a step further. But was it at all necessary that this should be so? Francis did not see any reason why the English legal system must be allowed to follow the British flag into Bengal. The autonomy of the native institutions could very well coexist with the sovereignty of His Majesty's Government in the country, and was in fact, its most indispensable condition. He and his partisans in the Council had often declared it as their 'most deliberate Opinion that Bengal is not tenable by Great Britain under any Form of Government which subjects the Natives generally to the British Laws or to the Jurisdiction of a British Court of Justice . . . We do not deny the Expediency of uniting every Branch of the Sovereign Power of the State in one Hand, nor do we conceive how such Sovereignty can exist but in his Majesty's person . . . But it does not appear to us that the Introduction of the British Laws or the Administration of any Laws in this Country by British Judges is a necessary Consequence of a Declaration of his Majesty's Sovereignty.'[255]

Weitzman, in commenting on Francis's objections to his opponent's judicial plan, says that 'in practice, they meant the denial to the State of the exercise of one of its most important functions – the administration of justice'.[256] The point, however, is that the physiocratic theory of state to which Francis subscribed did not attach much

[253] *Ibid.*, p. 505.

[254] *Ibid.*, p. 433. For a similar statement, also see *Sir Philip Francis's Minutes*, Introduction, p. vii.

[255] Majority Letter to Lord North, 16 May 1776. Public Records Office, T.49/10, no. 49.

[256] Weitzman, op. cit., p. 64.

importance to the administration of laws as the means of justice. The physiocrats insisted on reducing legislative activity to a minimum and on doing away altogether with what their best modern interpreter has called 'les chicanes de la jurisprudence et de la procedure'.[257] Quesnay had warned the sovereign power to be on guard against any possible abuse of positive laws which, he said, must in any case be subordinate to the 'primitive laws of society' derived from Nature itself.[258] To the extent that Francis believed the traditional form of Indian government to have been based on such 'primitive laws of society', he was being strictly logical in resisting all attempts to import positive laws from an alien source. He therefore looked upon any deviation from the 'Ancient Constitution' as harmful, while Hastings considered it as an indispensable measure of reform. Underlying this difference there was a fundamental opposition between two political theories professing very contrary views of law.

The other form of interference which Francis equally regretted was the employment of Europeans in the revenue administration of Bengal. This, he thought, was one of the many deplorable consequences of the Company's decision 'to stand forth as Diwan'.[259] The authorities at home simply did not understand that it was impossible to govern a country like Bengal 'without the Intervention of the Natives' and that the Europeans were incapable of conducting 'the Detail of Government'.[260] For his own part, he proposed a complete Indianization of the service in that very important branch which was concerned with the management of the revenues. The experience of others who had conquered and successfully ruled the country in the past, justified such a policy. 'When Nadir Shah separated four great Provinces from the Empire', he wrote to Lord North, 'he not only

[257] Weulersse, *Les Physiocrates*, p. 187.

[258] 'Despotisme de la Chine', section 19. *François Quesnay et la Physiocratie*, t. II, pp. 927–8.

[259] To H. Strachey, 23 November 1775. *Francis MSS* 53 (49) 15.

[260] To Clive, 21 May 1775. *Ibid.*, 47 (36) 59. To Lord North, 21 November 1775. *Ibid.*, 47 (36) 82.

left the Natives undisturbed in the Possession of their Lands, but would not suffer a single Persian to be employed in the Collection of Revenues. By this Policy, he certainly did not mean to relinquish any of his rights as Conqueror or Lord Paramount. The consequence was that his Tribute was well paid, and the Country flourished . . . If you mean to keep Bengal, whether for the Nation or the Company, you must not suffer a single European to be concerned in the Collection or Management of the Revenues.'[261] This, of course, could not be done at once. Otherwise, a very large number of Europeans would be suddenly thrown out of employment, and they might succeed in defeating the measure itself by resisting it. With a correspondent who had apparently been pressing for such a policy, he therefore urged moderation, but at the same time firmly pointed out that his plan, which was then already laid before the Council, was 'calculated to remove them by Degrees from any Share in the Collections, or Influence over the internal Government of the Country'.[262] The argument against employing the natives, he knew, was the familiar one of their alleged dishonesty. To this his answer was to doubt, in the first place, the assumption that the Europeans were more honest. 'From the extraordinary decline of the Revenue, since we took the direct Management of it into our own Hands, it seems probable that white Collectors are not much honester than black ones.'[263] Besides, if the native officers were found guilty of embezzlement, it would be easier to punish them than Europeans committing the same offence. But apart from all other considerations, he said, tying it up with the entire problem of economic drain, 'it makes a wide Difference to Bengal, whether Embezzlements are committed by Natives, who keep the Produce of their Roguery in the Country, or by Europeans who carry it away'.[264]

The difficulties in the revenue administration arose not merely from the employment of Europeans, but also, in a technical sense,

[261] To Lord North, 13 January 1775. *Ibid.*, 47 (36) 47.
[262] To Rous (Private), 22 June 1776. *Ibid.*, 77 (31) 8.
[263] To Clive, 21 May 1775. *Ibid.*, 47 (36) 59.
[264] To H. Strachey, 23 November 1775. *Ibid.*, 53 (49) 15.

from 'the inextricable perplexity of Mofussil accounts'. The English had taken over the system of revenue accounting from the Mahommedans. But the native terms, units, calendar and languages used for this purpose were all unfamiliar to them. Hastings was certainly not at his most knowledgeable when in his minute of 12 November 1776 he spoke of these accounts being 'kept with a regularity and precision unknown in Europe'. To this Francis retorted by a reference to an official admission of difficulty by the President and Council themselves in 1772, and to the proposal for reform made by the Committee of Circuit.[265] For once, facts were on his side.

What made the revenue records read like 'a separate Science' was, in the first place, 'a confused and affected Reference to different Oeras and to different Systems of dividing the Year'.[266] Francis wanted the Bengali and Persian modes of time-reckoning to be replaced 'by an Act of Power' in favour of the Christian calendar, 'so that the ruling power and the subjects might compute by one and the same measure of time'.[267]

By far the worse source of confusion was, however, the use of the Bengali and Persian languages in official accounts. Here, too, the remedy proposed by Francis was radical and far-sighted, though rather ahead of his times. He recommended the introduction of English as the official language for the government of Bengal. The sanction behind such a measure was simply their right of conquest, the right which, he believed, the Mughals themselves had used in promoting Persian to a similar status during their rule. However, it would not be necessary, he hoped, to force the language on the natives. They would be persuaded to learn it in their own interest, and this would

[265] *Sir Philip Francis's Minutes*, pp. 131–2, 161–2. The recommendations of the Committee of Circuit were not followed up, nor were those of Francis himself. Shore who had mastered the native accounts better than most other Englishmen of his time, wrote in his famous minute of 18 June 1789: 'Even the ablest and best will acknowledge that the perplexed details of the accounts of the ryots in Bengal, cannot be understood, without the assistance of the natives versed in them' (Firminger, vol. II, p. 51).

[266] To Lord North, 24 February 1775. *Francis MSS* 47 (36) 48.

[267] *Letter from Mr Francis to Lord North*, p. 49.

make their employment in the administration all the more effective. The idea occurs very prominently in two of Francis's letters to Lord North in 1775 and 1777, and in view of its great importance for the history of Indian education would perhaps be best stated in his own words.

> The English Language must alone be used in all accounts with the Government: as Conquerors we have a right to impose any Condition on the People which may be essentially necessary to the preservation of the Conquest. But it is unnecessary for us to impose it by Authority. The People are sensible of the great Advantage of learning English, and are universally desirous of possessing it. It is highly to the Interest of Government, in every Sense, that this Desire should be encouraged and assisted.[268]
>
> If with the Christian oera, the English language could be introduced into the transaction of business, as the Persian was by the Mughal Conqueror, I conceive it would be attended with convenience and advantage to Government and no distress or disadvantage to the natives. To qualify themselves for employment, they would be obliged to study English instead of Persian. If schools were established in the districts, with proper encouragement to the masters, a very few years would produce a set of young men of business, whose example and success would spread, and graft the institution gradually into the manners of the people. The natives would soon end it as one of the most effectual barriers against the oppression of Europeans. Every man then would be able to speak for himself, and every complaint would be understood.[269]

Francis thus was no orientalist in the sense that Warren Hastings and Sir William Jones were. 'Barbarous and unknown' were the words he used for Bengali and Persian, a description faintly echoing the Roman concept of the world beyond the imperial frontiers. He was, in this respect, Macaulay's precursor. He anticipated the latter by about sixty years in laying down for India a pattern of cultural development which prevailed until the middle of this century, and has, on the whole, survived even the withdrawal of British power

[268] To Lord North, 24 February 1775. *Francis MSS* 47 (36) 48.

[269] *Letter from Mr Francis to Lord North*, pp. 49–50.

from the country. What these two men had in common was not merely their contempt for the native languages, but even to some extent the technique of promoting the official alternative. Francis's idea of 'grafting the institution gradually' with the help of a network of schools is very reminiscent of Macaulay's 'filtration theory'. The important difference was that the latter intended English to be the medium of a broad liberal education, while for his predecessor it was to serve mainly as an instrument for the training of a large administrative cadre. History, however, was on Francis's side, and as it turned out, Macaulay's system succeeded more as a measure of mass recruitment of graduate clerks, 'young men qualified for business', than as the agent of Western enlightenment for the vast majority of the Indian people.

The ban on the employment of foreigners in the revenue service was for Francis only the first step towards the removal of European influence in the government of Bengal. This had to be followed up by firm measures against colonization. Speaking in terms of the useful distinction made by Richard Pares between 'colonies of exploitation' and 'colonies of settlement',[270] it would perhaps be correct to say that Francis did not deny the importance of the former in a very limited sense. As it has been discussed earlier in this chapter, he admitted the need for European enterprise in the plantation type of agriculture devoted primarily to commercial crops. But even then he regarded this only as a minor supplement to native cultivation. His insistence on restricting the European farmers to waste lands makes it quite clear that he had never wanted the colonies of exploitation to predominate.

In any case, his opposition to colonies of settlement was emphatic and unequivocal. It had fed deeply on the eighteenth-century French tradition of anti-colonialism, best expressed in two famous botanical analogies: one by Montesquieu comparing an empire to a tree and colonies to its branches which, if allowed to grow too much, would

[270] Pares, *The Historian's Business*, p. 56.

only drain the sap from its trunk for nourishment, but produce nothing but shade; the other by Turgot who spoke of colonies as fruits which are attached to the tree only so long as they are not mature enough. Between them, there was a whole school of opinion led by such stalwarts as Mably, Voltaire and Raynal who denounced colonialism.[271] Francis had all the authority of the *philosophes* on his side when he wrote that after the formal assumption of sovereignty by His Majesty's Government in Bengal 'our colonising here would then be as unnecessary with respect to the Security of our Conquest, as it would be dangerous if not fatal to the Mother Country.' Thus in a letter to Lord North on 24 February 1775.[272] For even less radical minds in England the events of the following year proved to be a confirmation of Turgot's pessimism. The loss of the thirteen colonies in America was for many the most conclusive evidence that colonial emancipation was historically inevitable and indeed, almost a law of nature. Adam Smith wrote of the colonies as a most unwholesome liability, and Josiah Tucker hailed the fiasco at Yorktown as 'one of the happiest events that ever happened to Great Britain'. Even Arthur Young who, unlike these, was not quite a free trader, lectured to the Abbé Raynal on the virtues of separatism.[273] Francis, therefore, was well on the side of the angels when in introducing the first edition of his *Original Minutes* in 1782 he went out of his way to warn the government against the possible dangers of a European settlement in Bengal.

> As a question at last, it deserves to be considered, whether it may not be essential not only to the internal prosperity of the country, but to its dependence on Great Britain, that the Europeans in Bengal should be limited to as small a number as the services of the Government will

[271] Montesquieu, *Lettres Persanes*, no. 121. Lokke. *France and the Colonial Question*, pp. 35–49, 70–5.

[272] *Francis MSS* 47 (36) 48.

[273] Schuyler. *The Fall of the Old Colonial System*, pp. 66–7. Bodelsen, *Studies in Mid-Victorian Imperialism*, pp. 13–14. Young, *Travels in France* (ed. Bentham-Edwards), pp. 261–2.

admit of . . . The increase of Europeans in Bengal . . . necessarily tends to fix them there for ever. They become colonists in effect; because, in a very great number, a great majority cannot hope or expect to return with fortune or independence to the mother country. Their connexions with it are gradually dissolved, and their attachment to it declines in the same proportion. When once they shall have multiplied to a certain point, it is in the course and nature of things, that Bengal will neither pay tribute nor obedience to England. We are not intitled to conclude from any experience that we actually possess, that Bengal may not be lost by other means besides those of a foreign invasion and conquest.[274]

It should be added that Francis's objection to colonies of settlement extended beyond his Indian career and beyond Bengal. He was one of those who in 1804 opposed all official grants to Wilberforce's settlement in Sierra Leone.[275] In India, this turned out to be still another issue of dispute between him and Warren Hastings. The latter had in his plan of April 1775 actually recommended European settlement in the Twenty-four Parganas, which he hoped would encourage 'an accession of inhabitants from foreign countries, and . . . in time become an addition of strength to the British Empire in India'.[276] But it was Francis's policy which came to stay in the Bengal administration when in 1789 Lord Cornwallis himself threw the full weight of his opinion in its favour.[277]

Francis was opposed to 'an addition of strength to the British Empire in India' not only in terms of an increase in the number of European settlers, but also territorially. He was to earn quite a reputation in later life as an avowed enemy of all wars and expansion. The conduct of his own nation in the Peninsular War was denounced by him as a series of mistakes, while at the same time he urged that someone must 'drive the French out of Germany,

[274] *Sir Philip Francis's Minutes*, Introduction, pp. ii–iv.

[275] *P.D.*, vol. II, p. 968.

[276] *Sir Philip Francis's Minutes*, pp. 4–5.

[277] To C.O.D., 6 March 1789. Ross, *Correspondence of Charles, First Marquis of Cornwallis*, vol. I, p. 550.

Holland, Flanders, and Spain, and shut them up . . . within their boundary as it was limited by the treaty of 1763'.[278] In the House of Commons he was the most relentless critic of Wellesley's campaigns against the Marathas.[279] Earlier, in 1792, Cornwallis, who knew his susceptibilities well enough, had wondered whether Francis might not take it upon himself to 'represent our interference in the affairs of Assam as a continuation of our spirit of ambition and conquest'.[280] But his record as a conscientious objector goes back to the time when he was a member of the Bengal Council. In almost every debate on foreign policy he condemned Hastings as a war-monger who had violated treaties contracted with the native powers and committed the Company to costly strife all over the country.[281] The only addition to British dominion he was happy about was that of Benares, because it was 'to acquire revenue without territory'. In the sense that Hastings had already invented the technique of expansion which Wellesley was to develop further by his system of 'subsidiary alliances' and that Francis was equally opposed to both, his anti-imperialism may be said to have been distinguished by a singular consistency which never weakened for a whole quarter of a century. By contrast, his own policy was one of deliberate self-containment: 'to preserve the peace of India within itself, to be content with what we possess, to adhere to our treaties with the country powers, and to convince them, by a fair and honourable conduct that we have really abandoned every idea of enlarging our establishment, or extending our influence in India at their expence.'[282]

What was the future of such an empire left to provide for itself among the alien people who were its constituents, insulated against any direct contact within the power that owned it, and strictly

[278] P. & M., II. pp. 368–9, 371, 377.

[279] Weitzman, op. cit., pp. 199–201.

[280] Cornwallis to Dundas, 10 December 1792. Ross, op. cit., vol. II, p. 187.

[281] Weitzman, op. cit., pp. 83–91.

[282] *Sir Philip Francis's Minutes*, Introduction, p. ii.

forbidden to expand itself? Francis had only the most pessimistic answer to offer. The dominion which England had acquired in Bengal was like a stranded whale washed ashore by the waves to the great embarrassment of its captors. In order to prevent it from doing any mischief, it had to be held fast to the ground by an intricate mesh of policy inhibiting all movement. But there was no doubt that the monster would perish in captivity. Francis was a prophet of doom in predicting that an empire like that must inevitably wither away. 'Bengal, even under the best European government', he said, 'must be from the necessary effect of its political situation, a declining country. The ruin of distant provinces, so circumscribed, might be accelerated by abuses, or retarded by prudence and honesty in the administration of its government; but sooner or later it must happen.'[283] Ironically enough, this was a perspective he shared in common with Hastings. Surely Firminger read too much into the latter's use of the expression: 'the British Empire in India'?[284] Francis, too, had used it on innumerable occasions and in precisely the same sense, that is, in the simple eighteenth-century meaning of the word 'empire' as a dominion. Francis, it has been said, did not realize that British 'paramountcy was inevitable' in India.[285] But nor did Warren Hastings. In a letter to Elliott, written on 10 February 1777, Hastings expressed his pessimism in exactly the same terms and almost the same words as his adversary. 'The dominion exercised by the British Empire', he observed, 'is fraught with many radical and incurable defects, besides those to which all human institutions are liable, arising from the distance of its scene of operations, the impossibility of furnishing it at all times, with those aids which it requires from home, and the difficulty of reconciling its primary exigencies with those which in all States ought to take place of every other concern, the interests of the people who are subjected to its authority. All

[283] *P.H.E.*, vol. 29, p. 1547. Also see *Sir Philip Francis's Minutes*, Introduction, p. v.

[284] Firminger, vol. I, p. ccxcvi, n.

[285] Weitzman, op. cit., p. 86.

that the wisest institutions can effect in such a system can only be to improve the advantages of a temporary possession, and to protract that decay, which sooner or later must end it.'[286] If in spite of this he still undertook measures that eventually helped in the progressive enlargement of England's empire in India, it was because as a practical administrator he was not, like Francis, prepared to sacrifice immediate interests for the sake of a philosophical attitude. As for the inevitability of imperial development, this was a nineteenth-century invention fondly ascribed to Hastings by his Victorian admirers, but of which he had not the slightest idea himself.

[286] Gleig, *Memoirs of the Life of Warren Hastings*, vol. II, pp. 149–50.

5

The Progress of the Doctrine

FRANCIS'S PLAN OF 1776 WAS defeated in the Calcutta Council. He returned home to England five years later. After that his name became associated with a number of lost causes like the impeachment of Warren Hastings, the reform movement and the agitation against slave trade. The notoriety he earned in these controversies appears to have obscured his Indian record in the minds of his contemporaries. Consequently, when his policy came to achieve its final legislative triumph in the Bengal Regulations of 1793, he had the mortification to see the bouquets being passed over his head to others. He therefore owed it to himself – modesty never being his strong point – to remind Parliament from time to time of his own claim to credit. Thus in 1792 on hearing from Dundas about the decision to make the Decennial Settlement permanent he said that 'he had earnestly recommended this plan himself, so long ago as the year 1776 . . . by which other persons had profited and for which he had never received either thanks or credit'.[1] Among these 'other persons' the one he considered most guilty of pirating his ideas was Lord Cornwallis. Speaking only a few months after the latter's death in favour of an official motion in Parliament for a memorial to the late Governor-General, Francis did not consider it in the least inopportune to refer to the Permanent Settlement of Bengal and ask the House to consider 'whether this is not the very

[1] *P.H.E.*, vol. 29, p. 1546.

plan which I proposed in 1776, and which Lord Cornwallis has done me the honour to adopt and execute'.[2] If any honour was done at all, it must have been quite unintended on the part of Cornwallis, who had an intense dislike for Francis.[3] But with all his senile and pathetic egotism and the bad taste of bargaining for acknowledgment *post factum* Francis was still quite right in regarding the new agrarian policy for Bengal as the fulfilment of his vision of 1776.

1. The Act of 1784 and the Dilemma of Macpherson's Government

To this end the contribution of Pitt's India Act was by no means decisive. If it helped at all this was only in a negative sense, that is, as an open admission of the failure of Hastings's system and of the need for a radical change. How exactly this change was to be brought about was nowhere stated in this Act except in very vague terms which fell short even of the provisions of Fox's abortive East India Bill. On the central question of land revenues, it went no farther than to express an undefined bias in favour of a permanent settlement with the zamindars. It gave no lead on the problems of hereditary rights and unalterability of the fiscal demand without which such a settlement could not possibly work.[4] In this sense the Act of 1784 was indeed, as

[2] *P.D.*, vol. 6, p. 123. About a year later Francis took it up again with the *Edinburgh Review* which had in the course of a book review mentioned Cornwallis and Shore as the architects of the Permanent Settlement. Francis wrote in protest: 'On the third of February 1806, when it was proposed in the House of Commons to erect a monument to Lord Cornwallis, the sole exclusive merit of giving the Natives a fixed and certain property in the Lands they cultivated, was attributed to him by Lord Castlereagh and Mr Charles Grant. If you will consult the debates of that day, you will see in what terms I asserted my original right to the principle and plan; which his Lordship received and adopted from *me*.' 'To the Authors of the Edinburgh, Review for April 1807', *Francis MSS* 54 (54) 58.

[3] For some of his uncomplimentary remarks about Philip Francis, see Ross, op. cit., vol. I, p. 409, and vol. II, p. 187.

[4] The Court of Directors were required by this Act to give orders 'for settling and establishing, upon principles of moderation and justice, according

Mill observes, even less than a palliative. To at least one sworn enemy of the plan for a permanent settlement, James Grant, it seemed at the time that the Act had called for no change at all in the existing policy, but on the contrary confirmed his own views[5] which, as we know, were opposed to everything that Francis stood for.

But such limitations did not prevent the Directors from using the Act of 1784 as the thin end of the wedge. In their letter of 12 April 1786, they reproduced all the more important points of Francis' criticism of the farming system and laid down the central recommendation of his plan of 1776 as the basis of a new policy. They referred to the country having been 'drained by farmers', the impoverishment of the zamindars, the ruinous drive for maximization of the revenue and its result – outstanding arrears. The failure of Hastings' five-year settlement was pointed out as a useful lesson. And from all this followed the first official directive to proceed to a permanent settlement: 'It is our intention that the Jumma now to be formed, shall, as soon as it can have received our approval and ratification, be considered as the permanent and unalterable Revenue of our territorial possessions in Bengal.'[6]

Meanwhile, within the Indian administration itself the idea of permanent settlement was making headway independently of what either Parliament or the Court of Directors had to say about it. During the last five years of Hastings's rule, when Francis had already left Bengal, the idea did not perhaps for obvious reasons openly manifest itself. But there can be no doubt about the fact that even then some of the ablest and most influential officers of the Company had already made up their mind about the superiority of the plan of 1776 to

to the laws and constitutions of India, the permanent rules by which the tributes, rents, and services of the Rajas, Zemindars, Poligars, Talukdars and other native landholders should in future be rendered and paid to the United Company'.

[5] Grant, op. cit., p. 13.

[6] Law, *Correspondence of the Honourable Court of Directors of the East India Company and of the Governor-General in Council respecting the Permanent Settlement of the Land Revenue*, p. 3.

the existing system. The most convincing evidence we have of this is John Shore's memorial of 13 January 1782 which he had drawn up for Macpherson.[7] Originally it was 'not meant for the public eye' and this for very good reasons. So long as Hastings remained in power, it would have been most unwise for an officer serving under him to come out with an explicit contradiction of his policy. Tolerance was certainly not one of his virtues. It was only after he left that Macpherson, who succeeded him in office, produced the document at a meeting of the Council in May 1785.

The two problems discussed by Shore in his paper are both indicated in its title: 'Remarks on the Mode of Administering Justice to the Natives in Bengal and on the Collection of the Revenues'. His censure of the existing system of government in all its important aspects, his

[7] *Proceedings, Revenue Department, G.G.C.*, 18 May 1785. The greater part of this memorial is still unpublished. Neither Hunter nor Firminger mentions it. Ascoli alone of all modern scholars seems to have been acquainted with this document: he quotes three lines from it without, however, a reference to his source (*Early Revenue History of Bengal*, p. 36). It was also known to John Stonhouse who refers to it in his anonymous pamphlet, *Thoughts on the Expedience of Settling Permanent Leases with the Landholders in Bengal, Bahar, and Orissa* (p. 42), published in 1792. Stonhouse was the Head Revenue Assistant to Thomas Law's friend, W.A. Brooke, Collector of Shahabad. The association suggests that during the early days of Cornwallis's rule those among the district officials who favoured a permanent settlement had already come to know all about the debates in Macpherson's Council and were looking upon Shore's minute as a kind a rallying point.

Shore's biographer too had seen the memorial and published three large extracts from it (Teignmouth, *Life of Lord Teignmouth*, vol. I, pp. 73–4, 485–8). But the title and the date he gave to the document both differ from those in the original. The title as given in the *Proceedings of the Governor-General in Council* is 'Remarks on the Mode of Administering Justice to the Natives in Bengal and on the Collection of the Revenues', and not as the biographer has it, 'Memoir on the Administration of Justice and Collection of Revenues'. The biographer's date is 1785; the correct date is 13 January 1782. For a detailed discussion of the origins and contents of this memorial, see R. Guha, 'An Administrative Blueprint of 1785', in *Bengal Past and Present*, vol. LXXIV, part 1, no. 138.

criticism of the Supreme Court of Judicature, his plea for a simple and despotic form of administration and the justification of reform as a defensive measure against foreign invasion and native rebellion are all reminiscent of Philip Francis. But it is on the problem of land revenue that their views show the greatest, though not complete, agreement. 'It is a very capital defect in this Government', says Shore, 'that no system is permanent.' So far as the system applied to the management of revenues, 'it is fundamentally bad'. He examines the apparatus of collections at central and local levels, and then goes on to recommend a new mode of settlement on the following lines.

> It may be pronounced that upon the whole the zemindars who have the greatest rights are also the properest persons for the management of the revenues of their own districts . . .
>
> I therefore propose that the settlement be made with the zemindars themselves and that the amount of the jumma be irrevocably fixed during the lifetime of the zemindar.
>
> The assessment should also be moderate, and in that case the zemindar should be compelled to pay it, taking upon himself all profits and losses. If the assessment is excessive there will be either a necessity to admit an abatement in case of loss, or the lands must be sold.

Francis would have approved of each of these proposals except one. There is no departure here from his own ideas about (a) the zamindars being the rightful proprietors, (b) the need for an unalterable revenue demand, and (c) the importance of a moderate assessment. Shore differed only by limiting the period of settlement to a lifetime.

It is by encouraging such bold thinking and bringing it out in the open that the Act of 1784 helped in the progress of the idea of permanent settlement. However, during the brief period which intervened between the proclamation of the Act in India and the arrival of the Directors' letter of April 1786, the ambiguities of the clause relating to zamindars were used in support of each of the rival schools of thought on this matter. The conflict between those who wanted to go forward to a conclusive deal in favour of the zamindars and those who for want of a better argument favoured a more conservative approach on grounds of expediency is clearly illustrated in a debate in Macpherson's Council in the summer of 1785.[8]

The occasion of the debate was a 'Plan for Collecting the Revenues' submitted by Charles Stuart, a member of the Council. In drawing up the plan, he said, he had 'attended to the spirit of the 39th Article of the late Act of Parliament in favour of the rights of Zemindars', and his recommendations bear this out. In the first place, he proposed that a revenue settlement should be made with 'every Zemindar who is not totally incapable', and in case of a zamindar being a minor or a female or otherwise considered incompetent, with a near relative or with an old servant of the family. Significantly enough, he did not ask, 'Who owns the land?' It is perhaps correct to interpret this silence to mean that by 1785 there were already a number of high officials in Bengal to whom the need for a zamindari settlement was beyond question. After the hopeless experience of the farming system they were convinced of the advantage of a change-over to what seemed at that time to be the only other alternative. They were eager to give this policy an immediate trial and did not find it necessary to seek legal or traditional justification in Hindu and Islamic law-books or in the opinions of RoyRoyans and Kanungoes. Among the officers trusted by Cornwallis to collect for him local data on which alone the final decision about a long-term policy was to depend, those who like Shore searched for precedents in native custom and history were far outnumbered by less academically inclined men like Stuart who were biased *a priori* in favour of the zamindars. No wonder that the information they produced was of a singularly one-sided character, enough to satisfy the Governor-General about the correctness of his predetermined course of policy but still found unconvincing by the astute President of the Board of Revenue.

Secondly, Stuart recommended that the settlement with zamindars should be permanent. It was to remain experimental for the first year only 'until we receive the orders of the Court of Directors

[8] *Proceedings, Revenue Department, G.G.C.*, 10 and 18 May 1785. For a discussion of this debate, see the article mentioned above.

upon the 39th Clause of the late Act of Parliament. But after that it will be proper to fix the Jumma unalterably during the lifetime of the zemindar.'

Thirdly, the rate of assessment for the new settlement should be the average of collections for the three years from 1773–4 to 1775–6. 'From the best information I have been able to obtain', he wrote, 'this was considered very equitable jumma.' He was, however, ready to allow a certain amount of flexibility in the rate of assessment and added a note to say that officers making the settlement need not be bound rigidly by this rate, but should only take the three years' average as 'the basis of all their settlements'.

Finally, Stuart proposed to enforce the payment of revenue in regular instalments (*kists*) on pain of public sale of a part of each defaulting estate.

A settlement according to these principles, he thought, would benefit both landlords and tenants. It would be in every respect superior to the existing policy based on short-term leases which tended to make the zamindar as oppressive as the ordinary farmer. 'At present', he observed, 'the Zemindar collects the utmost his country can produce, and consequently rackrents his tenants. Could he be assured that Government would not raise their demands upon him, it would be his interest to encourage improvements. He would grow rich himself. The people under him would be happy.' The classic illusion of the Permanent Settlement! As is well known from subsequent developments, nothing of the sort happened. The zamindar did indeed grow rich but only at the expense of the people under him. For neither Stuart's plan nor its perfected prototype of 1793 provided any effective safeguard for the peasantry against rack-renting.

The Governor-General's reply to this plan was weak and unconvincing. But its interest lies precisely in its half-hearted conservatism. Macpherson said that he knew about the controversy between Hastings and Francis, who 'patronised different and opposite systems', and John Shore's memorial of 1782 had indeed been written for him. But he did not want 'any sudden or abrupt changes.' He was shy of originality, and preferred to drift until more specific instructions were sent from England. 'When I succeeded in February last to the charge of my present office', he said, 'I laid down as a general and necessary principle to avoid innovation in the system of government, to endeavour to conduct the public affairs in the train in which they had devolved upon me.' But he would not insist even on this. Should the majority of the Council differ with him and consider Stuart's plan good enough for immediate adoption, he would not, he said, stand in their way, but give them his entire support in spite of all personal disagreement. As an example of vacillation this has no parallel in the history of the omnipotent governor-generalships of the eighteenth century. But it shows, above all, the dilemma of an administration which had lost all initiative in the face of a radical change.

A government thus divided in its interpretation of the Act of 1784 could hardly be expected to guide policy with firmness and decision. The revenue settlement of the year immediately following the Act was, therefore, full of inconsistencies. To begin with, the Committee of Revenue formulated six guiding principles for the settlement of 1785–6 and forwarded them for the approval of the Governor-General in Council.[9] Here the Committee proposed a settlement with the zamindars for an initial period of one year 'with an assurance however that the duration of it shall be extended from year to year so long as he continues to pay up his stipulated revenue'. But this apparent bias in favour of the zamindars was counterbalanced by the recommendation that lands which had been settled with ijaradars the previous year should be 'kept on the same footing'. The Committee, of course, adds in anticipation of doubt that 'the proportion of land thus possessed in farm by persons not being zemindars is at present small' – a most amazing statement – and that 'the Hon'ble Board may rest satisfied that it shall not be unadvisedly augmented'. Reduced to plain language the Committee's proposal amounted to a limited extension of zamindari settlement at the expense of the *khas*

[9] Letter from Committee of Revenue to G.G.C., dated 31 March 1785. *Proceedings, Revenue Department, G.G.C.*, 22 April 1785.

sector directly under official management, but without any substantial modification of the farming system. But even this modest concession in principle was apparently not allowed by the Committee to influence its practice. For in almost every case demanding a revision of settlement for the ensuing year the Committee firmly set aside the claims of the zamindars and recommended either direct management or farming.

On being taken up for consideration by the Council these proposals touched off a fresh round of controversy there.[10] Its decisions showed how on a vital economic problem the Act of 1784 had set the cabinet in total opposition to its most important subordinate department. The latter had suggested the exclusion of zamindars in every case where a settlement had to be revised. The districts affected were Bishnupur, Chandradwip, Jahangirpur, Jalalpur and Nadia. In each case the Council reversed the decision in favour of the hereditary proprietors or their nearest kin. But any impression this might give of unanimity at the leading centre of the government or of its firmness must be at once corrected by a reference to the debate itself and its self-contradiction on matters of policy. On 6 June 1785 Governor-General Macpherson and his colleagues met to consider two documents each of which demanded, in its own way, an answer to questions raised by the recent Act. The first was a letter from the Committee of Revenue containing two sharply formulated queries:

> 1st – Whether the Rule . . . prescribed in favour of the Zemindars is to be considered as ipso facto annulling the engagements entered into last year, by which the faith of Goverment stands pledged to many farmers not being Zemindars to continue them under certain conditions in the possession of their respective farms, those conditions having been on their parts truly and completely fulfilled?

[10] The sources for this and the subsequent paragraph are: letter from the Committee of Revenue (25 May 1785); letter from F. Redfearn, Collector of Nadia (29 May 1785); minutes of Mr Stables and the Governor-General; and the Council's letter to the Committee of Revenue in *Proceedings, Revenue Department, G.G.C.*, 6 June 1785.

> 2ndly – 'Whether the Committee are to exercise a discretionary power of excluding the Zemindars from the management of their lands, where these may be deemed wholly unqualified for the trust?

The other document before the Council was a letter from the Collector of Nadia. Less circumspect than the Committee of Revenue in his bias for a settlement with ijaradars, he had sent up to the Council two statements entitled 'Objections against putting the Zemindar of Nuddea in Possession' and 'Reasons for Continuing the Present System'. The zamindar, he argued, was bankrupt, oppressive and deceitful. The farmers, on the contrary, were 'in general very responsible men' who had been paying to the government at a progressively increasing rate every year. He, too, took up the point of honour emphasized by the Committee of Revenue that 'the faith of Government is solemnly pledged for the continuance of the present farmers from year to year for 4 more years'.

In the debate which followed contrary inclinations clashed exactly as they had done in the Council less than a month before over Stuart's plan. Only it was Mr Stables this time who came forward as the spokesman of the positive view. 'The Act of Parliament', he said, 'has stepped in favour of the Zemindars . . . To let the lands in farm ought to be in the last extremity.' He saw nothing in the given circumstances to justify the exclusion of the zamindar of Nadia. To this Macpherson replied by expressing his doubt about the competence of the zamindar, but added characteristically that since Mr Stables wanted the 'experiment', he would not oppose a settlement with the Raja of Nadia. On the basic questions raised by the Committee of Revenue, too, he was not very helpful, saying, as he did, two contradictory things in the same breath: first, 'that every farmer possessing under the Company's seal a farm granted to him for a fixed period of years . . . cannot be legally dispossessed of his farm, nor is it the meaning of the Act of Parliament that such engagements should be broken'; and secondly, 'that the engagements to farmers which were not for more than one year, and which only contain a clause for continuation from year to year . . . are not to stand in opposition to the claims of the zemindars'. But what was to happen if an engagement with farmers contained an element of each of these conditions, which were by no means mutually exclusive? The case of the Nadia farmers was evidently one where the government had committed itself to continue the leases from year to year for a fixed period of five years. Did not, then, the Governor-General contradict himself by authorizing a settlement with the zamindar ? He did, and the farmers knew it. So we find them pressing home their demand for retention in a statement addressed to the Council and claiming compensation to the amount of Rs 400,000 in case the government should decide to cancel their leases. Happily for Macpherson the dilemma was resolved by the zamindar himself declining the settlement[11] and thus leaving in this particular district the loose ends of the Act of 1784 dangling in the air for still another term.

2. Lord Cornwallis and the Idea of Improvement

Exactly eight weeks after Cornwallis's arrival in India Shore wrote the following epitaph on Macpherson's regime: 'Never was any administration so thoroughly despicable as his: a total want of energy, dignity, and common sense distinguish it. Evasion was substituted for decision; caution and hesitation, instead of action. Natives and Europeans universally exclaim that Lord Cornwallis's arrival is the salvation of the country.'[12] It is difficult to say how the natives actually felt about all this; they had seen quite a few changes of command since 1765 without particularly benefiting from any of them, and how after all, in terms of their own experience, was Macpherson's rule

[11] For the petition signed by twenty-two farmers of Nadia, the names of the parganas represented by them and the Council's final resolution adopted after the zamindar's withdrawal, see *Proceedings, Revenue Department, G.G.C.*, 22 June 1785.

[12] To W. Bensley (13 November 1786). Teignmouth, op. cit., vol. I, pp. 128–9.

any worse than Hastings's? Property had been equally insecure under both. If it was true, as Shore himself was to point out in his celebrated minutes three years later, that the natives had no confidence left in the government whatsoever and would not trust even a declaration of Permanent Settlement, then it could not be that in 1786 they had looked upon the new Governor-General as a messiah. Shore was, however, quite right in representing, in the manner he did, the widespread sense of past exasperation and actual relief among the senior European officials in Bengal at that time. They all hailed the arrival of Cornwallis as the signal for decisive action. Decision was badly wanted indeed. For in spite of the Act of 1784, in spite of the Directors' letter of 12 April 1786, there was no sign yet of a sharp and complete break with the past. Even as late as 21 August 1786, that is only three weeks before Cornwallis was to disembark, the Council had written to the Court expressing great satisfaction about the state of the revenues and promising, evidently under Grant's influence, a still higher rate of assessment in the future.[13] Such notions inherited from the 1770s had to be rejected once for all, the dead roots of the farming system removed from the administration, and the foundations of the new order laid down with a firm, determined hand. For Shore and his colleagues 12 September 1786 was the first historic date in a reformed calendar.

For an assignment like this Cornwallis was admirably suited, if not by any remarkable understanding of the issues involved, at least by temperament. Resoluteness was his most outstanding quality. The strategy had been clearly laid down by Parliament and the Court of Directors and even some important details of tactical direction indicated. True he had no knowledge of the terrain at all, but he could depend for that on his highly experienced staff. All he had to do was to assume command, organize the administration into a task force, and throw them into action. The way he set about his work

[13] Letter no. 12 in *General Letters to the Court of Directors, Revenue Department*, vol. 6.

and the single-minded zeal with which he pressed forward to his objective – the declaration of Permanent Settlement – shows that having lost a campaign in America, he was determined to win the one on his hands in India. Already by December 1787, he was confidently writing to the home authorities about 'the permanent arrangement intended in the ensuing year'.[14] But unforeseen difficulties were in his way. The accounts which he had ordered to be collected as early as February 1787 were not ready even at the beginning of the fiscal year 1788-9, and 'it was with real reluctance', he reported, 'we found ourselves under the necessity of postponing the arrangement till the ensuing year'.[15] Then Shore suddenly fell ill, and since no policy could be formulated without his active participation it looked for a while as if the timetable was going to be completely upset.[16] But the cloud passed. We learn from the next letter home that Shore had recovered in time to deliver his long-awaited minute on the subject of settlement, and now that everything was in order the Governor-General had no doubt that he could 'proceed without delay to carry into execution such resolutions as may be finally determined upon for the conclusion of the Settlement without Waiting for the expiration of the present Bengal year'.[17] But again he proved too optimistic. When the document on which he had counted so much was taken up by the Council for discussion next month, it became quite clear that his views on the subject of Permanent Settlement were fundamentally opposed to those of his chief adviser. In his two minutes of 18 September 1789 Shore insisted that the government must not commit itself to any permanent arrangement except on the basis of further experience and that meanwhile it should proceed to a settlement with the zamindars for ten years only. Cornwallis had

[14] Letter no. 25 of 15 December 1787. *Ibid.*

[15] Letter to Court of Directors, 6 November 1788. Ross, op. cit., vol. I, p. 548.

[16] Letter to C.O.D., no. 31 of 10 March 1789. *General Letters to the Court of Directors*, vol. 6.

[17] Letter to C.O.D., no. 32 of 10 August 1789. *Ibid.*

not expected the brakes to be suddenly applied in this fashion. He had no patience for any further delay. 'What is the experience that is wanting,' he asked, 'and what, by delaying a permanent settlement for a few years, would probably be improved?' To postpone it in favour of a decennial lease, he said, would ruin and impoverish the country. His own judgment coincided with his sense of mission as he affirmed: 'As I have a clear conviction in my own mind of the utility of the system, I shall think it a duty I owe to them (that is, the Court of Directors), to my country, and to humanity, to recommend it most earnestly to the Court of Directors to lose no time in declaring the permanency of the settlement . . . and not to postpone for ten years the commencement of the prosperity and solid improvement of the country.'[18] The differences were referred to the home authorities. Meanwhile, the argument went on in the Council. In a further statement Shore developed what had at the outset looked like a modest amendment, into a devastating attack on the very fundamentals of the policy. Cornwallis, however, remained unshaken. 'I will not call it ten years settlement', he said.[19] Eventually, three years after the controversy had begun, the Directors in their despatch of 19 September 1792 gave their verdict. 'We shall be happy', they said in concluding that letter drafted for them by Pitt and Dundas, 'that Lord Cornwallis . . . sees no reason to deny himself the happiness of announcing a new constitution to so many millions of the Asiatic subjects of Great Britain.'[20] In March 1793 the decennial settlements of Bengal and Bihar were declared permanent.

The determination with which Cornwallis pursued the aims of the policy set out for him by the Court of Directors has sometimes been interpreted in a manner that does him little justice. He has far too often been portrayed as a machine operated by remote control

[18] Minute of 18 September 1789. Firminger, vol. II, pp. 510–15.

[19] Letter to N. Smith, 9 November 1789. Ross, op. cit., vol. I, p. 462.

[20] For the authorship of this letter, see Kaye, *The Administration of the East India Company*, p. 183n.

from Leadenhall Street, as a mindless giant whose only function was to execute his masters' orders. To some extent this prejudice must have been the product of a mental comparison which all students of the period are inclined to make between him and the two other men whose names are closely associated with the policy of Permanent Settlement: that is, Philip Francis and John Shore. Both were distinguished by their originality. This was a quality for which Cornwallis was never known, and even his contemporary admirers had noted it.[21] But mediocrity does not necessarily mean vacuity. He concentrated on carrying out the given policy not because he had no ideas of his own, but because they did not contradict it. He defended it against Shore not by loading his argument with the weight of his authority, but on the strength of his convictions. He genuinely believed in the correctness of the plan for Permanent Settlement because it conformed to his own experience and his understanding about the needs of an agrarian society. Mill puts his finger on the right spot, but as usual ruins his argument by the use of exaggerated language, when he suggests that Cornwallis was in this respect inspired by 'aristocratical prejudices'.[22] This phrase has provoked many writers to bark up the wrong tree in Cornwallis's defence. Some have weakly suggested that after all he only reflected an attitude almost universal in the Bengal administration at that time; others have gone to the extent of maintaining that he had no such inclinations at all. To take one author each from the last century and this, Wilson and Weitzman may be said to represent the first view, and Law and Ascoli the other.[23] But what are all these apologetics for? To say that Cornwallis's opinions were shared by others in the Company's service is no answer to Mill. To say, on the other hand,

[21] See, for instance, Law, *A Sketch*, p. xiv.

[22] Mill, *The History of British India*, vol. V, pp. 340–1, 348, and Book VI, Ch. V *passim*.

[23] Wilson's note in Mill, vol. V, p. 348. Weitzman, op. cit., p. 197. Law, *Correspondence*, pp. 66, 68, 70, 72. Ascoli, op. cit., p. 67.

that Cornwallis was not biased in favour of the zamindar class would be to suggest that he advocated a permanent settlement merely for practical reasons as just the best policy, and this of course cannot be proved: had this been so, he would have no ground whatsoever for difference with Shore.

One has only to turn to his recorded statements to see how, in fact, he wanted a *restoration* of the native landed aristocracy. The good society in which he believed was of the same pyramidal structure as the one outlined by Francis, consisting of 'a regular gradation of ranks' with the propertied class holding the vital middle position. This assumption underlies much of what he has to say against Shore's view that the zamindars were worthless and incompetent. Cornwallis did not deny the fact, but maintained that their degeneration was the result of the existing system which had deprived them of property and thereby ruined their potentialities; 'under the influence of another, founded upon very different principles' they were sure to improve.[24] Even more explicit on this point was his letter of 2 August 1789 to the Court of Directors. He wrote,

> ... independent of all other considerations, I can assure you that it will be of the utmost importance for promoting the solid interests of the Company, the principal landholders and traders in the interior parts of the country should be restored to such circumstances as to enable them to support their families with decency, and to give a liberal education to their children according to the customs of the irrespective castes and religions – that a regular gradation of ranks may be supported, which is nowhere more necessary than in this country for preserving order in civil society.[25]

Thus there can be no doubt with which particular class Cornwallis most sympathized. It is, however, far more important to point out that in pleading for the zamindars he assigned to them a function altogether

[24] Minute, 3 February 1790. Firminger, vol. II, p. 532.
[25] Ross, vol. I, p. 554.

different from their traditional role in Indian society. Thomas Law wondered why Cornwallis should be suspected of having favoured the aristocracy when, in fact, he took away from the zamindars many of their former prerogatives such as 'the power originally exercised of collecting transit duties, and all kinds of impositions, and of deciding in civil cases'.[26] The truth is that he wanted to reform the old Bengali zamindar by depriving him of his feudal privileges and to convert him, by education and the gift of property, into an improving landlord after the contemporary English model. In this respect, again, his policy was a faithful, if not conscious, imitation of the plan of 1776; only he developed the anti-feudal implications of Francis's ideas to their logical conclusion. The way in which the doctrine of Permanent Settlement shed all its earlier ambiguities and within fifteen years emerged as a clear definition of capitalist aims in agriculture provides still another historical argument against the notion, held by writers like M. Beer,[27] that the physiocrats, like the devil himself, had their feet turned backwards.

It was from a purely physiocratic position that Cornwallis, like Pattullo and Francis before him, proceeded to argue the case in favour of Permanent Settlement. Agriculture, and not commerce, he said, was the primary source of Bengal's wealth. His statement on the subject in a letter written to the Court of Directors a fortnight before the formal proclamation of Permanent Settlement must be regarded as a measure of the decline of mercantilist influence on Indian economic policy since Hastings's time. 'Although agriculture and commerce promote each other', he wrote, 'yet in this country, more than in any other, agriculture must flourish before its commerce can be extensive. The materials for all the most valuable manufactories are the produce of its own lands. It follows therefore that the extent of its commerce must depend upon the encouragement given to agriculture, and that

[26] Law, *Correspondence*, p. 68.

[27] *An Inquiry into Physiocracy*. See particularly Chapter I for Beer's characterization of physiocracy as a plea 'for a return to the pre-industrial era'.

whatever tends to impede the latter, destroys the two great sources of its wealth.'[28]

The declaration of Permanent Settlement, he thought, would act as a radical incentive to agriculture. It would restore confidence in property and induce large investments of capital in land. Even as early as November 1789 he mentioned with great enthusiasm a report from Bihar that one of the wealthiest men in a certain district had already offered to purchase some lands.[29] This for him was a straw in the wind. If the mere possibility of a Permanent Settlement could produce such confidence, what great prospects might not open up when a formal announcement was made. Surely Shore was carrying his scepticism too far when in spite of such good omen he insisted that under the circumstances a declaration of Permanent Settlement would hardly restore the zamindars' faith in the government. Cornwallis, on the contrary, had no doubt at all that 'the grant of these lands at a fixed assessment will stamp a value upon them hitherto unknown'.[30] This confidence never flagged, and throughout this period he went on insisting that the Directors had only to signal their assent and the doors of a fabulous land-market would be thrown open to them and all the dormant resources of native capital brought to play. 'Landed property will acquire a value hitherto unknown in Hindoostan and the large capitals possessed by many of the natives in Calcutta which are now employed in usury or monopolizing salt and other necessaries of life will be appropriated to the more useful purposes of purchasing and improving lands.' Thus he wrote in his despatch of 12 April 1790.[31] Three years later on the eve of the historic proclamation, it was

[28] To C.O.D., 6 March 1793, para. 17. *General Letters to the Court of Directors, Revenue Department*, vol. 7. The idea, though not so clearly stated, occurs already in his minute of 3 February 1790. Firminger, vol. II, p. 541.

[29] Ross, vol. I, p. 462.

[30] Minute, 3 February 1790. Firminger, vol. II, p. 538.

[31] Para. 3. *General Letters to the Court of Directors, Revenue Department*, vol. 7. Also see letter dated 12 December 1792, para. 7. *Ibid.*

still the same unwavering optimism repeating itself in the same vein: '. . . there is every ground to expect that the large capitals possessed by the natives . . . will be applied to the purchase of landed property as soon as the tenure is declared to be secure, and they are capable of estimating what profit they will be certain of deriving from it, by the public tax upon it being unalterably fixed.'[32]

It was Cornwallis's idea that in this great agrarian revolution the zamindars should be both harbingers and principal beneficiaries. Secure in their proprietary rights they would have no hesitation in investing their wealth in land. Since the demands of the government upon them would be moderate and subject to no further alteration, they should in their own interest apply their profits to improve agriculture. 'Improvement' was a key word which frequently occurred in his minutes and correspondence. The two great objects of improvement that he had in mind were the cultivation of waste lands and the care of irrigation works. The Permanent Settlement, he predicted, would 'be the means of bringing into cultivation the very great proportion of desolate land which is to be found in almost every district' and enable 'the proprietors of the soil . . . from the profits arising from their estates to keep the embankments and reservoirs in proper repair'.[33] The cumulative result of all this would be a rise in population which the country, still suffering from the effects of the famine of 1770, so badly needed. In short, under the new economic conditions created by the Permanent Settlement, the zamindars were sure to find the 'spirit of industry and economy' of great advantage to themselves. He had, therefore, no doubt that they would turn into 'economical landlords and prudent trustees of public interest'. Shore, who had a more intimate knowledge of native society, found this image of the zamindar so utterly unrealistic that he had great difficulty, one feels from his minutes, in resisting the temptation to make fun of it. Cornwallis, on his part, knew the English landlord too

[32] Letter of 6 March 1793, para. 22. *Ibid.*

[33] Letter of 12 April 1790, para. 3. *Ibid.* See also letter of 25 January 1792, para. 8. *Ibid.*

well not to maintain that proprietorship called for enterprise; the *idea* of the zamindar as entrepreneur had, therefore, to fit the idea of property. Philip Francis's great invention had at last found a governor willing to support it by his own enthusiasm and the necessary legal sanction.

3. Thomas Law and the Doctrine in its Final Form

Cornwallis could never bring himself to admit that his policy was in fact a realization of Francis's plan of 1776. However, on many occasions he acknowledged his debt to Thomas Law in most generous terms. 'You may be assured', he wrote to Law in 1794, 'that I shall never cease to acknowledge with gratitude the lights I received from you respecting the Mocurrery system and permanent settlement.'[34]

Thomas Law belonged to that group of highly talented Collectors of Bihar who, much more readily than their colleagues in the rest of the Presidency, took their cue from the Act of 1784 to proceed towards a long-term settlement with the zamindars. Why Bihar, rather than Bengal, should have turned out to be the first testing-ground of Permanent Settlement is a question deserving consideration on its own merit. It will suffice here only to indicate that the answer must be sought in the morphological differences between their respective land systems of which Shore wrote so acutely in his first minute of 18 September 1789. Bengal had a much higher proportion of large estates than Bihar and as a result was more severely affected by the agrarian policies of Warren Hastings. To clear a way there through the ruins and rubble of all the vast dilapidated zamindaries and establish a permanent arrangement was indeed a formidable task. In Bihar, on the other hand, it was easier to make a fresh start simply because, with all the numerous transfers of smallholdings which took place there under the farming system, the basic structure of landed property remained unchanged. The high wind, they say in Bengal, hits only the trees, but spares the grass.

[34] Letter of 14 April 1794 quoted in Law, *Correspondence*, pp. 9–10.

Whatever the reason, the Bihar officers were the first to come forward with proposals formulated in terms of the new policy. As early as March 1786, that is even before the Directors' letter explaining the Act of 1784 had been despatched, the Council received and forwarded to the home authorities a memorandum from William Young,[35] who had just retired from service, communicating many observations respecting the Bahar province drawn from his own experience, and concluding with offering terms 'for the farm of the whole province for 20 years.'[36] By the end of the next year the Board of Revenue had before them a recommendation from Thomas Law that some of the lands within his collectorate should be settled with farmers for life at a reasonable rate instead of being leased out to the highest bidders. The 'experiment', as he called it,[37] did not

[35] The memorandum, dated 4 March 1786 and addressed to G.G.C., is recorded in *Proceedings, Revenue Department, G.G.C.*, vol. 96.

[36] To C.O.D., 23 March 1786. *General Letters to the Court of Directors, Revenue Department*, vol. 6. William Young was one of those district officials who responded with enthusiasm to Philip Francis's plan of 1776. He and three other members of the Patna Council – I. Sage, E. Law and E. Golding – signed a letter addressed to the Governor-General in Council on 21 May 1776 saying that they would be happy to try a mukarari settlement in Bihar. *Francis MSS* 77 (31) 3. Francis kept in touch with him and in his letter of 5 July 1778 congratulated Young for his enquiries into the state of the revenue administration. 'The Result of your Researches', wrote Francis, 'confirms me in almost all the general opinions, which I had formed long ago on the Subject of the Revenues, and on which I drew up a Plan for a Permanent Settlement early in the year 1776.' *Ibid.*, 51 (41) 41.

[37] In *An Answer to Mr Princep's Observations on the Mocurrery System* (pp. 4–5) Law describes how he came to launch the experiment. 'It was a painful observation of the evils of this [farming] system', he writes, 'that encouraged me to persevere for the attainment of a better . . . I went not on, urged by zeal alone, without having entered into the minutiae of the whole system. I translated numberless Canongoey papers, and Ryot's accounts, and every one shewed me that the Ryot always ended the year in debt, and that he was often obliged to sell his plough and cattle; I began therefore the experiment of the Mocurrery settlement in a few Pergannahs, and had the satisfaction of finding that it succeeded even beyond my expectation. From all my investigations, I found the Zemindars, Proprietors of the land; if

receive the Board's sanction at that time.[38] But soon things started moving. Throughout the following year we find him engaged in a lively correspondence with Shore about the need for a permanent settlement with the zamindars, and by 1789 he had got the Council to approve of his mukarari plan for Bihar.[39] The success of his plan made a great impression at all levels of the administration. The glowing terms in which W.A. Brooke, Collector of Shahabad, wrote about it is a measure of its influence on other district officials.[40] It went a long way in confirming the Governor-General in his ideas about the soundness of his own policy, and Law was rewarded by a seat on the Board of Revenue. A still greater tribute was paid to the power of his experiment when Shore, who contested all its major principles, singled it out for a devastating attack in one of his minutes.[41] Ill health forced Law to resign and leave India early in 1791, and the language of high commendation in which his colleagues bade him

---

however, they had not been Proprietors, it would in my opinion have been advisable to establish landholders.'

[38] Law's letter to the Board, 21 November 1787, and the Board's reply, 27 November 1787. *Proceedings. B.O.R.*, 27 November 1787.

[39] G.G.C. to C.O.D., 10 August 1789, paras. 6–7. *General Letters to the Court of Directors, Revenue Department*, vol. 6.

[40] Brooke's letter (1 April 1789) quoted in Law, *A Sketch*, pp. 38–40. John Stonhouse who was Brooke's assistant at Shahabad, wrote a pamphlet in 1792 in support of the plan for Permanent Settlement.

[41] In his *Heads of a Proposed Speech by a Proprietor upon the Policy of Renewing the Company's Monopoly etc.*, published in 1793, Law says how he 'greatly promoted the perpetual land-tax and the abolition of all feodal tolls, duties and impediments' (pp. 15–16). In the British Museum copy of this pamphlet (Cat. No. C.T. 75 [5]) there is a marginal note against these words in Law's own hand. It reads: 'I obtained this tho' opposed by Sir John Shore, Mssrs. Stuart etc.' In his tract, *An Answer*, published the following year, he came out with an explicit reference to Shore as the person 'who at first entertained not the most favorable opinion of the plan' (p. 23). For a further discussion of Shore's opposition to the Permanent Settlement, see Chapter 6 below.

farewell at that time was repeated three years later in the Council's despatch to the Court of Directors.[42] But his reputation exceeded the limits of mere administrative achievement. He had a particularly good record of service to his credit and was often complimented on it by his superiors including Shore, his severest critic. It is only when one finds Cornwallis himself acknowledging Thomas Law as 'the founder' of the Permanent Settlement[43] that one comes to realize his importance as the man who not only carried out pioneering tests for the new policy, but also armed the Governor-General with arguments to defend it against Shore.

There was much that was common between Law and Francis in their general approach to agrarian problems. Law in all his policy statements made very much the same use as his predecessor of the principles of European political economy and applied them without qualification to Indian conditions. His printed works and minutes still in manuscript are littered with quotations from Francis's favourite authors – Montesquieu, Blackstone, Turgot, Adam Smith. He had also the same passion for reasoning by deduction and the same disregard for concrete historical and geographical differences between Bengal and – to name some of the areas actually covered by his generalizations

[42] See the Council's Resolution of 21 January 1791 quoted in *Proceedings, B.O.R.*, 26 January 1791; and letter to C.O.D., 29 December 1794, para. 58 in *General Letters to the Court of Directors, Revenue Department*, vol. 7.

[43] Cornwallis's letter to Law (28 March 1796) quoted in Law, *Correspondence*, p. 10. To other contemporaries too Law was known as the brain behind the Permanent Settlement. His name figures prominently in most of the pamphlets written in this period on the land question in Bengal whether by supporters of this policy like Stonhouse or by its opponents like Neild and Prinsep. Law himself recorded his claim to credit in a number of statements in all the three pamphlets he wrote on Indian affairs after 1792, viz. *An Answer, Heads of a Proposed Speech and Correspondence.*

– Bihar, France, Spain, England, Turkey and America.[44] His language itself was at times highly evocative of the abstract manner of Philip Francis as, for instance, in the following definition of what for both was the common 'philosophy' of Permanent Settlement.

> The basis of prosperity is laid by fixing the land-tax. The exclusive right to surplus produce is the only incitement which acts constantly and universally – the only spring which keeps human labor in motion. The violation of this fundamental maxim of agrarian policy constitutes the chief objection to the holding of land by the State, by the King, by Corporate bodies etc. All manufacturers etc are maintained by the produce of the earth, which the proprietors will increase in proportion to demand. Thus the human species will multiply to the utmost . . .[45]

The real importance of Law's contribution to the doctrine of Permanent Settlement, however, lies not in what he had in common with Francis, but where he exceeded the latter. He purged the doctrine of the feudal alloy implicit in its original conception and interpreted it *exclusively* as a policy of capitalist development in agriculture. He acknowledged that 'much merit is certainly due to Mr Francis for his sensible minutes'; but the latter, he thought, had not gone far enough and had, in fact, favoured '*restoring the old feodal system*' by pleading for the zamindars' right to criminal jurisdiction. 'If Mr Francis's system had been adopted', he wrote, 'the Zemindars would have been confirmed in *prejudicial prerogatives*, and might have entered into formidable combinations, when the *policy* of government should have required the resumption of criminal jurisdiction, or their *necessities* compelled increased taxation.'[46]

Underlying this criticism was a certain view of Indian history. Cross-examined by Shore he had to admit that the phrase 'laws and constitutions of India' mentioned in the thirty-ninth article of the

[44] His minute on the Tehsildary question shows that he had evidently no respect for the nice distinctions made by Shore between Bengal and Bihar. *Proceedings, B.O.R.*, 29 October 1790. The American analogy occurs in his *Correspondence* (p. 70) and the others throughout the text in *A Sketch*.

[45] Law to B.O.R., 13 June 1789. *Proceedings, B.O.R.*, 3 August 1789.

[46] *A Sketch*, pp. ii–v, viii–ix.

Act of 1784 was only 'a general expression', and that until recently the country had known no 'regular system of revenue'.[47] This did not prevent him from assuming in all his policy statements that agrarian relations under the old Hindu and Mahommedan governments had been feudal in the precise European sense of the word. Kings, zamindars, ryots all fitted into a familiar pattern as he wrote: 'The "Maharajah" under Hindoo Government taxed his Liege . . . the Mussulman Government observed the same principles, and when refractory Zemindars refused the Tribute, the Emperor gave the Estate to a favorite Officer . . .'[48] And again, 'My opinion is that the Zemindar is indisputable proprietor of the soil, and the Ryot but a vassal or peasant.'[49] The abuses resulting from such a system had always been a matter of great concern for him. Even as early as 1784 we find him begging the Board of Revenue for powers to abolish a whole list of imposts at Gaya described by him as harmful and 'non-productive',[50] and the abolition of 'feodal taxations' figured prominently in his mukarari settlement four years later.[51] European examples came easily to his mind. Was it not a fact that in France and Spain, too, there were social and economic factors comparable to those in Bengal and people suffered in much the same way? Was it not true, on the other hand, that Scotland 'which has flourished since the union by annihilation of the feudal tenures, vassalage, &c has improved rapidly'?[52] The theme of a parallelism between medieval Britain and Bengal before the Permanent Settlement and of

[47] *Ibid.*, pp. 127, 131.

[48] Letter to B.O.R., 9 January 1788. *Proceedings, B.O.R.*, 19 August 1788.

[49] Law, *A Sketch*, p. 133. Also see *ibid.*, p. 52, for a characterization of the former regime as 'the feudal Mogul Government'. Its relationship with the zamindars is thus described by him in *An Answer* (p. 2): 'Formerly, the Zemindars, like feodal lairds, used to pay a certain tribute to the sovereign.'

[50] Law's letter to B.O.R. (13 November 1784) quoted in *Proceedings, B.O.R.*, 3 March 1785.

[51] Law, *A Sketch*, p. 70.

[52] *Ibid.*, p. 44.

the corrective influence of reform in both cases appears thus in his pamphlet written in answer to John Prinsep:

> Formerly the Lairds in Scotland and Barons in England . . . exercised the power of imposing fines and held Courts of Justice; but these injurious rights have been taken away, and the proprietary rights remain. The same has been done in Asia.[53]

In other words, it was his policy to render feudalism harmless, to liquidate 'the dangerous influence of feudal Rajahs and Nabobs'[54] without actually depriving them of their property.

Law was convinced that the economic result of this reform would be to usher in an immense quantity of capital into land and particularly to encourage 'the wealthy and creditable' from other parts of the country to 'bring their capitals into these provinces'.[55] The idea, as we have already noticed, is as old as Dow's *Dissertation*, and figured prominently in Francis's thesis. The latter, however, was not clear about its implications, and when confronted with them, reacted most unfavourably. In a speech in the House of Commons in 1792 he expressed his satisfaction that the policy originally recommended by him had at last been adopted by the government of Bengal, but deplored the phenomenal sale and transfer of lands that it had brought about.[56] Fifteen years later it was still his opinion 'that the plan itself has not completely succeeded and that its benevolent purposes have been defeated', because 'the Landed property of Bengal changes hands every day from the families of the old Proprietors to a new set of men, who may be called the moneyed interest of Calcutta, such as Shroffs, Banyans and other Natives employed in the collection of the Revenue or in Stations of great personal Favour'. His social bias thus contradicted the logic of his economics, and it was with the genuine incomprehension of a physiocrat that he wrote in 1807:

53 *An Answer*, p. 26.
54 *A Sketch*, p. 44.
55 *Ibid.*
56 *P.H.E.*, vol. 29, pp. 1546–8.

'I never meant that *my* plan should have been executed in this manner.'[57]

There was no room for such anomaly in Thomas Law's view of the Permanent Settlement. On the contrary, he regarded the sale of property as the engine which would keep the land-market going. One of the worst features of the farming system was that it made it necessary for the government to prohibit unauthorized sale of estates 'lest farmers should be collusively defrauded of their revenue by Zemindars alienating their property', and consequently, 'the estates are clogged and rendered of little value'.[58] He warned the government that 'restraint upon the ready transfer of property must cause its depreciation', recommended 'that all formal Zemindary Sales . . . be valid without impediment',[59] and at the right moment in course of an argument in the Board of Revenue produced a telling quotation from Blackstone in support of this view.[60] Once, under the impact of the Permanent Settlement, land had turned into a commodity, it was to be allowed all possible freedom of exchange.

Nor, like Francis, was he inhibited by sympathy for those among the ancient proprietors who might fail to adapt themselves to the severities of the new climate of competition. The principle of natural selection was implicit in the law of the market: only the fittest must survive. 'Government may safely authorize Zemindars to dispose of their estates', he said; 'changes can only be beneficial; for the ignorant,

[57] 'To the Authors of the Edinburgh Review for April 1807'. *Francis MSS* 54 (54) 58.

[58] Law, *A Sketch*, p. 56.

[59] *Ibid.*, p. 220.

[60] T. Law's minute in *Proceedings, B.O.R.*, 7 June 1790. After Law the economics of the land-market became so firmly integrated with the policy of Permanent Settlement that we find even such minor advocates as Stonhouse repeating the argument thus: 'The State can have no Interest in prohibiting the Sale of Land as heretofore. Facility of Transfer augments its Value to the Proprietor, and by necessary Consequence, adds to the Security of Government.' *Thoughts on the Expedience of Settling Permanent Leases*, etc., p. 50.

extravagant, or indigent, will sell to the able, prudent, or wealthy, who will improve the lands and add to the stock of labour.'[61] Thus for the first time the Permanent Settlement was envisaged as something that must not *necessarily* be a zamindari settlement. Of all the protagonists of that policy he was indeed the only one who did not insist on the restoration of the old zamindars. He expected the mechanism of sales to operate in such a way that in course of time all but those who had the necessary entrepreneurial abilities would be eliminated from proprietorship, and 'a class of native gentlemen proprietors' would emerge to take their place.[62] This idea, first formulated by him in 1788, was repeated almost in the same words more than thirty years later when he wrote again on the same subject.[63] Meanwhile he had emigrated to America, and his experiences there provided for him further justification of the policy he had initiated in Bengal so long ago.[64] In a pamphlet published during a short visit to England in 1825

[61] Law, *A Sketch*, p. 56. The idea frequently occurs in Law's correspondence. Even if an estate fell into arrear not because of the zamindar's incompetence, but in consequence of a natural calamity like flood or drought, or simply because the government had overassessed it, 'the proprietor', he mercifully pleaded, 'should be at liberty to resign the estate' (*ibid.*, p. 95). Shore considered this as amounting to saying that 'the estate of the proprietor may be forfeited without any fault on his part' (Firminger, *Fifth Report*, vol. II, p. 519). He was 'not sure that in authorizing the settlement made by Mr Law, we have not given sanction to an act of injustice' (*ibid.*, p. 517).

[62] Law, *A Sketch*, p. 51.

[63] Law, *Correspondence*, p. 25.

[64] In both the *Dictionary of National Biography* and the catalogue of the Library of the British Museum Law is referred to as 'Thomas Law of Washington'. This is quite appropriate considering that he spent the greater part of his life, in fact the last forty years, in that city, where he made a reputation for himself as a financier, speculator, 'economist and industrialist, who by marriage was connected with Washington's family and had by his talent earned the admiration of Thomas Jefferson (see Clark, *Greenleaf and Law in the Federal City*, pp. 233–44, 328–9). Both the fortune and the experience gained in India were useful to him in his American career. He invested the wealth of a nabob in plots and houses in Washington (*Gentleman's Magazine*, New Series, vol. II, p. 437), applied his enthusiasm for sugarcane

he wrote: 'In the United States public land is sold that proprietors may be created.'[65] This was intended as an argument against the ryotwari plan. What lay behind this statement was, however, the conviction that he had himself been justified in counting on the land-market of Bengal to produce a new pattern of proprietorship based on enterprise rather than ancestry. By a few firm strokes he completed and brought up to date the image of an Indian bourgeoisie already sketched in rough, uncertain outline by Philip Francis.

The concept of the gentleman-farmer is further strengthened by his emphasis on 'improvement'. In this respect, too, he set the tune for Cornwallis. Under the farming system, he said, there was no incentive at all for the landlord to 'build, dig wells, plant trees, and to improve a village, lest the Aumils should proportionably assess him.'[66] He also knew from his own experience how difficult it was to persuade the government to finance such public works. Once in 1787 he had, as Collector of Bihar, sanctioned a sum of ten thousand rupees for embankments (*golundazey*) in an area severely damaged by flood. He could not depend on the local farmers to invest in projects like this, because their leases were soon due to expire, and of course 'without the hopes of being repaid or continued in their farms, it cannot be expected from them.' The Board of Revenue, however, refused to authorize the expenditure. 'Every assistance to cultivation being for the benefit of the farmer', they said, 'we deem it incumbent on him not the Government to make the Golundazey.' This was followed within a month by still another request from Law for an additional grant of 2,250 rupees as agricultural loan to the ryots to be used for further

plantation in Bihar to build a sugar refinery in Washington (Clark, op. cit., pp. 245–6), and drew upon his knowledge of the economic problems of Lord Cornwallis's government in Bengal to support his agitation for a national currency in the country of his adoption (Law, *An Address to the Columbian Institute on the question 'What Ought to be the Circulating Medium of a Nation?*, p. 16).

[65] Law, *Correspondence*, p. 70.

[66] Law, *A Sketch*, pp. 50–1.

extension of sugarcane growing; this, he had pointed out, would increase the area under cultivation from 250 bighas to 1,125 and the revenue from 1,500 rupees to 6,750 – an increase of four hundred and fifty per cent in each case. Here again the farmer had refused to advance the money, and the government's reaction to Law's proposal proved to be no more favourable than on the previous occasion.[67] Eventually, after much haggling, he did elicit from the government a reluctant and partial approval of his budget of improvement, but the experience – and this was by no means exceptional – had confirmed his view that under the old system agriculture was nobody's business; the administration passed on the responsibility to the lessees and they returned the compliment; in the end, nothing ever got done.

The Permanent Settlement was to put an end to this state of affairs once and for all. 'The superior production of English estates over those of France and other countries', he said on the authority of Arthur Young, was owing to 'the greater capital employed in husbandry'.[68] In Bengal, too, the same cause must produce the same result, that is, 'new inhabitants, aqueducts, wells, embankments, and every mark of industry.'[69] The new proprietors, he was sure, would be prepared 'from self-interest' to introduce 'emulous improvements' in their estates.[70] 'Every man will lay out money in permanent structures, as such works enhance the value of his estate and promise future benefit.'[71] As an example he cited the case of Raja Mitrajit Singh, a zamindar of Bihar, whose property had passed into the hands of 'an out-bidding farmer.' But thanks to the mukarari system, wrote Law in 1794, 'that young Zemindar is now in possession of his estate, is building houses, making roads, and extending cultivation.'[72]

[67] Law to B.O.R., 27 November 1787, and B.O.R.'s reply, *Proceedings, B.O.R.*, 7 December 1787. Law to B.O.R. and enclosures, 20 December 1787, and B.O.R.'s reply, *ibid.*, 8 January 1788.

[68] Law, *Correspondence*, p. 7.

[69] Law, *A Sketch*, p. 81.

[70] *Ibid.*, p. 44.

[71] *Ibid.*, pp. 50–1.

[72] Law, *An Answer*, p. 13.

He even predicted the possibility of a limited development of manufacture, though only as an ancillary of the basic enterprise in land.[73] Above all, he expected a tremendous increase in the output of cash crops. Under the farming system rents were so high for lands growing commercial crops that the peasant was obliged to fall back on rice cultivation, for which – and he was generalizing here on the basis of his Bihar experience – the farmers accepted rent in kind. Under the new settlement, the landlords, in their own interest, 'will promote emulative encouragement by lowering the high rates of the first produce'. He calculated how by reducing the rent on lands that grew articles like cotton, sugarcane, opium, etc., the proprietors could most profitably change the crop-pattern in their estates. He tried this out himself in the districts under his charge and obtained phenomenal results. In one pargana sugarcane had increased from 100 bighas to 1,000, in another from 10 to 200, and for the entire area under his mukarari system he reported by the end of 1788 a trend towards a hundred per cent increase in sugarcane and cotton.[74] His initiative had changed the crop-pattern beyond recognition in those parts of Bihar where he happened to serve. He could never insist enough on the great possibilities this would have for India's export trade, particularly in sugar. He was delighted to see American ships taking in cargoes of sugar at the Calcutta port. 'Why should not the Company do this, I asked?'[75] He actively participated in the controversy on this question during the 1790s: Bengal sugar, he insisted, was much better and cheaper than the west Indian product, and could therefore be more profitably imported by Britain. His horizon of capitalist development under the Permanent Settlement was thus stretched far beyond the limits of a purely Indian market for agricultural goods.

But perhaps his most far-reaching, and as it turned out to be, perfectly utopian, idea was to introduce in Bengal technological improvements similar to those which had accompanied the agrarian

[73] Law, *A Sketch*, p. 52.
[74] *Ibid.*, pp. 60–3, 73.
[75] *Ibid.*, Preface.

revolution in England. 'Let me here, whilst it is in my memory, recommend', he wrote in 1825, 'that all the instruments of agriculture lately invented in Europe should be sent out to the several presidencies in India, and that each of them should have a farm similar to that of Rambouliet established by Napoleon for the instruction of the cultivators. This has rendered much useful exemplary information . . .'[76] This was the language of an old man developing further the logic of his youthful vision of capitalist prospects in Indian agriculture. He was blissfully unaware that during the thirty-two years since it was launched the Permanent Settlement had gone off the orbit he had so neatly calculated for it, and that his 'gentlemen proprietors', *nouveaux riches* though they mostly were with no claim to noble descent, had proved themselves to be exceedingly fond of the traditional ways of estate management: far from imitating the model landlords of Arthur Young, they were happy to be living off the fat of the land, but comfortably away from it. It was the France of the *ancien régime* and not the England of Townshend and Tull that still remained a more authentic parallel for Bengal.

Fully conforming to his concept of the Permanent Settlement were Law's ideas on taxation and commerce. Here, too, there was much common ground between him and Francis, but, again, Law improved on the latter both in emphasis and implication. There was also some characteristic difference in the way their respective views on the subject were formed. Francis's objection to indirect taxes was, in the true physiocratic manner, a corollary derived from his basic agrarian thesis. But from what we know of Thomas Law from his early correspondence with the Board of Revenue, it appears that even before the mukarari plan had emerged in his mind he was already busy clearing the thick undergrowth of imposts obstructing internal trade. The prohibitory regulations of the government were, of course, very helpful in such an undertaking. But one had to be careful enough to recognize the abuse in all its protean shapes. Thus, within

[76] Law, *Correspondence*, p. 55.

a fortnight of their abolition in 1784 the species known as rahadary duties reappeared in Law's district 'under the name of Gunge duties'. Still a junior official in charge of the minor collectorate of Rotas, he reported at that time: 'I have removed as many impediments as occurred, conscious that my hilly district can only be benefited by the policy of encouraging Beoparries to transport the produce of the land to Benares and Patna.'[77] His vigilance never slackened in this respect. He was personally responsible for weeding out this pest from every district of Bihar where he happened to be posted, and many ancient encrustations broke up under his blow.[78]

However, it was not so much by the vigour of his individual efforts as by fighting for a general policy on inland duties that Law contributed most. He soon found out that at the root of the problem lay certain privileges connected with landownership: the zamindars claimed and most profitably exercised a right to levy duties and tolls on the sale and transport of goods, thus extending their control of landed property to the entire field of commerce. Here again France provided the appropriate analogy. Arthur Young found the indirect taxes under the *ancien régime* too numerous and too complex to be intelligible to Englishmen.[79] At about the same time his compatriots serving in India were busy tackling as a matter of ordinary routine longer lists of far more curious items of inland customs and excise duties. The economic consequences were also not very different for

[77] Law to B.O.R., 11 October 1784. *Proceedings, B.O.R.*, 9 September 1785.

[78] In his *Letters to the Board submitting by their requisition a Revenue Plan for Perpetuity* he quotes a whole list of such imposts from the *Ain-i-Akbari.* One of these was 'Nekass (a tax on the sale of cattle)'. There is a note in pencil against this item in Law's own hand in the margin of an India Office Library copy of this book (V. 1172). It reads: 'I obtain'd the abolition of this when Judge at Patna.' A summary of the measures he introduced in Gaya 'to investigate and abolish the numerous extortions and oppressions that existed in that town' will be found in 'Abstract of Gaya Proceedings' in *An Answer*, pp. 62–72.

[79] Young, *Travels in France*, pp. 317, 319.

the two countries even in detail. Law's reference to a specimen of the Zemindars' impositions which in three days' journey raise the price of commodities from 100 to 150 per cent'[80] is reminiscent of the fate of that bottle of Bordeaux wine which, thanks to *aides* and *traites*, had its price doubled by the time it reached Paris.[81] Like Francis, he, too, sought in French therapy a cure for Bengal's ailment. There are in Law's writings many admiring references to the *économistes*, and he wrote in conscious imitation of their doctrines in urging the government '*to abolish* all internal duties' and replace them by one single tax. This, he predicted, must result in a 'great increase of commercial intercourse and prosperity'.[82]

What Law wanted to achieve by this reform was to press the anti-feudal edge of the Permanent Settlement to its logical limit: that is, to deprive the zamindars not only of their right to collect *abwab* and *mathote* from the peasants, but also of their claim to sayer from traders and shopkeepers. In his own mukarari plan for Bihar these two aspects were completely integrated into a single act of policy, and in spite of Shore's disagreement[83] he succeeded in winning Cornwallis over to his side. The Sayer Regulations of June 1790 were primarily his work, both conceived and formulated by him. It was stated there that 'it has been determined to take from the landholders the power of imposing and collecting duties altogether, and to exercise this privilege hereafter immediately and exclusively on the part of government'. Clearly these Regulations were intended to undermine the economic basis of the old zamindari system and thereby make it easier for the new class of proprietors to take over; by emancipating trade from feudal impediments these measures were designed to make the market safe for the increased agricultural output which must result from 'improvements'; in short, they were to ensure that nothing hindered the turnover of

[80] Law, *A Sketch*, p. 181.

[81] Hazen, *The French Revolution*, vol. I, p. 70.

[82] Law, *A Sketch*, pp. 186, 187.

[83] Shore wanted the government to assume the right of collecting customs duties, but 'with respect to tolls levied upon the purchase and sale of goods', he said, 'the amount may safely perhaps be trusted to the proprietors of the villages'. *Ibid.*, p. 112.

capital invested in land. When, as an old man, Law wrote again on the subject in 1825, he was happily convinced that these aims had been fully realized, and in self-gratification quoted Lord Moira's testimony that thanks to these Regulations 'commercial capital and enterprise have been turned towards the land'.[84] He was then far too removed from Indian realities to be able to grasp that for native capital, under its new predicament, this was more a sign of retreat than of advance; for, between 1790 and 1820, all perspectives in Indo-British economy had been revolutionized by free trade.

Or, was he not consistent after all in his own way? Had he not himself envisaged the opening up of the Indian market for free trade as early as 1792 when he wrote *A Sketch*? One of the many positive results of the Permanent Settlement he predicted was the creation of a new range of needs arising from a higher standard of living and greater purchasing power. The idea had already occurred to Pattullo and was, indeed, destined to figure prominently in the early nineteenth-century literature on free trade.[85] Law himself expected the gentlemen-proprietors 'who will gradually have established themselves in good houses with the various comforts of life'[86] to set the pace for new economic demands. These could be best satisfied by 'the exportation of foreigners', mainly British.[87] To make this possible the Company must 'rise superior to the narrow views of merchants, and adopt an enlarged policy', he wrote, propping up his statement by copious

[84] Law, *Correspondence*, p. 59.

[85] For Pattullo's views on the subject, see above p. 54. For an early nineteenth-century specimen in the literature on free trade, see W. Lester, *The Happy Era of One Hundred Millions of the Human Race, or the Merchant, Manufacturer, and Englishman's Recognised Right to an Unlimited Trade with India* (pp. 39–40), and especially the following passage: 'We should not only see the palaces of the Rajah, and the houses of the Vakeels, Aumils, Shrofs, and Zemindars, furnished and decorated with the produce of English arts and manufactures, but the Ryots . . . may, like the British farmers, have a taste for foreign produce, as soon as they can acquire property enough to procure it.'

[86] Law, *A Sketch*, p. 51.

[87] *Ibid.*, p. xxv.

extracts from Adam Smith.[88] Monopoly had to go. In particular 'the company must allow private ships to go under their passport'. If they still wanted to retain their lead in the carrying trade 'let them obtain it by superior terms, but not by monopoly'. They might continue to bring home 'their tributary investments', but in all other respects, 'the private trade of Asia . . . should be free'. English traders should be encouraged to take their goods to India 'if the company cannot afford to export any articles, or have not sufficient capital, their resources being appropriated to armaments'.[89] The natives, on their part, would be given reciprocal opportunities to send exports to England. It was, indeed, the aim of Law's customs reform to promote both internal and foreign trade of Bengal. During the earlier period of British rule, he regretted, 'the line has never been drawn between goods brought for sale . . . and those meant for exportation'; they were all equally subject to imposts. He quoted Adam Smith's observation on the Alcavala of Spain that 'nothing could be produced for distant sale' under such an obstructive regime of duties.[90] Now that these were abolished, he was sure that 'the natives will be industrious and happy, whilst they find a mart for super-abundance'.[91]

All this sounds very fair and reads almost like the preamble of a model commercial treaty based entirely on considerations of mutual benefit and reciprocity. However, the heads-I-win-tails-you-lose principle underlying it becomes clear when one looks more closely into the specific recommendations Law made for Indian exports. There was not one article of manufacture on his list except sugar, which England had to get in any case from the West Indies. For the rest it was all agricultural products (including raw hides and skins). The most offensive of all items, textiles, was omitted in favour of cotton.

On this as on most other questions Law preferred to express his own ideas by quoting someone else. In his work *A Sketch of Some Late*

[88] Law, *Heads of a Proposed Speech etc.*, pp. 3–4, 8, 10, 17–18.

[89] Law, *A Sketch*, pp. xxxv–xxxvi.

[90] *Ibid.*, pp. 171–2.

[91] *Ibid.*, p. xxv.

Arrangement in Bengal he published the text of a letter from a private British trader with whom he evidently was in complete agreement. The letter reads in part as follows:

> Without purchasers for the surplus produce of the soil and manufactures, the spirit of industry and improvement which your excellent Mocurrery system is formed to excite . . . will, I fear, languish into indifference . . .
>
> The wants of the natives of Hindostan, it is said, are but few . . . The experience of past ages contradicts this assertion; for the wants of all men increase in proportion to their means . . .
>
> Ensure then to the Hindostanny produce of his labour or ingenuity; teach him to exchange the surplus for his own benefit in multiplying his enjoyments . . .
>
> What prospect does this open to the consumption of the manufactures of Great Britain, provided they could be introduced at a reasonable rate, and paid for with the produce of Bengal!
>
> All this, to my mind, seems easy of attainment, by allowing an unrestrained intercourse; but whilst the trade is restricted to the Company's ships, no extension can be hoped for . . .
>
> . . . in such articles as cotton, sugar, hides and skins, hemp, grain, and there is no limiting the extent to which the exports [from Bengal] might rise. This would also turn the industry of the country into a channel, of all others most advantageous to England, and lessen the rivalship that its cloths hold with our rising and extensive cotton manufactures . . . I trust that the partial interest of ship-owners will not be allowed to operate long against the mutual benefit of both countries.
>
> If a remittance [of surplus revenue] is the only reason for continuing the [Company's] monopoly, a free trade would open multifarious and secure channels for any sum that the government might want to remit, which would operate in the hands of the merchant-remitter as an encreased capital employed for the benefit of the country.
>
> To this would be added the excess of capital in England, which would gradually withdraw itself from various existing trades there that are overrun by the number of competitors, and pour its creative and enlivening influence over the East, where it could be employed so much more advantageously . . .[92]

[92] *Ibid.*, pp. xxvii–xxix.

This letter was written in July 1790. It illustrates very well how already at this date far-sighted Englishmen like Law and his correspondent had adapted the doctrine of Permanent Settlement to that of Free Trade. Originating as only a secondary notion tagged on to Dow's mercantilist thesis, the idea of Permanent Settlement had thus within twenty years reached the highest point of contemporary economic thought. But it could go no further. After the first three decades or so of its existence as a policy it was to turn back on its course to degenerate into an apologia for the quasi-feudal land system in eastern India during the remainder of British rule. It is easy to understand, in retrospect, why this had to happen. Conceived, in its final form, as a policy of capitalist enterprise in agriculture, the Permanent Settlement needed a sovereign home market for its potentialities to mature to their full extent. Under the circumstances, however, this was not feasible. For the progress of the Industrial Revolution in England was at the same time pressing its own demands on India: 'the excess of capital in England', mentioned by Law's correspondent, was only too eager to 'pour its creative and enlivening influence over the East'. In the unequal contest that followed, the weaker capitalism had to yield. During the nineteenth century India gradually emerged as a vast agrarian hinterland of the British Empire. Correspondingly, the Permanent Settlement, too, assumed the character of a pre-capitalist system of landownership, mocking its own original image as visualized by Philip Francis and Thomas Law.

6

First Doubts

One firm voice of dissent that was raised against the policy of Permanent Settlement in its hour of triumph was John Shore's. He had hailed the appointment of Cornwallis with great enthusiasm, but after three years of collaboration emerged as his most formidable critic. Their controversies have been analysed and commented upon by many historians. What, however, needs still to be sufficiently emphasized is that in opposing the Governor-General in the way he did, Shore revolted against the entire system of Philip Francis and consequently against his own inherited and long-cherished notions. Considered in this light much of what has been written on the subject would perhaps be found wanting in probity. There are some writers who on the strength of his agreement with the theory of zamindar-ownership have related him directly to the Francis tradition, and in their hands his differences have been reduced to the size of a mere administrative detail. This view, ably represented by Miss Weitzman, is best formulated in her *classic* understatement: 'The debatable point was only that of permanence.'[1] Others like Ascoli have formed their estimate of Shore on the basis of the rival minutes of 1789–90,[2] and as a result missed the important

[1] Weitzman, op. cit., p. 197.
[2] Ascoli, op. cit., pp. 63–70.

point about the progressive development of his scepticism and his eventual self-contradiction. Either way his emphasis on experience has been valued only for what it was worth in producing a wise quantitative amendment. From such interpretations it hardly emerges that in fact what Shore did was to use experience as a solvent of dogma and thereby question the very first principles of the plan of 1776.

It has already been noted that during the 1770s Shore had managed to remain independent of both the rival factions in the Council.[3] But in his ideas he was certainly closer to Francis than Hastings. This was known to all including Hastings himself. The malicious imputation of Captain Price that Francis's minutes were actually written by Shore is of no value at all except as indicating a contemporary awareness of their partial agreement on certain matters. Shore himself provides more direct evidence on the subject in a letter he wrote to Ducarel in 1789. 'My ideas concur with those of Mr Francis', he said; 'but the length of time which has elapsed since the proposal of his Plan requires a modification of it, now necessary.'[4] This was an acknowledgment of his debt to Francis as well as of his doubts. For what he euphemistically described as 'modification' amounted, in fact, to an antithesis.

In many aspects of personal development and attitude the two men were in perfect contrast to each other. Francis had been primarily a politician. Shore, on the contrary, was shy of politics. As a clerk in Lisbon the young Francis had been impatiently longing for the hub of London's public life. Shore on his return to England in 1790 had quietly retired to the countryside and withdrawn himself altogether even from Indian affairs.[5] For Francis every pawn-move on the Indian chessboard was directly related to his grand political strategy; every detail of his participation in the government of Bengal was charged with an element of ulterior political motive. To Shore, however, the business of administration was altogether divorced from politics. They were for him two very different professions and almost mutually exclusive. 'We are all too busy to give our time to politics', he wrote

[3] See p. 56, n. 129.

[4] To G.G. Ducarel, 15 February 1789. Teignmouth, vol. I, p. 166.

[5] To Goodlad, 13 January 1791. *Ibid.*, p. 207.

from Calcutta in 1793. 'In England they are the sole occupation of many. Here they come in as secondary objects of concern.'[6] Francis, in whatever he did at home or abroad, gravitated towards Parliament. Shore viewed Westminster with a mixture of distrust and diffidence. He promised to his friend Wilberforce that he would 'never attempt to mix in the goodly society of which you are a member', and went on to draw a firm line of distinction between administrator and politician thus: 'A man may make a tolerably good Governor-General, and an inefficient Member of Parliament. Our habits are deliberative, not oratorical.'[7] The Governor-Generalship of India was for Francis the highest political prize: he regarded his appointment to the Bengal Council as only a base camp to organize the resources for an assault on the summit. Shore was actually Governor-General, 'King of Bengal' as Francis would have said, when with all the great power at his command he still modestly wanted to keep his role limited to that of a mere official.

This is not to suggest that Shore had no political opinion of his own. He had. Only these were informed with that supreme quality which was so important for a good administrator but useless to a politician: his judgment, as he himself recognized, was too 'deliberative'. A reference to his views on two of the most outstanding questions of the 1790s will bear this out. He was one of those early enthusiasts of the French Revolution whom Burke and the Reign of Terror had turned into a critic. He hated 'the diabolical principles of Robespierre's gang', ridiculed the revolutionary 'madness of the French at Chander-nagore', despised the National Assembly for its 'want of ability'. But while he drifted away from the republican position, he was still careful not to identify himself with the cause of legitimacy. He was far too aware of the evils of the old order in France to want it restored. He spoke with concern about the counter-revolutionary preparations going on at Coblentz and hoped that 'the spirit of Freedom' would defy 'a successful invasion by the pupils of Despotism' and oppose it by 'a firmer union of the democrats'. He objected to

6 To Charles Grant, 21 October 1793. *Ibid.*, p. 262.

7 To Wilberforce, 25 October 1795. *Ibid.*, p. 345.

the French Revolution only so far as it had some undesirable repercussions in England. He asserted again and again in his letters that he was 'too much a citizen of the world' and had 'too much humanity' not to wish the French success in the way they wanted to work out their destiny. Only they had inspired too many madmen on this side of the Channel who wanted 'to see real comfort sacrificed to ideal perfection, the wisdom of ages renounced for the quackery of new political experiments, or, in other words, the Constitution overturned'. He was thus not so much against the French Jacobins as against their English imitators who wanted the nation to abandon the shade and security of its ancient oak for the pursuit of a mirage of reform. Even on this latter issue, however, his position was not an unqualified one. He was genuinely convinced of the superiority of the English Constitution to all others, but did not deny that it could do with some useful amendment. Only 'the proper time, mode and quantum of improvement' had to be carefully considered. For, as he put it, 'We are something like the natural situation of Holland: a rat may let in an ocean.' It was not the demand for reform that he opposed, but the precipitate form which he thought the movement had assumed in the hands of agitators.

Reconstructed thus from bits and pieces of his correspondence between 1791 and 1795[8] – for Shore would not, of course, discuss politics except incidentally – his views appear to be placed at a neatly calculated middle point equidistant between Burke and Francis. They also illustrate his geometry of decision-making on any problem where two positions were given at opposite extremities. In such cases he would, depending on his actual inclination at the time, take off from an initial point proximate to either pole (on the French Revolution the point of departure was close to the left; on the reform movement,

[8] Teignmouth, vol. I, p. 208; and the letters reproduced there as below: to A. Caldecott, 31 December 1791 (pp. 215–16); to Lady Shore, 14 April 1793 (pp. 242–4); to J. Blackburn, 14 October 1793 (pp. 257–8) and 12 May 1795 (p. 327); to C. Grant 21 October 1793 (pp. 261–2) and 7 March 1795 (pp. 313–16); to F. Baring, 1 January 1795 (pp. 311–12). Also, see extract from his journal (*ibid.*, p. 266).

close to the right), and then by a series of deliberate moves in the other direction finally correct the balance. As a result his argument, unlike Francis's, was seldom carved out of a single piece. It was, on the contrary, built up as a structure carefully propped on conditionals which admitted of no generalization on its face value. General conclusions, he noticed, were far too often deduced from particular instances, and this, he thought, was not 'fair argument'. In his first minute of 18 September 1789 he sharply pulled up a Bihar officer for having based his universal condemnation of the zamindars on one individual sample of worthlessness.[9] By the same logic he could have demolished the entire edifice of Francis's plan had he wanted to do so.

As an administrator responsible for the execution of policy he also regretted the tendency of formulating a general principle without a thought about its applicability. 'To establish general principles as a rule of practice is the most important', he said; 'but it will still be more satisfactory to point out and superintend the application of them.'[10] It was precisely on this ground that he took his stand in his final statement of 1789 against the declaration of Permanent Settlement. He did not, he said, object to the 'general principles' cited by the Governor-General, 'but the application of them must be directed by circumstances of time and situation'.[11] Thus he sought to correct the policy of Cornwallis by the same modifying formula he had proposed earlier for that of Francis. He had no use for the timeless, universal categories of either. For himself, 'in innovating great principles' he would only 'take experience for our guide',[12] and once principles were thus determined they had again to be passed through the same crucible: 'Experience must be the test of all measures.'[13]

His approach to policy was, therefore, essentially tentative and experimental. He would give his support to any experiment even if

[9] Firminger, vol. II, p. 481.
[10] Minute, 18 June 1789. *Ibid.*, p. 67.
[11] Minute, 21 December 1789. *Ibid.*, p. 519.
[12] *Ibid.*, p. 523.
[13] Minute, 18 September 1789. *Ibid.*, p. 481.

he had doubts about its success. He had, as he said in his minute of 21 December, serious and fundamental objections to Law's mukarari settlement of Bihar. Yet, he added, 'I am not sorry that it had been executed. The experiment will give rise to a further experience, which may assist in determining upon the general question.'[14] Any impression that this might give of a lack of strength on his part will, however, be altogether wrong. His biographer speaks of his firmness in adhering to decisions taken, and the history of his controversy with Cornwallis is sufficient proof of it. Only the positive content of each decision had to be 'tempered by cautious conditions'.[15] To the difficulty of such a task he was admirably matched both by temperament and intellect. A satirist had most aptly described him as 'a good man, but as cold as a grey hound's nose'.[16] A characteristic reserve, one is almost tempted to call it coolness, combined with a sound respect for facts kept him firmly rooted to the ground. Unlike Francis he was not discouraged by details and minutiae. On the contrary, when he mentioned[17] that he had compared four manuscript copies of the *Ain-i-Akbari* before deciding that Grant had misread the Persian word *rubba* for *reia*, he was merely speaking of a routine act of meticulousness. This could have easily degenerated into a sort of petty clerical obsession but for all his genuine and abundant humility which was in such striking contrast to the intellectual arrogance of Francis. He knew how to value other people's judgment. It was his habit to circulate his drafts and invite criticism before finally pronouncing on a problem.[18] In his last note in reply to Cornwallis he said that he was not 'ashamed to distrust my own knowledge, since I have frequent proofs that new enquiries lead to new information'.[19] It was humility such as this that greatly added to the power of his scepticism. His faculty of doubting and his sense of experience had certainly matured with age, but the

[14] *Ibid.*, pp. 523–4.
[15] *Ibid.*, p. 520.
[16] *Ibid.*, p. xii n.
[17] To Rous, 22 February 1789. Teignmouth, vol. I, p. 170.
[18] *Ibid.*, pp. 76–7.
[19] Firminger, vol. II, p. 520.

same qualities are already apparent in some of his earliest Indian observations. He was only twenty-one and had been three years in the country when he wrote to his mother from Murshidabad:

> The immense number of things to be remarked cannot be ascertained by one view: the first idea I form, appears, on retrospect, to be always imperfect, and often erroneous. I endeavour therefore, by observations founded upon a more intimate knowledge, to amplify those remarks which are cursory, and correct those which are false. As to facts, I never assert the authenticity of them, unless I have previously received conviction; but with regard to speculative points, I must beg your indulgence for representing them differently, occasioned by the different points of view in which they are offered to my sight.[20]

One can hardly improve upon this as a definition of his approach to the problems debated seventeen years later in the Calcutta Council. On many of the more important issues he set out from an initial position close to the 'speculative points' represented by Francis, but allowed himself to be guided by the dialectic of experience to very different conclusions.

On the question of revenue settlement he began, as Francis did, by asking who owned the lands. Unlike Francis, however, he did not turn for an answer to works in English, French and Latin, but to the ancient and medieval Indian literature in Sanskrit, Arabic and Persian and the living knowledge of the people in Hindustani and Bengali. He had a small farm of his own and derived from its management some first-hand, if elementary, information about native husbandry and customary tenures.[21] In course of his official duties he mastered the complex arithmetic of Persian revenue accounts. From all this he was convinced that 'upon the whole', as he cautiously put it in his memorandum of 1782, it was the zamindars who had 'the greatest rights'. Only the evidence for it was far too various, far too insufficient, and above all far too difficult to interpret in clearly differentiated terms of principle and practice to serve as a foundation of policy.

[20] To his mother, 1 April 1772. Teignmouth, vol. I, pp. 38–9.
[21] *Ibid.*, p. 33.

In the first place, he had found out that under the Mahommedans the rights and functions of the zamindars were not always the same in one part of the country as in another. In his first minute of September 1789 he had many valid and acute observations to make on the differences between the zamindars of Bihar and Bengal. 'In all speculations regarding the Zemindars', he warned Rous, 'you must be careful to distinguish Bengal from all other parts of the Empire. There was most certainly a difference in the practice and principles of Finance here.'[22] The logic of this view was to doubt the assumption, common to both Francis and Cornwallis, that the zamindars were an undifferentiated category and had uniform rights.

Secondly, he was utterly dissatisfied about the inadequacy of evidence. To try to glean information on the subject from native literature was 'to hunt out three grains of wheat amidst a bushel of chaff'. To Rous who was apparently at this time writing his dissertation on landed property, he said, 'You are not, I think, likely to get more information on Zemindary rights.'[23] Cornwallis, too, wrote to the Court of Directors in the same desperate terms: 'It does not appear to us that any further lights into the rights of the zemindars can be obtained by a profest investigation into them . . . The fact as far as we are informed is that the Oriental historians nowhere treat the subject professedly, and all that can be gleaned from a research into them can only be obtained by inference from a very few facts, and which are rarely sufficient to repay the time and attention necessary for the investigation.'[24] It speaks a lot about the difference between

[22] To Rous, 22 February 1789: Teignmouth, vol. I, p. 169. In striking contrast to this was Francis's remark protesting that Hastings should want the settlement for the period beginning in 1777 to be made in Bihar independently of that for Bengal. 'No ostensible reason can be assigned to justify this Distinction', he wrote to Ellis (6 January 1777), 'since every Argument that can be supposed to apply to one part of the provinces holds equally valid with respect to all the rest.' – *Francis MSS* 49 (38) 66.

[23] Teignmouth, vol. I, p. 169.

[24] G.G.C. to C.O.D., 10 August 1789. Para. 79. *General Letters to the Court of Directors, Revenue Department*, vol. 6.

them that in spite of such an utter lack of evidence five weeks later Cornwallis pressed for an immediate declaration of 'permanency' based on zamindari rights and Shore still remained unconvinced.

Thirdly, it was not the paucity of evidence so much as its ambiguity that made it difficult for Shore to accept a settlement concluded with the zamindars on so-called legal grounds. Landed property under the Mughals, he admitted, belonged to the zamindars; but it did not necessarily follow that they had any rights derived from proprietorship. What looked like rights in principle was easily subverted by the practice of an arbitrary government. 'My opinion is decided that the Zemindars were the hereditary proprietors of the soil', he said, 'but that the Sovereign claimed what portion of the rents he pleased. The Zemindars were thus far left at his mercy.'[25] The moderation of the later Mughals from Akbar to Aurangzib was only a matter of personal benevolence having nothing to do with the problem of ownership. The idea of proprietary rights, he shrewdly suspected, was an English notion wrongly applied to the historical circumstances of medieval India. 'A property in the soil', he said, 'must not be understood to convey the same rights in India as in England; the difference is as great as between a free constitution and an arbitrary power.'[26] Thus he questions the basic historical concept underlying the plan of 1776, and then in another statement extends the logic of this objection to the structure of agrarian relationship designed on that concept. His judgment on this point in his minute of 21 December 1789 anticipates all subsequent criticism of the Permanent Settlement as a whig doctrine of landownership imposed on India. He writes:

> The most cursory observation shows the situation of things in this country to be singularly confused. The relation of a zemindar to government, and of a ryot to a zemindar, is neither that of a proprietor nor a vassal; but a compound of both. The former performs acts of authority unconnected

[25] To Rous, 22 February 1769. Teignmouth, vol. I, p. 169.
[26] Minute, 18 June 1789. Firminger, vol. II, p. 83.

> with proprietory right; the latter has rights without real property; and the property of the one and the rights of the other are, in a great measure, held at discretion. Such was the system which we found, and which we have been under the necessity of adopting. Much time will, I fear, elapse before we can establish a system, perfectly consistent in all its parts; and before we can reduce the compound relation of a zemindar to government, and of a ryot to a zemindar, to the simple principles of landlord and tenant.[27]

Francis had conceived of the agrarian relationship in Mughal India as primarily feudal; he had wanted to replace it by a model derived from contemporary England. Shore rejected both this interpretation of history and its implications for policy. Beyond the little that was common between them in their agreement about the need for a zamindari settlement, there lay a world of difference on the question of rights. For Francis, happily, what he thought was legally valid, coincided with what he considered expedient: there was indeed no scope for a conflict between the two in a mind as monolithic as his. Shore, however, appears to have foreseen the possibility of a contradiction between right and policy. He, therefore, prepared himself in advance to treat each of these problems independently of the other, if necessary. 'The general question', he wrote, 'may with propriety be divided into two parts: of right and policy. If the former can be clearly ascertained, it will probably tend to elucidate the latter; which, at all events, deserves a separate consideration.'[28] Thus in his minute of 2 April 1788; that is, long before the signal for controversy went up in the Council. It was not intuition but the logic of his method that required the formulation of a rule to deal with such an eventuality. The occasion arose for its use when in summer next year he set about collecting his ideas into a definitive statement 'premising that I pretend only to state facts', found it impossible 'to reconcile the principles of right with the practice of an arbitrary government',[29]

[27] Firminger, vol. II, p. 520.
[28] *Ibid.*, p. 737.
[29] Minute, 18 June 1789. *Ibid.*, pp. 80, 83.

and was therefore obliged to indicate a solution only in terms of expediency. 'We have admitted the property in the soil to be vested in the zemindars', he said; and 'although it should be proved, under the Mogul system, to have belonged to the sovereign, which I deem impossible, the Company ought in my opinion to relinquish it.'[30] In other words, even if on historical grounds the zamindars were found to have had no right of ownership, under the changed conditions of British rule, he thought, it would be simply good policy to invest them with property.

The two considerations which, for Shore, were most relevant to a policy of settlement were the need (a) to restore confidence in property, and (b) to uphold the government's right of intervention in the zamindars' affairs. For Francis the second of these two considerations did not exist at all, while the very small measure of agreement which apparently existed between them on the first, was in fact only a common point of departure in different directions.

Shore believed, as Francis did, that the farming system had destroyed all sense of security in property, and that it should be the aim of the new settlement 'to establish a principle of giving confidence to our subjects'.[31] But he was not sure that confidence could be created by decree. Francis and Cornwallis had both based their policies on the assumption that a legal enactment in favour of permanent, hereditary rights would immediately inspire the zamindars with a sense of security and responsibility. Shore had no such faith in the miraculous powers of property. The farming system, he argued, had made the native proprietors cynical. For over twenty years they had 'subsisted upon annual expedients' As a result they were inclined to doubt the sincerity of any official declaration in favour of permanence. 'Some

[30] *Ibid.*, p. 61.

[31] *Ibid.*, p. 65. It should be noted, however, that Shore's condemnation of the farming system was more moderate and qualified than Francis's. He admitted that as a direct form of settlement it had certain administrative advantages (*ibid.*, p. 39), and that in Bihar it 'had been of considerable value in ascertaining the resources of each estate (Ascoli, op. cit., p. 64).

time will now be required to convince the zemindars that we are serious.' In the last analysis, nothing but time and experience could impress them about the stability of the new deal.[32]

Besides, there was the question of competence. The zamindar whom gift of property was expected to convert into a responsible and improving landlord was, after all, an abstraction. Did he really possess any of those qualities of enlightenment, characteristic of the contemporary English country gentleman, which Francis and Cornwallis had attributed to him? Shore knew the Bengali zamindars far too well to have any illusions about it. 'If a review of the zamindar of Bengal was made', he observed in his minute of June 1789, 'it would be found that very few are duly qualified for the management of their hereditary lands; and that, in general, they are ill-educated for this task; ignorant of the common forms of business, and of the modes of transacting it; inattentive of the conduct of it, even where their own interests are immediately at stake, and indisposed to undertake it.'[33] This view of the utter worthlessness of the native aristocracy recurs in all his more important statements. In fact, he often cited the authority of Francis himself to prove the need for re-educating the zamimdars.[34] It is this particularly negative estimate of their character, rather than the opinions of European authors quoted by Francis, that convinced Shore about the advantage of splitting up the larger estates in favour of petty proprietors who, he thought, could be trusted for 'a more prudent, economical, or equitable management'.[35] He was by no means convinced that a declaration of Permanent Settlement would by itself act as an incentive for a class of proprietors so utterly incompetent as the native landlords were. 'We know from experience what the zemindars are', he wrote; 'and I am not inclined, in opposition to that experience, to suppose that they will at once assume new principles of action, and become economical landlords and prudent trustees of

[32] Firminger, vol. II, pp. 113, 489–90, 515–16.

[33] *Ibid.*, p. 40 and *passim.*

[34] *Ibid.*, pp. 72, 75, 77.

[35] *Ibid.*, pp. 103–4.

the public interest.'[36] Thus, in spite of what he had in common with Francis in posing the problem of security, he was unable, on grounds of experience, to accept the latter's solution.

The other important consideration of policy was, for Shore, the need for State intervention. The government's right to intervene in the affairs of the zamindars was to be exercised, in the first place, in the form of an investigation of their resources. Francis was outraged at the very idea of an official enquiry into the value of the estates. Cornwallis, too, had no use for it: 'what is the experience that is wanting?' he asked in exasperation. For some time Shore himself seems to have been unable to make up his mind about this matter, and his opinion took a definite shape only during the controversies of 1789, making it necessary for him to modify or even reject some of his earlier views. As late as in his minute of June that year he wrote: 'We may fairly disclaim the idea of pursuing measures calculated to afford us a more accurate valuation of the lands, when attended with risque to the principle we assume, and the argument which rests upon the advantages to be derived upon the investigation loses much of its force.'[37] This was, in fact, essentially the same kind of argument which Francis had used against the Amini Commission: that is, an 'inquisition' into the value of the estates must undermine confidence in property. But even in this minute this was not quite the last thing Shore had to say on the subject, and on further consideration, he went on to qualify the statement in a manner that almost amounted to self-contradiction. After reiterating the argument mentioned above against the harmful consequences of local investigation, he added: 'Yet if this argument were urged to its utmost extent, the zemindars ought not to be called upon for any accounts . . . I can never allow that government should concede this point to them.'[38]

The reason why he thought the government must not surrender its right of enquiry into the value of the zamindari estates was that it

[36] *Ibid.*, p. 520.
[37] *Ibid.*, p. 102.
[38] *Ibid.*, p. 116.

would otherwise deprive itself of all claim to any future increase in land revenues. On this point he was against permitting the zamindars 'too much lenity'. Neither justice nor policy demanded, he said, that the government should submit to a permanent loss.[39] Even in the minute of June 1789 he had, therefore, thoughtfully laid down that the zamindars must be made to submit to official scrutiny the resources of all newly established villages; otherwise, he feared, the government might forfeit its claim amounting, in course of time, to anything up to twenty-five per cent of its revenues from certain estates.[40] He was also not altogether opposed, as Francis had been, to the idea of imposing a progressive addition (*russud*) to the amount of revenue due from an estate, not of course, as the Committee of Circuit had done, every year throughout the entire period of settlement, but only during the first few years.[41] In his final minute he clearly comes out with the idea that to insist on a permanent assessment would be to condemn the government to making a permanent sacrifice of its legitimate income. 'A temporary sacrifice may be made to inspire confidence', he said, 'but to consent to a perpetual loss, whilst it can be regained without injury or injustice, is certainly not advisable.'[42]

But it was not merely in its own interest that the government must reserve the right to investigate the value of the estates. It was a right that had to be exercised in order to ensure equality of assessment. This was an idea which Francis had found quite unacceptable. The incidence of fiscal demand, he most correctly observed, could not be evenly distributed without a most accurate survey of all existing properties. 'The idea is insupportable, and will not bear an argument', he concluded. In fact, he was convinced that an equitable assessment was not 'indispensably requisite'.[43] Shore held the diametrically opposite view 'that equality in taxation is of great importance, and,

[39] *Ibid.*, p. 66.
[40] *Ibid.*, p. 116.
[41] *Ibid.*, pp. 66–7.
[42] *Ibid.*, p. 523.
[43] *Sir Philip Francis's Minutes*, pp. 151–2.

in justice, all the subjects of a State should contribute as nearly as possible in proportion to the income which they enjoy'.[44] Since the settlement was to be made on the basis of incomplete information, the initial assessment could not help being unequal. But not to correct it in the light of further investigation would not merely perpetuate injustice, but create serious administrative problems: 'it may be found impracticable to collect it', he said drawing evidently upon the experience of the Hastings era.[45] In order, therefore, to achieve 'a more correct distribution' he would empower the government with the right of investigation, not as Francis said in his exaggerated manner, 'into the actual value of every man's estate', but 'in partial instances'.

A second and equally important right of intervention Shore wanted for the government was to regulate the zamindar's relation with the ryot. 'With respect to the ryots', he wrote, 'their rights appear very uncertain and indefinite.'[46] He mentioned seven different ways in which the landlords oppressed them.[47] In spite of this, however, he was not sure of 'the policy and propriety' of admitting 'the right of the government to interfere in regulating the assessment upon the ryots'. This might be justified in some extreme cases, but as a matter of exception rather than of rule. In June 1789 he was still inclined to maintain that the zamindar's dealings with his ryot was his own business and the government should better leave them to work these out as best as they could. 'The regulation of the rents of the ryots', he wrote, 'is properly a transaction between the zemindar or landlord and his tenants, and not of the government.'[48] This, clearly, was the *laissez-faire* policy Francis himself had advocated. Six months later, however, in his final minute Shore came out with a complete repudiation of his former view. He had already made up his mind by that time about the advantages of postponing a permanent settlement.

[44] Firminger, vol. II, p. 519.
[45] *Ibid.*, pp. 522–3.
[46] *Ibid.*, p. 84.
[47] *Ibid.*, p. 55.
[48] *Ibid.*, p. 93.

There was nothing, therefore, to prevent him from speaking up for intervention between zamindar and ryot. 'The necessity of some interposition between the zemindars and their tenants is absolute', he wrote. 'If the assessment of the zemindarries were unalterably fixed, and the proprietors were left to make their own arrangements with the ryots without any restrictions, injunctions or limitations, which indeed is a result of the fundamental principle, the present confusion would never be adjusted.'[49] Thus in contradicting himself he severed at the same time one of the last links that in terms of ideas had bound him to the Francis tradition. He had no regrets about sacrificing 'a fundamental principle' to the dictates of policy.

It was in the light of these two principal considerations of policy that Shore approached the problem relating to the period of settlement. The need to create confidence among the native proprietors required that the term of settlement should be as long and as far approximating permanence as possible. The need for further knowledge of the value of the lands demanded, on the contrary, that the settlement should be of the shortest duration: the sooner a term ended the easier it would be for the government to apply the experiences of the period just concluded to the conduct of policies during the next term. For Francis the first alone of these two considerations had been valid. His only concern was the problem of confidence; for this the logical solution was a permanent settlement. Shore had undertaken a more complicated task. He had to evolve a formula capable of resolving the mutually contradictory demands of confidence and experimentation in terms of time; that is, to decide upon a period of settlement long enough to reassure the men of property, but requiring no sacrifice on the part of the government of its right of intervention. The mean he worked out was a settlement for an initial period of ten years to be followed by subsequent settlements of equal or progressively longer duration until a point was reached when the government would be in a position to consider the question of a permanent arrangement in

[49] *Ibid.*, p. 520.

the light of all the experience acquired in the process. It was Shore's opinion that the progress from a decennial to permanent settlement should be on the following lines:

> I consider this [that is, the decennial settlement] as a period of experiment and improvement during which . . . we are to give confidence to the zemindars and procure a simplification of the present complicated rental of the Ryots. The foundation of this improvement is to be laid in regulations to be established, and the proposed reform depends upon the execution of them, without which, I may venture to predict, no assessment can be permanent. If at the end of the fifth, sixth, or any subsequent year, not exceeding the eighth, of the assessment, it shall be found that the desired improvement has been accomplished, that the relative rights of talookdars, ryots and zemindars are rendered definite and precise, and that the country flourishes under the prescribed regulations and the superintending care of the revenue officers, the settlement may again be extended, to any period of ten or twenty years. The doubts which I have suggested, will then be brought to a test. The question of a perpetual assessment may then be agitated with more accurate information.[50]

There is very little that is common between such a notion of Permanent Settlement and what Francis had professed. It is no longer that definite and rounded-off end product of a syllogism, but only a receding horizon pursued by spurts of experience, a perspective valuable only for the sake of the efforts it was expected to inspire. No one was more aware than Francis himself of the difference between his own version of the policy and Shore's. He took it upon himself to correct the mistake the *Edinburgh Review* had made in regarding Shore as an architect of the Permanent Settlement.[51] 'With respect to the

[50] *Ibid.*, p. 522.

[51] This letter, which has already been quoted in part earlier, was written in protest of an article in the *Edinburgh Review* of April 1807 (pp. 27–40) where the author, commenting on Colebrooke's *Remarks on the Husbandry and Internal Commerce of Bengal*, described the Permanent Settlement as 'a measure which constituted the great object of the successive administrations of the Marquis of Cornwallis, and of Lord Teignmouth'. The draft of Francis's letter which I have used, is catalogued in the India Office Library as *Francis*

part taken in this transaction by Mr Shore, now Lord Teignmouth', he pointed out, 'you are completely misinformed. Tho' he professed to approve of the principle, he resisted the measure to the utmost of his power, and in fact was an adverse party to Lord Cornwallis on that subject.' He cited an extract each from Shore's minutes of 18 May 1785 and 21 December 1789, the earlier of the two statements signifying assent to the principle of Permanent Settlement and the other opposing precipitation of the measure.

The 'modifications' Shore proposed to the plan of 1776 thus ended up in a double contradiction – contradiction of the plan itself as well as of his own views formerly based on it. In both respects his attitude looks forward to important developments in the future. Every single point he made in his minutes was echoed and often literally reproduced in the great debate on Permanent Settlement which was to begin almost before the ink had dried on the proclamation of 1793. His emphasis on experience, too, anticipated the outlook and method of Munro and his associates.[52] His deviation from the doctrines of Philip Francis was, in fact, the sign of a coming revolt against the entire eighteenth-century tradition in the Company's Indian administration.

MSS 54 (54) 58, but apparently the *Edinburgh Review* never accepted it for publication.

[52] Stokes, *The English Utilitarians and India*, pp.19, 23.

Appendix

THE EXTRACTS REPRODUCED below constitute Chapter IV of the document included among the John Rylands Library collection of the Pitt Papers[1] as 'Abstract of the Several Plans transmitted relative to the future Government of Bengal and the other British Settlements in India'. The circumstances of its origin are thus described in *Historical View of Plans for the Government of British India etc.*:[2]

> Scarcely had the supreme power been given to the presidency of Bengal, and the supreme court of judicature been established, when parties, in that settlement took a decided form. Whatever was proposed by one, was opposed by the other . . . These circumstances, however, have had one use; each party was suggesting plans for the better government of India, and regulation of our trade to the East Indies; and all were sending them home as proofs of their zeal in the service, and of the local information which they had acquired . . . Mr Lind, a counsellor at law was employed to examine these plans and opinions, with directions to reduce them to order and to state the result of the whole.

The 'Abstract' is arranged in six chapters, each beginning with a question followed by two sections, 'Abstract' and 'Remarks', and concludes with a chapter containing general observations under the heading 'Additional Remarks'. The leading questions are formulated as follows:

I. On what political principle Bengal, Bahar and Orissa can be held by Great Britain?

[1] There are two copies of this document in the John Rylands Library, catalogued as English MS. nos. 215 and 935.

[2] Pp. 70–1 and 71 note.

II. In whom is to be vested the supreme executive power?
III. By what persons and under what restrictions is the power of subordinate legislation to be hereafter exercised?
IV. Of the territorial revenues: Under what title and in what manner are they to be collected?
V. How are the other revenues to be collected?
VI. How, and by what courts should justice be administered?

The persons whose views the document as a whole takes into account are Warren Hastings, Sir Elijah Impey, Robert Chambers, General Clavering and Philip Francis; but the opinions of the last two alone are considered in Chapter IV.

The original contains many marginal notes referring by serial number and paragraph to the various official papers from which the abstract was made. These have been omitted from the text given below, but all footnotes have been retained as in the original.

Abstract

'*Of the Territorial Revenues: Under what Title and in what Manner are they to be collected?*

Upon these questions General Clavering and Mr Francis are very full. Both seem to consider them as of the highest importance. Both repeatedly declare, that upon a proper decision of them will depend the future happiness of the people, and the future value of the acquisition of this country to Great Britain.

Mr Francis begins his first plan by stating, that the Company very early embraced a very erroneous opinion; vizt. that, by the constitution of the Mogul Empire, the sovereign is *proprietor of the soil.* He points out the ill consequences which have followed from the Company's adopting this principle. To this he attributes the unreasonable exactions of revenues; the racking and distressing of the people, to pay more than they were able; and a consequent diminution in the real collections, proportionate to the increase in the nominal Jumma. In a word he represents the Company as living upon their capital; the country as impoverished and depopulated; and the system hitherto pursued, as calculated only to serve present exigencies, at the risk of future, but certain, ruin.

He proceeds afterwards to trace the ancient policy of the Government; with respect to the holders of land; and the ancient mode of collecting the territorial revenues of Government; to mark the deviations from them; and the consequences of these deviations.

His narrative, he says, is supported by the records of the Khalsa; by the information of some of the oldest servants in the revenue offices; and by other authentic documents.

It begins by the conquest of Bengal in the year 1573 by Akbar and informs us:

> 'That in this reign Rajah Toorel Mull, a famous financier formed the Jumma bundy or establishment of rent for all India.
>
> That the principle of this settlement was to leave the lands to their proprietors, the Zemindars; and to establish moderate permanent Jummas, or quit rents, to be paid by each of them to Government.
>
> That the Jumma of Bengal, including five circars of Orissa, was one crore forty nine lacks sixty one thousand and four hundred and eighty two rupees; and a fraction.
>
> That this Jumma differs but little from the Jumma under Soujah Gawn, in 1728; but that it is a crore less than the lands of Bengal were assessed at, in the settlement for the year ending in 1775.
>
> That a record was formed of this Jumma called Tumar; so that Tumar Jumma means the rent of the roll; and it is called ausil, or original Jumma, with reference to all subsequent alterations or additions.
>
> That at the same time a Tukseem, or division accompt of the whole Subah, was formed, showing the constituent part of each Zemindary; such as Pergunnahs, villages etc with the proportion of the general quit rent payable by each.
>
> That the hereditary office of canongoes was established to keep the accompts of the Tumar and Tukseem.
>
> That in all transfers of property among the Zemindars, the new Sunnuds or grants are taken out upon the Tumar Jumma.
>
> That the jaguires of the royal officers or Munsubdars, were granted as portions of the Jumma.
>
> That from thence to resum or fees of the canongoes are still calculated.
>
> That disputes concerning the limits of landed property are still decided by reference to the Tukseem.'

Having given this account of the formation of the Tumar and Tukseem Jumma, Mr Francis goes on to state the mode of collection, which, by his account, was very simple. The Zemindars, he says, for the most part, paid the rents at the treasury. Collectors were only sent on default of payment, to levy the rents due to government by distress, or a temporary attachment of the lands.

With respect to the Ryots Mr Francis says – that it is not ascertained, whether the Zemindars were required by Government to give pottah or leases to them, or whether the grant of leases was a voluntary security. But, he says, that in all the pottahs, the first thing specified is the *Ausil, or the original* ground rent, considered as the proportion of the original Tukseem, to be paid by that particular tenant, and upon which all other taxes, or impositions are calculated; whether permanent, *Aboab*, or occasional *Muthote.* That the pottahs express no term of lease: but that, by custom, the Ryot cannot be dispossessed, so long as he pays his proportion of the general rent.

Mr Francis further observes, that scarce any alteration was made in the settlement formed upon this simple principle, till the conclusion of Soujah Cawn's government about 1739 or 1740.

That during that period, however, the Subahdar did frequently extort, or received, more money from the Zemindars, either by violence or by way of free gift; but that the Jumma was invariable.

The first very material alternation made in the establishment was, as Mr Francis observes, by Alverdy Cawn, who cut off the son of Soujah Cawn, and usurped the government. But at that time the wealth of the Zemindars was so great, that they assisted him, during his wars against the Mahrattas, with a crore and a half of rupees. But he and Serajah Dowlah were the first who added to the Jumma, the *Aboabs* or permanent taxes; thereby swelling the rent roll, and increasing the ground rent, and hence this evil, he says accrued, that all occasional taxes became permanent.

Having shewn what was the Jumma of the *whole province* at its original settlement, by Akbar, Mr Francis proceeds to shew what was the Jumma of the *Dewanny Lands* only with the appropriations of it, under Soujah Cawn, and what it was under Alverdy Cawn; Serajah Dowlah; and Cossim Alli; upon which last Jumma our first settlement appears to have been made.

The Jumma of these lands under *Soujah Cawn* was one crore, one lack, thirty eight thousand and six rupees and a fraction.

Under Serajah Dowlah it was one crore, thirty eight lacks, twelve thousand, four hundred forty three rupees, and a fraction.

Under *Cossim Alli* it amounted to one crore, eighty six lacks, fifty nine thousand, seven hundred and twenty rupees, and a fraction.

The net rent proposed to be raised by the settlement of 1776–7 was one crore, seventy seven lacks, seventy three thousand, seven hundred and seventy five rupees and a fraction.

The sum *actually collected* was one crore, thirty eight lacks, twelve thousand, four hundred and forty three rupees, and a fraction.

But if the ancient establishment had been altered by Alverdy Cawn, Cossim Alli, as Mr Francis informs us shook them from their foundation; and with them overthrew the rights and property of the Zemindars. But his reign, he adds, was marked by pillage and rapine, and murder; and concluded by carrying off immense treasures, when he was driven from the country.

The country, Mr Francis informs us, was in this situation when the Dewanny was ceded to the Company: ancient establishment overthrown; many of the Zemindars dispossessed, and reduced to beggary, and the wealthy families brought to ruin.

In this situation, Mr Francis says that even the ancient revenues which had before been collected with ease could not now be realised without new taxes, expedients, and measures of rigor. That such measures could not but precipitate the ruin of the country, yet that the successive administrations, instead of lowering the demands of Government, in point either of revenue or investment have gone on increasing them in proportion as the ability of the country decreased.

The sudden and unexpected increase of investments forced the servants of the Company, or at least gave them a pretext, to have recourse to monopolies; oppressive to the manufacturer, destructive of emulation, and consequently of industry; and which, excluding the Indian markets from sharing in the produce of Bengal, drove the other Indian states to establish manufactures at home.

The increased demand of revenue introduced the system of farming. Men of low rank and desperate fortune were employed as *Aumib* or collectors; they farmed the revenues of a district, at a stipulated price; where the produce of the land was not sufficient to furnish for contract, they laid *Aboab and Muthoote*. The Ryot seeing no end to the demands sought expedients to procure, or extort abatements in the Ausil: then the farmer when the crop was on the ground, laid another Muthoote, or else the improved lands were made to pay for the deficiency of lands unimproved. Still he says the sums assessed could not have been raised but for sources now dried up. For many of the natives, he says, then enjoyed offices the emoluments of which they spent in the respective districts: the Shroffs made loans to the Zemindars, which have never been repaid; and the fines in the criminal courts, or Aboab Phoujadaree, contributed to the general fund.

The decline of the country, Mr Francis observes, was frequently represented by Mohammed Reza Cawn, as well as by the most intelligent servants of the Company; who joined in representing the necessity of employing the Zemindars, and leaving something to the natives. But it being suspected that Mohammed Reza Cawn wished only to cover his own oppressions by those representations, Supervisors were appointed for the express purpose of learning and reporting the condition of the provinces, the state of trade, the mode of administering justice and collecting the revenues. From these reports it was intended to form a general plan for the future government of the country.

But this design, he says, was frustrated. For the Supervisors having procured accurate accounts of the *Hustaboods*, or valuation of the whole rents including the profits of the farmer, Zemindar, Talookdar etc.; the whole of these profits were swept into the treasury; and an institution, calculated to deliver the natives, was made a new instrument of oppression.

The Committee of Circuit which succeeded the appointment of Supervisors had for its profest object as Mr Francis informs us, an increase of revenues; and he adds, that the distress of the country, engaging many adventurers to offer to farm the lands at an exorbitant price, facilitates the increase of nominal rents. But he says the increase was *only nominal*: as the ballances, or parts of the rent not realised but remain due from the farmers since April 1772, amount to at least a crore of rupees. He mentions, what indeed is too obvious not to be at once perceived, that there is a wide difference between fixing a moderate rent, from which the tenant is to expect no abatement, and fixing an extravagant rent from which the tenant is to extort all the abatement he can.

The conclusions which Mr Francis draws from this long detail are:

That the Company levies higher rents from the country, labouring under great disadvantages, than it ever paid to its former governors in its most flourishing condition.

That the desire of increase inflexibly pursued, is ruinous to the country, and will be found to be the worst economy.

That the want of a fixt Jumma has rendered the land of no value, and taken away the only incitement to improve them.

That the employment of farmers, throwing the profits of collection into the hands of strangers resident at the capital, is a further cause of oppression and depopulation.

That less lands being now cultivated than heretofore, taxes are of course increased on what remains in a state of cultivation.

That needy adventurers have been encouraged to farm all the lands at exorbitant prices: and at the same time the Zemindars have been so disgusted, that, if not employed, they have done all they could to depopulate the country and embarrass Government; and where employed, have been rendered rapacious and unthrifty farmers.

That the lands being assessed at their utmost produce in the most favorable seasons, the income of Government must be precarious.

That the confusion arising from the abatement in the Ausil and the accumulated taxes renders the leases of the Ryots unintelligible; and opens a door to innumerable frauds and oppressions.

That even the Governor General, who made the last settlement, acknowledges, that the farmers engaged for a higher revenue than the districts could afford.

Upon the above recapitulation of facts, and the conclusions drawn from them, Mr Francis grounds the following propositions for the future settlement of the territorial revenues in Bengal, Bahar and Orissa.

That the Jumma be fixed once for all; made matter of public record; known to the people to be permanent and unalterable; and a condition annexed to the lands themselves, independent of any consideration of who may be the immediate or future possessors.

That the whole demand upon the country including Ghazipore, be founded upon an estimate of permanent services, under the general heads of civil, military, investments, contingencies.[3]

[3] Nos. 18, 19, 20 contain two estimates of services, and ways and means: with remarks thereon, upon these estimates an unappropriated ballance would remain of rupees 37,99,043:15 for unforeseen events. But General Gavering . . . thinks many of the articles of services calculated on too narrow a scale, and objects to the remissions of 10 per cent allowed in the collections. But if that allowance of

That in the distribution of the assessment, every possible relief be given to the Dewanny lands on account both of their distance from the capital, and the present poverty of the inhabitants.

That the particular regard be had to the distant provinces, and those which have few resources and manufactures.

That the medium of the actual receipts of the last three years be the rule of assessment.[4]

That the inequalities which might be found in such an assessment would neither be so burthensome, nor alarming; nor perhaps dangerous as an attempt – probably fruitless, of being more accurate by causing a Hustabood, or actual admeasurement and valuation of all the lands to be taken.

That the gross sum be collected, as well for the revenues, as all charges incident to it, being once ascertained, each Zemindary be assessed its proportion; and that sum be declared the quit rent of those particular lands in perpetuity.

That this distribution be called the *Tumar Jumma*, a name sanctified among the natives as conveying the idea of security.

That no temporary contributions be added to the Jumma on any pretence, or under any exigence of government.

That a new Tukseem be also formed.

That these records be carefully preserved in the Khalsa and translated into English.

That the head cutchery of each district[5] have an authenticated copy of its particular Tukseem for the inspection of all persons interested.

That the due discharge of the quit rent be the tenure by which the Zemindar holds his lands.

---

10 per cent should be struck off, so much will be added to the ways and means. In these estimates too the civil establishments seem to be carried too high.

[4] There seems a contradiction, or at least a confusion, in this part of the plan. Mr. Francis probably means that the medium of the actual receipts for the three last years will give the sum to be collected; that such sum will answer all the services, and have the unappropriated balances, stated in the last note, and in the papers there referred to; that to render this tax more equal regard should be had to the particular circumstances here mentioned.

[5] Mr. Francis calls a *district* that portion of lands which is under one Supervisor.

That in default of payment, a part of the Zemindary be sold to make good of the deficiency.

That this condition be expressly inserted in every *Caboleat* or grant to the Zemindars.

That in case of a sale for default of payment, if any ballance remains after the payment of the quit rent the proprietors have credit for the same. That in every sale of a Zemindary for default of paymt. a preference to be given to the next heir.[6]

That in case a Zemindar should be incapable of managing his lands, a Dewan or steward of sufficient ability and good character, be appointed to act for him: to be answerable to Government for the rent due to government, without whose approbation the Dewan should not be dismissed: but to be answerable to his master; to have no claim on the estate: and to be incapable of becoming a purchaser, in case of the sale of the Zemindary of which he is Dewan.[7]

That a new law of inheritance or rather stat[ute] of distribution be made, by which all Zemindaries producing more than two lacks each to government shall be divided among all the sons; but the others shall be vested in the eldest son, chargeable with the maintenance of the younger sons.[8]

That the Zemindars, having no heirs of their own blood, be not permitted to adopt heirs to inherit their real property.[9]

That a court of wards be established for the care of estates of which the incumbents are minors, idiots or females.[10]

That the Jumma once reduced, and the management of their lands being restored to the Zemindars, the allowance now made them in lieu of their Zemindaries, be stopt.

That to obviate the vexatious consequences of any inquisition into

[6] Sir John Clavering conceives that this might open a door to frauds.

[7] Sir John Clavering thinks this appointment of Dewan to be an expedient at once burthensome and dangerous.

[8] Sir John Clavering thinks this a dangerous experiment, and yet does not deny what the Governor General, as well as Mr. Francis, has frequently observed: that it is the interest of Government that the great Zemindaries be divided.

[9] This restriction Sir John Clavering considers as cruel and oppressive.

[10] This institution, Sir John Clavering thinks, is liable to great abuses; and opens a field to plunder and oppression.

ancient titles: and at the same time to relieve the Zemindars against modern and notorious usurpation of lands, held as charity lands, under the title of pretended gifts; a term of prescription be fixed for the quiet possession of all lands, held as charity lands under gifts real or pretended.[11]

Having thus secured the rights of the Zemindars, Mr Francis goes on to make a similar provision for the Ryots.

And on this head he proposes, that government prescribe a form for the Pottahs, which in the course of a given time, each Zemindar shall be bound to give to his tenants or Ryots.

That the lease be granted either for the term of his own quit rent that is so long as his rent remains the same; or for a term of years.

That the form of the lease be as simple as possible: stating only so much per Bega, for every cultivated Bega, varying according to the produce and quality of the soil, and of the situation of the lands; without any mention of *Aboab* or *Muthoote.*

That on the demand of the Ryot, the Supervisor of the district do cause such a pottah to be given, properly authenticated by himself, the Canongoes, and the officers of the Cutchery.

That every Ryot, on completing his annual payments, may demand a signed account of his Jummabundy from the Zemindar or his agent with a release at the foot of it.

These are opinions of Mr Francis and Sir John Clavering on this important question a question upon which Sir Elijah Impey is totally silent.

Remarks

Upon these propositions it is submitted,

That in theory at least they appear unexceptionable; equally favorable to the interests of the lord, the tenant in chief, and the under tenant; calculated to give general security, and to impress a general sense of that security, and consequently to excite general industry and diffuse general happiness.

That the facts adduced, and the vouchers by which they are supported, prove that the practice of near two centuries, from Akbar to Cossim Alli has added the testimony of experience in its favour.

[11] Sir John Clavering recommends delicacy and caution in the resumption of any charity lands.

That the fixation of the Tumar and Tukseem is not meant to restrain the Zemindar from increasing his rent in proportion as *he* improves the land, but only to fix the portion of public contributions to be paid by each tenant for his respective portion.

That the fixation of the Tumar is not to preclude Government from levying extraordinary aids on extraordinary exigencies; but only to fix, in the first instance, what each landholder is to contribute towards the ordinary and permanent services; and what proportion he should contribute towards the extraordinary and contingent demands.

Advantageous however as this mode of collecting the territorial revenues may be; though the interest of Government, as well as the happiness of the people, seem to require, that the Zemindars should be restored to their leases; still it is submitted, that there are three ways in which this may be effected.

> 1st. It may be expressly declared in the Act of Parliament, that the Zemindars shall be so restored to their lands, and the Ryots to their leases.
>
> 2ndly. The Act may simply empower the Governor and Council, so soon as they think it can be done with safety to restore them.
>
> Or, lastly: The Act may be totally silent upon it, and it may be left to his Majesty to give it in instruction to adopt so salutary a measure.

The first of these ways would, it is submitted, give to the people the strongest sense of security, and therefore be the most likely to excite industry. But yet by confirming the power the Governor and Council, by the express directions of an Act of Parliament, it may be attended with inconveniencies which are not foreseen; more especially as Mr Francis himself states, that the late oppressions have so sunk the spirits, diminished the weight and impaired the influence of the Zemindars that they can only gradually be restored to their ancient rights, or called to the discharge of their ancient duties.

The 3d. it is submitted, will not give the same sense of security, and therefore will not be so powerful a spur to industry.

But it is submitted that the 2d. whilst it would give the same sense of security as the first, would stand clear of the inconveniencies attendant on it, leaving so much to the discretion of the Governor and Council, especially at the beginning, *when only* much discretion on this point need be allowed.

Glossary

Abwab	Taxes imposed under the Mahommedan Governments in addition to the regular assessment on the land. Miscellaneous cesses, imposts and charges levied by the zamindars and public officers.
Amil, Aumil	A collector of revenue employed by the Government or by a revenue-farmer.
Bandobast, Bundobust	Settlement of revenue to be paid by the zamindar, renter, or farmer to the Government, or by the tenant to the zamindar.
Banya, Banian	A native cashier or man of business in the service of an European officer or trader.
Barkandaz, Burkundaz	Armed guard, escort or watchman.
Bigha	A measure of land varying in extent in different parts of India. In Bengal the standard *bigha* contained 1600 square yards, or a little less than one-third of an acre.
Dadni, Dadney	Paying in advance to labourers or manufacturers. Hence – merchant, that is, a native trader with whom the East India Company had a contract for the supply of goods for investment against a sum of money pain in advance.
Dalal	A broker.
Dastak, Dustruck	A document authorizing the free transit of certain goods and their exemption from inland duties.
Etmam	From *Ihtiman*: the jurisdiction of a zamindar over certain variable divisions of a province. An estate.

Golandazi, Golundazey	An advance made by the Government or the zamindar to the ryots to enable them to carry out urgently needed repairs in embankments, etc.
Gyrhest	From *Grihastha*: literally, a householder. The word as used in the text means a cultivator, a husbandman.
Hastobud, Hustabood	A comparative account showing the present and past produce of an estate. A detailed statement of any land yielding revenue.
Ijaradar	A revenue farmer. The renter of a village or an estate at a stipulated rate.
Jagir	A tenure common under Mahommedan rule, in which the public revenues of a given tract of land were made over to a servant of the state.
Jama, Jumma	The total amount of rent or revenue payable by a cultivator or a zamindar.
Jamabandi, Jummabundy	Settlement of the amount of revenue assessed upon an estate, a village or district. An annual statement of revenue due from any estate.
Kachari, Cutcherry	A landlord's office. An office where any public business is transacted.
Kanungoi, Canoongoey	Appertaining to a *Kanungo*, a key officer at the village and district levels who had it as his duty to keep a record of all circumstances and documents relating to landed property and the collection of revenue.
Katkindar, Cutkinadar	An under-farmer or under-rented holding under the revenue-payer to the zamindar.
Khas	Estates managed directly by the Government or lands from which the officers of the Government collected the revenue without the aid of any intermediate agency like that of the zamindar.
Kist	An instalment of revenue or rent due from a zamindar or ryot.

Lakh, Lack	One hundred thousand.
Mathaut, Mathote	An extra or occasional cess or tax imposed upon the cultivators for some special purpose, or under some incidental pretext either by the government, or its officials or the zamindar.
Mofussil accounts	Accounts relating to the gross amount of revenue payable to the zamindar by the subordinate cultivators, and through him to the government.
Molungee	A labourer engaged in the manufacture of salt.
Mukarari, Mocurrery	A proprietor's tenure held a fixed and permanent rate of revenue.
Paik	A footman. An armed attendant.
Pargana, Pergunnah	A fiscal district usually comprising many villages.
Patta, Pottah	A deed or document recording the terms on which a cultivator or under-tenant holds his land.
Ryot	A cultivator. A peasant.
Ryotwari	A settlement of revenue made by the government with each actual cultivator of the soil without the intervention of a third party.
Russud	A gradual increase in the amount of revenue assessed.
Sanad, Sunnud	A grant. A document conveying such grant under the seal of the ruling authority.
Subhankari	Arithmetical rules used in the traditional mode of accounting, measurement, etc. in Bengal.
Talukdar, Talookdar	A landholder who, in Bengal, is regarded as infrior to a zamindar, but not necessarily dependent on the latter. Hence – i, – y.
Wakf	An endowment for religious or charitable purposes.
Zamindar, Zemindar	A landholder. Hence – i, – y.

Bibliography

A. Unpublished Records

1. *Records Room of the Government of West Bengal, Calcutta*
   (I) Proceedings of the Board of Revenue.
   (II) Proceedings of the Governor-General in Council.
   (III) Letters from the Court of Directors.
   (IV) Letters to the Court of Directors.

2. *India Office Library*
   (I) The *Francis MSS.**
   (II) Clive – Verelst Correspondence.
   (III) Home Miscellaneous.

3. *British Museum*
   Additional MSS: The Hastings Papers.

4. *Public Record Office.*
   Treasury: The East India Papers.

5. *John Rylands Library, Manchester.*
   The Pitt Papers.

*References to documents belonging to this collection have been made according to the enumeration given in Kaye and Johnstone, *Catalogue of Manuscripts in European Languages belonging to the Library of the India Office*, vol. II, part II. The first figure indicates the serial number of the volume to which the document belongs; the second, within brackets, the old serial number which has been revised by Kaye and Johnstone; and the third, the location of the document itself within the volume. I have avoided reference by page in all cases except where the documents are not serially arranged.

B. Published Works

Acton, *Lectures on Modern History* (London, 1906).

Ascoli, F.D., *Early Revenue History of Bengal and the Fifth Report,* 1812 (Oxford, 1917).

Auber, Peter, *Rise and Progress of the British Power in India.* 2 vols. (London, 1837).

Baker, David Erskine, *Biographia Dramatica* (London, 1782).

Becker, Carl L., *The Heavenly City of the Eighteenth-Century Philosophes* (Yale, 1959).

Beer, M., *An Inquiry into Physiocracy* (London, 1939).

Biographie Universelle: Nouvelle Edition (Paris, 1843).

Black, George F., 'The Surnames of Scotland. Their Origin, Meaning and History'. *Bulletin of the New York Public Library,* vol. 50, no. 2 (February, 1946).

Blackstone, William, *Commentaries on the Laws of England.* 4 vols (Oxford, 1765–9).

Bodelsen, C.A., *Studies in Mid-Victorian Imperialism* (London, 1960).

Bolts, William, *Considerations on India Affairs, particularly respecting the present state of Bengal and its dependencies* (London, 1772).

Boulanger, Nicolas-Antoine, *Recherches sur l'origine du despotisme oriental* (London, 1762).

———, *The Origin and Progress of Despotism in the Oriental and other Empires of Africa, Europe and America* (London, 1764).

Bourde, André J., *The Influence of England on the French Agronomes* (Cambridge, 1953).

Briggs, Asa, *The Age of Improvement* (London, 1959).

Brougham, Henry Lord, *Historical Sketches of Statesmen who flourished in the Time of George III.* Second Series (London, 1839).

Brown, Philip Anthony, *The French Revolution in English History* (London, 1918).

Burke, Edmund, *Correspondence of the Right Honourable Edmund Burke.* Vol. III (London, 1844).

Butterfield, H., *The Whig Interpretation of History* (London, 1931).

Cambridge History of India. Vol. 5.

Chattopadhyaya, Bankimchandra, *Anandamath* (In Bengali).

Clark, Allen C., *Greenleaf and Law in the Federal City* (Washington D.C., 1901).

Cobban, Alfred, *Edmund Burke and the Revolt Against the Eighteenth Century*. Second edition (London, 1960).

Cobbett's Parliamentary Debates.

Colebrooke, Sir James Edward, *A Digest of the Regulations and Laws, enacted by the Governor General in Council for the civil government of the territories under the Presidency of Bengal* (Supplement . . . completing each article of the Digest to the close of the year 1806). 3 vols (Calcutta, 1807).

D'Alembert, *Morceaux choisis de Tacite*. T. 1 (Paris, 1784).

De Pinto, Isaac, *An Essay on Luxury* (London, 1766).

Dictionary of National Biography.

Dow, Alexander, *The History of Hindostan,* from *the* earliest account of time *to the death of Akbar; translated from the Persian of Mahummud Casim Ferishtah* . . . together with a Dissertation concerning the Religion and Philosophy of the Brahmins. With an appendix containing the History of the Mogul Empire from its decline in the reign of Mahummud Shah to the present time. Vols. 1, 2 (Vol. 3. The History of Hindostan from the death of Akbar to the . . . settlement of the Empire under Aurungzebe . . . A dissertation on the origin and nature of despotism in Hindostan . . . An enquiry into the state of Bengal.) 3 vols (London, 1768–72).

———, *Zingis, A Tragedy* (London, 1769).

Edinburgh Review. April 1807.

Encyclopaedia of the Social Sciences.

Febvre, Lucien, *La Terre et l'Evolution Humaine: Introduction Geographique a l'Histoire* (Paris, 1922).

Felling, Keith, *Warren Hastings* (London, 1954).

Ferguson, Adam, *Essay on the History of Civil Society*. Fifth edition (1782).

Firminger, Walter Kelly, *The Fifth Report . . . on the affairs of the East India Company . . .* 1812. 3 vols. Edited by W.K. Firminger (Calcutta, 1917).

Forrest, George W., *Selections from the Letters, Despatches, and Other State Papers preserved in the Foreign Department of the Government of India,* 1772–1785. 3 vols. Edited by G.W. Forrest (Calcutta, 1890).

———, *The Administration of Warren Hastings, 1772–1785* (Calcutta, 1892).

Francis, Philip, *Heads of Mr Francis's Speech in reply to Mr Dundas on the 23d. of April 1793* (London, 1793).

———, *Letter from Mr Francis to Lord North, late Earl of Guildford.*

———, *Original Minutes of the Governor-General and Council of Fort William on the settlement and collection of the revenues of Bengal, with a plan of settlement recommended to the Court of Directors in January 1776* (London, 1782).

———, *Philip Francis's Speech in the House of Commons on Tuesday, 7 March, 1786* (London, 1786).

———, *Popular Topics* (London, 1784). Published anonymously.

———, *Reflections on the Abundance of Paper in Circulation and the Scarcity of Specie* (London, 1810).

———, *Sir Philip Francis's Minutes on the subject of a Permanent Settlement for Bengal, Behar and Orissa.* Edited by Romesh C. Dutt (Calcutta, 1901).

———, *The Francis Letters.* Edited by Beata Francis and Eliza Keary. 2 vols (London, 1901).

———, *We have been all in the Wrong* (London, 1785).

Francisque-Michel, Xavier, *Les Ecossais en France, les Francais en Ecosse.* 2 vols (London, 1862).

Furber, Holden, *John Company at Work* (Cambridge, Mass., 1948).

Fyfe, W.H. (tr.), *Tacitus: The Histories.* 2 vols (Oxford, 1912).

Gentleman's Magazine. New Series, vol. II (1834).

George, M. Dorothy, *English Political Caricature.* 2 vols (Oxford, 1959).

Ghosh, Jamini Mohan, *Sannyasi and Fakir Raiders in Bengal* (Calcutta, 1930).

Gibbon, Edward, *The History of the Decline and Fall of the Roman Empire.* Edited by J.B. Bury. 7 vols (London, 1898).

Gide, Charles and Rist, Charles, *A History of Economic Doctrines* (London, 1960).

Gleig, G.R., *Memoirs of the Life of Warren Hastings, first Governor-General of Bengal.* 3 vols (London, 1841).

Gordon, T., *The Works of Tacitus.* Vol. I: 'Political Discourses' (London, 1728).

Graham, Henry Grey, *Scottish Men of Letters in the Eighteenth Century* (London, 1901).

———, *The Social Life of Scotland in the Eighteenth Century*. 2 vols (London, 1899).

Grant, James, *An Inquiry into the Nature of Zemindary Tenures in the Landed Property of Bengal* (London, 1790).

Grant, Michael (tr.), *Tacitus: The Annals of Imperial Rome* (Penguin Books, 1956).

Guha, Ranajit, 'An Administrative Blueprint of 1785'. *Bengal Past and Present*, vol. LXXIV, part I (January–June 1955).

———, 'Chirasthayee Bandobaster Sutrapat' (in Bengali). *Parichaya* (Calcutta, Magh 1362–Ashadh 1363).

———, 'Report on an Investigation of the Gauripur Raj Estate Archives'. *Report of the Regional Records Survey Committee for West Bengal, 1955–56* (Calcutta, 1956).

———, *West Bengal District Records (New Series): Burdwan Letters Issued, 1788–1800.* Edited by R. Guha and A. Mitra (Calcutta, 1956).

Halévy, Elie, *England in 1815.* Second edition (London, 1949).

Handley, James E., *Scottish Farming in the Eighteenth Century* (London, 1953).

Hansard, *The Parliamentary History of England from the Earliest Period to the year 1803* (London, 1815–20).

Hazard, Paul, *La Pensée Européenne au XVIIIéme Siecle*. 2 tomes (Paris, 1946).

Hazen, Charles Downer, *The French Revolution*. 2 vols (New York, 1932).

Heckscher, Eli Filip, *Mercantilism*. 2 vols (London, 1935).

Higgs, Henry, *The Physiocrats* (London, 1897).

Hill, Christopher, *Puritanism and Revolution* (London, 1958).

Hobbes, Thomas, *Leviathan* (Oxford, 1946).

Holzman, James M., *The Nabobs in England* (New York, 1926).

Hume, David, *The Letters of David Hume*. Edited by J.Y.T. Greig. 2 vols (Oxford, 1932).

Hunter, William Wilson, *A Statistical Account of Bengal*. 20 vols (London, Edinburgh, 1875–7).

Institut National d'Etudes Démographiques (ed.). *François Quesnay et la Physiocratie*. 2 tomes (Paris, 1958).

Journal de Commerce. February and March 1759.

Journal of the House of Commons.

Kaye, John William, *The Administration of the East India Company* (London, 1853).

Keynes, John Maynard, *The General Theory of Employment, Interest and Money* (London, 1936).

Koebner, R., 'Despot and Despotism: Vicissitudes of a Political Term'. *Journal of the Warburg and Courtauld Institutes,* vol. XIV, nos. 3–4, pp. 275–302.

Law, Thomas, *A Sketch of some late Arrangements and a View of the rising Resources* of *Bengal* (London, 1792).

———, *An Address to the Columbian Institute on the question 'What Ought to be the Circulating Medium of a Nation?'* (Washington, 1830).

———, *An Answer to Mr Princep's Observations on the Mocurrery System* (London, 1794).

———, *Correspondence of the Honourable Court of Directors of the East India Company and of the Governor General in Council respecting the Permanent Settlement of the Land Revenue* (London, 1825); to which is appended 'Remarks on the Ryotwarree and Mocurrery Systems'.*

———, *Heads of a Proposed Speech by a Proprietor upon the Policy of Renewing the Company's Monopoly etc.* (London, 1793).

*I have used the India Office Library copy (T. 5161) of the book. In the Library of the British Museum the part entitled 'Remarks etc' is treated as a separate work (Catalogue No. 8158.b.1) published in 1820 and 'without a title page'. This description is misleading. It was Law's intention that the two parts should be read as complementary to each other. In the India Office Library copy the section containing official correspondence follows the essay 'Remarks etc'. In the author's own manuscript notes serving as a preface to this copy it is explained how the two sections came to be arranged in this way and why the sequence should be reversed. 'I recommend the perusal of the latter part first', writes Law, 'as it conveys all the reasoning of the Court of Directors and of Marquis Cornwallis in favor of the permanent System called *Mocurrery.* These added documents I had an opportunity of seeing after I had finished my Contrast of that and the Ryotwarree System. The latter has been introduced to supercede the former, after experiencing the beneficial effects of the former.'

———, *Letters to the Board submitting by their requisition a Revenue Plan for Perpetuity* (Calcutta, 1789).

Lecky, William Edward Hartpole, *A History of England in the Eighteenth Century.* 7 vols (London, 1892).

Lester, W., *The Happy Era to one hundred millions of the human race; or the Merchant, Manufacturer, and Englishman's recognized Right to an unlimited trade with India: with the rise, progress, and approaching death of the East India Company's claimed rights; shewing the time when their charter was no monopoly* (London, 1813).

Locke, John, *Two Treatises of Government* (New York, 1947).

Lokke, Carl Ludwig, *France and the Colonial Question: A Study of Contemporary French Opinion, 1763–1801* (New York, 1932).

Macaulay, Thomas Babington, *Critical and Historical Essays.* 2 vols (Everyman's Library).

Malcolm, John, *The Political History of India from 1784 to 1823.* 2 vols (London, 1826).

Manuel, Frank E., *The Eighteenth Century Confronts the Gods* (Cambridge, Mass., 1959).

Marshman, John Clark, *History of India.* 3 vols (London, 1871).

Martineau, Harriet, *British Rule in India* (London, 1857).

Marx, Karl, *Theories of Surplus Value* (London, 1951).

Maverick, Lewis A., *China a'Model for Europe* (Texas, 1946).

Meikle, Henry W., *Scotland and the French Revolution* (Glasgow, 1912).

Mill, James, *The History of British India.* Fifth edition with notes and continuation by H.H. Wilson. 10 vols (London, 1858).

Milton, John, *The Works of John Milton.* 18 vols (Columbia edition, 1931–8).

Montesquieu, *Oeuvres Complètes.* 3 tomes (Paris, 1950).

Moon, Penderel, *Warren Hastings and British India* (London, 1947).

Murphy, Arthur, *The Works of Cornelius Tacitus.* Vol. I (London, 1793).

Namier, Lewis, *The Structure of Politics at the Accession of George III.* Second edition (London, 1957).

[Neild?], *Summary Remarks on the resources of the East Indies; written prior to the introduction and institution of the decennial leases to Zemindars, and intended as a contrast to the pamphlet of Mr Thomas Law, entitled*

'Rising Resources', published in support of the Mocurrery System, planned by that gentleman and adopted by Lord Cornwallis . . . By a civil servant long employed in the Revenue and Judicial Departments. (London, 1792?).

Observations sur la Physique, sur l'Histoire Naturelle et sur les Arts (Journal de Physique). T.I (Paris, 1773).

Pares, Richard, *The Historian's Business and Other Essays* (Oxford, 1961).

Parkes, Joseph and Merivale, Herman, *Memoirs of Sir Philip Francis.* 2 vols (London, 1867).

Pattullo, Henry, *An Essay upon the Cultivation of the Lands, and Improvements of the Revenues of Bengal* (London, 1772).

———, *Essai sur l'Amelioration des Terres* (Paris, 1758).

Plumb, John Harold, *England in the Eighteenth Century* (Penguin Books, 1950).

Plutarch, *Plutarch's Lives.* 3 vols. (Everyman's Library).

Prinsep, John, *Observations on the Mocurrery System of Landed Property in Bengal originally written for the Morning Chronicle under the signature of Gurreeb Doss, with replies* (London, 1794).

Records of the Government of Bengal, *Letter Copy Book of the Supervisor of Rajshahi at Nator* (Calcutta, 1925).

———, *Proceedings of the Committee of Circuit at Krishnagar and Kasimbazar*. 8 vols in 3 parts (Calcutta, 1926–7).

———, *Proceedings of the Controlling Council of Revenue at Murshidabad.* 12 vols (Calcutta, 1919–24).

———, *The Letter Copy Books of the Resident at the Durbar at Murshidabad, 1769–1770* (Calcutta, 1919).

Roll, Erich, *A History of Economic Thought* (London, 1949).

Ross, Charles, *Correspondence of Charles, First Marquis Cornwallis.* Second edition. 3 vols (London, 1859).

Rouse, Charles William Boughton, *Dissertation Concerning the Landed Property of Bengal* (London, 1791).

Rousseau, J.J., Oeuvres de J.J. Rousseau. T.III: *'Traduction du Premier Livre de l'Histoire de Tacite'* (Paris, 1796).

Schumpeter, Joseph A., *History of Economic Analysis* (New York, 1955).

Schuyler, Robert Livingstone, *The Fall of the Old Colonial System* (New York, 1945).

Sen, Navinchandra, *Palasir Yuddha* (in Bengali).

Sen, S.R., *The Economics of Sir James Steuart* (London, 1957).

Sinha, J.C. 'Economic Theorists among the Servants of the John Company, 1766–1806'. *Economic Journal*, March 1925.

Sinha, N.K., *Fort William India House Correspondence, 1767–1769*, vol. 5. Edited by N.K. Sinha (Delhi, 1949).

Society of the Friends of the People, *Proceedings of the Society of the Friends of the People; Associated for the Purpose of obtaining a Parliamentary Reform in the year 1792* (Strand, 1793).

———, *Rules of the Society of the Friends of the People in Southwark*, 25 April, 1792.

Somerville, Thomas, *My Own Life and Times, 1741–1814* (Edinburgh, 1861).

Stokes, Eric, *The English Utilitarians and India* (Oxford, 1959).

[Stonhouse, John], *Thoughts on the Expedience of Settling Permanent Leases with the Landholders in Bengal, Bahar, and Orissa* (London, 1792).

Sutherland, Lucy S., *The East India Company in Eighteenth-Century Politics* (Oxford, 1952).

Tacitus. See D'Alembert, Fyfe, Gordon, Grant, Murphy, Rousseau.

Tawney, R.H., *Business and Politics under James I* (Cambridge, 1958).

Teignmouth, *Memoir of the Life and Correspondence of John Lord Teignmouth*. 2 vols (London, 1843).

The Universal Jewish Encyclopaedia (New York, 1939).

Thomson, Charles W., *Scotland's Work and Worth*. 2 vols (Edinburgh, 1909).

Veitch, George Stead, *The Genesis of Parliamentary Reform* (London, 1913).

Verelst, Harry, *View of the Rise, Progress and Present State of the English Government in Bengal, including a reply to the Misrepresentations of Mr Bolts and other writers* (London, 1772).

Viner, Jacob, *Studies in the Theory of International Trade* (New York, 1937).

Vinogradoff, Paul, *Villainage in England* (Oxford, 1892).

Voltaire, *Essay sur l'Histoire Générale et sur les Moeurs et l'Esprit des Nations depuis Charlemagne jusqu'à nos jours.* 7 tomes (Geneva, 1756). 8 tomes (Geneva, 1761–63).

———, *Fragments sur l'Inde* (Paris, 1773).

———, *L'Orphelin de la Chine* (Paris, 1763).

Weitzman, Sophia, *Warren Hastings and Philip Francis* (Manchester, 1929).

Weulersse, Georges, *La Physiocratie à la fin du regne de Louis XV, 1770–1774* (Paris, 1959).

———, *La Physiocratie sous les ministères de Turgot et de Necker, 1774–1781* (Paris, 1950).

———, *Les Physiocrates* (Paris, 1931).

———, 'Economics: The Physiocrats', in *Encyclopaedia of the Social Sciences.*

Wolf, A., *A History of Science, Technology, and Philosophy in the Eighteenth Century* (London, 1938).

Young, Arthur, *Young's Travels in France.* Edited by M. Bentham-Edwards (London, 1913).

Index

(Italics indicate location in both text and footnote on the same page; 'n' indicates location in footnote only)